P9-DUR-806

THUCYDIDES

888.2
H783

THUCYDIDES

Simon Hornblower

WITHDRAWN

The Johns Hopkins University Press
Baltimore

171352

LIBRARY ST. MARY'S COLLEGE

First published in 1987 by
The Johns Hopkins University Press
701 West 40th Street
Baltimore, Maryland 21211

© 1987 by Simon Hornblower

All rights reserved. No part of this
publication may be reproduced, stored in a
retrieval system, or transmitted, in any
form or by any means, electronic, mechanical,
photocopying, recording or otherwise, without
the prior permission of the publisher.

Library of Congress Cataloging-in-Publication Data

Hornblower, Simon.
Thucydides

Bibliography: p.
Includes index.
1. Thucydides.   2. Greece—Intellectual life—To 146 B.C.   I. Title.
DF229.T6H67.1987   938′.0072024   87-4213
ISBN 0-8018-3529-1

Printed in Great Britain

Contents

Preface

This book had its origin in an Oxford graduate seminar given by Edward Hussey and myself in summer 1981, on 'Thucydides and the Sophists'. With one exception, the papers in that seminar series were given by Hussey or me. The exception was Colin Macleod's 'Thucydides and Tragedy', which has now appeared in Macleod's posthumous *Collected Essays* (see p. ix below). Hussey's own views on the sophists will be developed by him in a book. I should like to thank all those who participated in the discussions, in particular Ewen Bowie, Miriam Griffin, Gregory Hutchinson, Oswyn Murray, Christopher Pelling and the late Tom Stinton (who also helped me by correspondence afterwards). Since 1981, David Lewis, Robert Parker and Richard Rutherford have kindly discussed particular issues with me and supplied me with valuable references.

I subsequently lectured for two years on Thucydides Book i to candidates for Honour Mods (a literary examination) and this clarified my thoughts on many issues.

I am deeply grateful to Hussey and Macleod for all that I have learned from them in different ways about Thucydides, and I should like to dedicate this book to Edward Hussey and to the memory of Colin Macleod.

In the actual writing of the book I incurred two further debts. Jasper Griffin read most of the typescript at the penultimate stage, and the enormously valuable and detailed comments of so accomplished a literary critic led me to rewrite the book, in particular by expanding what was too elliptically put, or by spelling out what was unspoken. But the book's defects remain at my door not his. Victoria Harris has also read, commented on, and much improved all the individual chapters at different times, and for this I am equally grateful; the same exemption clause however applies.

The aim of the book is to place Thucydides in his intellectual setting. There are several general books on Thucydides or on the

Peloponnesian War. There are several other books which treat
Thucydides in relation to a particular aspect of intellectual life.
But there is none, I think, which tries to put him in his
fifth-century intellectual context as a whole, in all its
inchoateness and variety. It is no use my apologising for making
incursions into areas some of which are new to me. According to
Polybius, the Roman writer Aulus Postumius apologised for
writing a history in imperfect Greek idiom and method, on which
Cato the Censor commented that it was like a boxer entering a
boxing-match or the *pankration* and apologising to the
spectators because he could not stand the fatigue or the blows. I
sympathise with Postumius but I agree with Cato.

Oriel College, Oxford   S.H.
15 September 1986

Abbreviations

Abh. = Jacoby, F., *Abhandlungen zur griechische Geschichts-schreibung*, ed. H. Bloch (Leiden 1956).

DK = Diels, H. & Kranz, W. (eds), *Fragmente der Vorsokratiker⁶*, 3 vols (Berlin 1952).

FGrHist = Jacoby, F., *Die Fragmente der griechischen Historiker*, 15 vols (Leiden 1923-1958).

HCT = Gomme, A.W., Andrewes, A. & Dover, K.J., *A Historical Commentary on Thucydides*, 5 vols (Oxford 1945-1981).

HRR = Peter, H., *Historicorum romanorum reliquiae*, 2 vols (Leipzig 1914², 1906).

IG = *Inscriptiones Graecae.*

Macleod = Macleod, C., *Collected Essays* (Oxford 1983).

ML = Meiggs, R. & Lewis, D., *A Selection of Greek Historical Inscriptions to the end of the Fifth Century BC* (Oxford 1969).

OGIS = Dittenberger, W., *Orientis graeci inscriptiones selectae*, 2 vols (Leipzig 1903-1905).

RE = Pauly-Wissowa, *Realencyclopädie der klassische Altertumswissenschaft*, 83 vols.

SEG = *Supplementum Epigraphicum Graecum.*

Strasburger = Strasburger, H., *Studien zur alten Geschichte*, 2 vols, ed. W. Schmitthenner & R. Zoepffel (Hildesheim 1982).

Syll³ = Dittenberger, W., *Sylloge inscriptionum graecarum³*, 4 vols (Leipzig 1915-1924).

Tod = Tod, M.N., *Greek Historical Inscriptions*, 2 vols (Oxford 1946, 1948).

Note on Thucydides' life and book

In the chapters which follow, knowledge is assumed of the information given below, and of the italicised terms; it seems preferable to give this briefly and all at once, rather than either providing a lengthy summary of Thucydides' book or explaining every expression like 'the Melian Dialogue' and where the section so referred to fits in, at the first appearance of the expression.

(i) Life

Thucydides was born in about the 50s of the fifth century BC. His father's name was Oloros, and this is evidence both of royal Thracian descent and of a blood tie with the politician and commander Kimon, whose grandfather's name was also Oloros; also with Pericles' political opponent Thucydides son of Melesias (Wade-Gery, *Essays*, 239ff. On the possibility of a distant relationship to the Pisistratid tyrants, see *HCT* iv 323). Thucydides was thus an aristocrat. Aristocratic values were inculcated in the gymnasia and in the drinking sessions called *sumposia*; for the relevance of this to Thucydides' writing see below, p.29.

Further evidence for the Thracian connexion is provided by Thucydides himself in Book iv (ch. 105) where he mentions that he had mining concessions in Thrace. He was thus a rich man, and this should be remembered when we consider his political opinions in Chapter Seven. He also mentions (ibid.) his political influence in Thrace: on this see below, p.166.

But Thucydides is a Greek name and Thucydides himself was an Athenian citizen. Attica, the territorial and political unit of which Athens city was the capital, was divided into 139 *demes* or constituent villages. These demes were established by the reformer Kleisthenes in the late sixth century, when the Pisistratid tyranny was replaced by a moderate democracy. The demes were of three kinds: city, coastal and inland. We know

1

(below, p.97 n.98) the name of Thucydides' deme: Halimous, a city deme in the 'Kleisthenic' sense but physically on the coast and about four miles from the city; it is roughly where the modern airport is. Many demes are just names to us, but Halimous happens to be a deme we know something about, from a fourth-century speech (Demosthenes 57) which deals with deme politics, specifically a dispute about citizenship rights, a matter regulated at deme level. The picture of Halimous, a 'medium-to-small' size deme, which emerges from the speech, is of an excitable and even quarrelsome community, vocal and politically alive. Unfortunately Halimous also happens to be the deme we know *most* about, so we cannot say for sure how unusual it was in this or any other respect. This is stressed in a recent book by David Whitehead, *The Demes of Attica* (1986), who points out that we cannot know if it was exceptional for demesmen to hold meetings in the city market-place, as the Halimousians do in the speech, rather than at some local venue; nor whether there was a tendency for deme politics to serve as apprenticeship for national politics; Whitehead thinks not. But more distant demes had their own theatres where meetings could happen (like Thorikos); and some demes were surely more boring places than others to grow up in. If we ask why and how Thucydides came to have the intense interest in politics which his writings attest, the early years in Halimous, with its – perhaps – exceptionally close relation to the city, are worth bearing in mind.

When the war began in 431 (see the following section) Thucydides started to write (i 1).

In the early 420s Athens was struck by an appalling plague, which Thucydides caught: ii 48.3. Not only his detailed description of its symptoms, but his fondness for seeing even strictly non-medical matters in medical terms (see below, pp.132, 173), can reasonably be ascribed to a natural amateur interest in a serious illness one has suffered from oneself. The experience was surely (in the vulgar sense) traumatic.

He served as commander or *strategos*, one of ten annually elected officers (below, p.157 n.6), in 424. (This is not likely to have been his first taste of responsibility. For a speculation that he had something to do with the 'purification' of Delos in 426, which he describes at iii 104; see below, p.184.) Military reportage surely affected his style: below, p.40.

As commander Thucydides was unlucky in his Spartan opposite number, the great general Brasidas. In the latter part of Book iv he tells, with remarkable detachment, of his own part in operations in the North Aegean in 424. He failed to relieve the valuable and important city of Amphipolis and was sent into exile in consequence. He says at v 26 that the leisure he now enjoyed (he does not add anything about his private financial means, though these were also surely relevant) enabled him to spend time with the other combatant side in the war, the Peloponnesians.

The second half of Thucydides' life is a biographical blank. The assumption that he remained at least based in Thrace is relevant to a number of the possible intellectual influences discussed in this book: the poet Euripides and Socrates' friend Agathon went to nearby Macedonia in the last decade of the century; another Socratic figure Kritias spent time in Thessaly in Central Greece; Democritus came originally from the Thracian town of Abdera, and was a contemporary of Thucydides. In an important article published in 1985, Edward Hussey has argued, as we shall see (p.129), for a particularly close connexion between the thought of Thucydides and Democritus. Andokides, the Athenian orator disgraced after a scandal in 415, visited Macedon among other places, and was a possible informant about the scandal, and other memorable events of 415, like the Sicily Debate. And it is interesting that Andokides (see D. Macdowell's edition of *On the Mysteries* p.21) wrote prose which hovers between amateurism and professionalism, as Thucydides hovers between the technical and the non-technical (below, p.107). Other Athenians like Konon (below, p.77) could have kept Thucydides in touch with Athenian politics. Finally, the medical writings of the Hippocratic doctors show many contacts with North Greek places like Thasos, which may be relevant to some of the points made below in Chapters Five and Seven. But books were reasonably widely obtainable in this period. Xenophon (*Anab.* vi 5) says that written books (cargoes, presumably: see Cawkwell's Penguin note; rather than the private libraries of sea-captains!) were among the items washed up on the shores of, precisely, Thrace, in about 400 BC, from shipwrecked vessels. The Thracians fought among themselves for such prizes. Thucydides no doubt found easier ways of keeping up with the literature in his subject.

He died around the end of the century or the beginning of the next; see Chapter Six below for a new piece of evidence from Thasos which may show, but probably does not, that he lived several years into the 390s.

(ii) The book

Books i–v 24 deal with the Ten Years War, or *Archidamian War*, of 431-421, between Athens and Sparta (the Peloponnesians were led by Sparta; the whole war – see below, p.7 – of 431-404 is called by convention the *Peloponnesian War*). This section of the whole war ended with the *Peace of Nikias*. The uneasy years 421-415 are dealt with in Book v 25-end; Books vi and vii describe the *Sicilian Expedition*, an invasion by Athens. The rest of the war is sometimes called the *Decelean War* after a fort in Attica, Decelea, which Sparta occupied in 413, or the *Ionian War*, because much of the fighting took place in the eastern part of the Mediterranean off Ionia. Thucydides dealt with only a small part of this final stage, in Book viii.

Book i begins with an authorial preface stating the magnitude of the theme; this is then developed in an amplification (*auxêsis*) called the *Archaeology*, a review of earlier and prehistoric Greek history designed to make the points that no earlier war was of much consequence, and to bring out the importance of sea-power. There follows a *Preface* on method (i 20-23) culminating in a statement of Thucydides' view of the deep cause of the war: see p.30 below, on i 23.6. Particular quarrels over Corcyra and Potidaea are then described (the *Kerkyraika* and the *Potidaiatika*). An important congress at Sparta is given in the form of the *Spartan Tetralogy* of speeches by two Spartans and delegations from Athens and Corinth (i 68ff.). Thucydides describes Athens' growth to a menacing level of power in the *Pentekontaetia* ('Fifty Years', theoretically 480-430, but actually cut short in the early 430s): i 89-117. Some unreasonable diplomatic demands by the two sides enable him to give, in a series of digressions, material about earlier episodes concerning a would-be Athenian tyrant Kylon, the Athenian Themistocles and the Spartan Pausanias. These are the *Pausanias and Themistocles Excursuses* (i 126ff.). Pericles' *First War Speech* ends the book (i 140ff.).

Book ii opens with some more authorial remarks on method

and dating, prompted by the Theban attack on Plataea. Athens' preparations for war enable Thucydides to give antiquarian material about early Athens (ii 15). Pericles delivers the *Funeral Oration* (ii 34ff.) over the war dead of the first year's fighting. Then comes *The Plague* which killed among others Pericles, so after *Pericles' Last Speech* we get *Pericles' Obituary*, a long and exceptionally important chapter (ii 65). Then comes more about Potidaea and Plataea, and some naval fighting by Phormio. The lengthy episode analysed in Chapter Eight below belongs here (429/8).

Book iii begins with the revolt from Athens of Mytilene on the island of Lesbos, causing the *Mytilene Debate* (iii 37ff.) at Athens between the advocate of harshness (Kleon) and his opponent (Diodotus): 427. Plataea is now taken, and we get a *Plataea Debate* in front of Spartan 'judges' (this is no real trial) between Plataeans and Thebans (iii 53ff.) Then comes the *Corcyra Stasis* section which for the purposes of the present book is one of the most important parts of all Thucydides, being sustained comment in his own person (iii 82ff.). '*Stasis*' is the Greek for factional strife. Some Sicilian and Central Greek episodes follow (427-5).

Book iv describes Athenian successes at Pylos in the West Peloponnese in the year 425 which lead to the *Pylos Debate*, a one-sided affair as Thucydides gives it, only the Spartan delegation being given a speech; Kleon (who resists the Spartan peace proposals) is denied one. Campaigning at Megara, Thrace, at Delium on the border between Athens and Boiotia, and the northern campaigning round Amphipolis (see Life, above) occupy much of the rest of the book; but the *Conference at Gela* (iv 58: 424) is a Sicilian episode which should be mentioned.

Book v gives the terms of the Peace of Nikias near the beginning. What immediately follows is some, frankly, rather tedious diplomacy in the Peloponnese, on which see p.139 below. The *Mantinea Campaign* (418) told the Greek world in plain terms that although Sparta had failed to smash up the Athenian Empire and 'liberate' Greece, and in that sense had definitely 'lost' the Archidamian War (see ii 8 for the aim) she was still militarily supreme (v 75). The *Melian Dialogue*, unique in form in all Thucydides, is what its usual description implies, an actual dialogue between Athenian and Melian representatives over the question of whether the island of Melos should submit to Athens

(416): v. 85ff. Wider imperial issues are ventilated (below, p.185).

Books vi and vii are almost entirely devoted to a description, in very high finish, of the *Sicilian Expedition* of 415-413. Passages we shall refer to frequently include the *Sikelika*, an antiquarian introduction (vi 2-5); the *Sicily Debate* at Athens (vi 10-23: Alcibiades and Nikias); a digression (54-59) about Harmodius and Aristogeiton, who killed the Pisistratid Hipparchus in 514 (this is prompted by the scandals of the *Mutilation of the Herms* and the *Profanation of the Mysteries*; see below, p.84. The connection is that Alcibiades was thought to be mixed up with the latter scandal at least, and his 'tyrannical' life-style awoke memories and fears of the Pisistratids.) Sicilian viewpoints are expressed in the *Camarina Debate* (vi 72ff.). Alcibiades, originally an Athenian general but now on the run because of the scandal of the Mysteries, makes a speech at Sparta (vi 89ff.).

Book vii has few speeches, but there is a *Letter of Nikias* to the Assembly at Athens near the beginning (vii 10ff.) which is a kind of speech. The *Fortification of Decelea* in 413 occasions some valuable comment of a financial nature (vii 27-29) by Thucydides, but the non-Sicilian digression ends not on this note but with an atrocious story about the butchering of the inhabitants of a place called Mycalessus in Boiotia, including the boys in a school, by some Thracian mercenaries whom Athens could no longer afford to pay. The Athenians in Sicily fare worse and worse; *Speeches by Nikias* (vii 61ff.; 77ff.) are noteworthy. The *Final Sea-battle* (vii 70-71), an intensely vivid piece of writing, comes in between.

Book viii gives the Athenian reaction to the defeat, and describes revolts in the empire; Persian interest is reported for almost the first time. But the main theme of the book is the oligarchic revolution at Athens, culminating in the coup of 411. Speeches are absent, but there is indirectly quoted comment by Alcibiades at ch.46 and by Phrynichus at ch.48. Valuable Thucydidean comments are at ch.68 (on Antiphon and others) and above all at ch.97, on the less extreme regime which succeeded the 400 oligarchs of 411. This regime is that of the so-called '5000'. Thucydides' narrative breaks off in 411. In ii 65 (see above) he has however anticipated the final Athenian defeat, as also at the important vi 15, a digression about Alcibiades.

Introduction
Thucydides and 'History'

Wars and the administration of public affairs, says Gibbon (ch. 9), are the principal subjects of history. This is a narrow definition, though many would still subscribe to it. The man most responsible for the view of history which it implies is a historian who in his work never uses the words 'history' or 'historian' (*historia* and *historikos*) at all.

Thucydides, as we have seen, wrote only one work, an unfinished account in eight books, breaking off in 411 BC, of the war of 431-404 BC between Athens and the Spartan-led Peloponnesian League. We call it the 'Peloponnesian War' because we see it from the Athenian point of view. (Thucydides was an Athenian, and, bias apart, he simply knew more about Athens than about Sparta; cf. v 68 for the difficulty of finding out about Sparta.) Arnold Toynbee correctly but cumbersomely called the war the 'Atheno-Peloponnesian War'; Thucydides has no one name for it: Toynbee-like, he refers to it on his first page as the war of the Athenians and Peloponnesians, but equally he can call it the war against the Athenians, or against the Spartans, depending on the context.[1]

So although, for instance, Crawley's admirable Everyman translation purports to be of a work called *The History of the Peloponnesian War*, neither 'History' nor 'Peloponnesian War' have any Thucydidean authority. This reminds us that Thucydides did not label his own work. It is we who have to do that, and we cannot answer the question 'What was Thucydides doing?' by saying 'He was a historian and so must have behaved in such-and-such a way'. That Thucydides did not call the Peloponnesian War by that name does not matter very much

[1] A.J. Toynbee, *Hannibal's Legacy* i, Oxford 1965, 1. For Thucydides' own usage see G.E.M. de Ste Croix, *The Origins of the Peloponnesian War*, London 1972, 294f.

except that it reminds us that there is no label on the work; that he did not call his work a 'history' matters very much indeed. It means that we have no easy clue as to the kind of enterprise he thought he was engaged in.

The verb *historein* simply meant 'to enquire', and naturally Thucydides has to express the thought 'inquire' sometimes. For his researches into early Greece he uses the word which means 'find', and for the contemporary narrative he uses the group of words which means simply 'collecting things and writing them down'. The standard Greek lexicon gives the meaning of the relevant noun as 'one who collects and writes down historic facts, historian'.[2] But we must disregard the words 'historic' and 'historian' in that definition, if we are interested in how Thucydides saw his task, because if one thing is certain it is that when Thucydides said that he collected and wrote things down, he did not know that this made him a historian. Why not? Because the words 'historian' or 'history' did not yet exist, as technical expressions for what Thucydides was doing.

Why does Thucydides avoid words formed from *historein*, 'to inquire'? Perhaps because of its associations with Herodotus, in many respects his only prose predecessor; their relation is treated further below. Thucydides certainly wished to distance himself in formal ways from Herodotus, to whom he owed so much. Perhaps the word *historia* meant 'Herodotus' and so was unacceptable.

But this is not very satisfactory. The real reason for Thucydides' avoidance of *historia* as a description of his own activity is surely that the word was not yet completely technical. Herodotus' opening sentence uses the word: 'This is the

---

[2] 'Finding' for early Greece (*heuriskô*): see, for example, i 20. 'Collecting' (from root *sungraphô*): this word had probably already been used, to describe his own writings, by the Sicilian writer Antiochus of Syracuse, who lived in the second half of the fifth century BC: see *FGrHist* 555 F1. However, it is not quite certain that this was Antiochus' own title, if indeed he had one, and the same is true of Hellanicus, whose *Attikê sungraphê*, or 'Athenian collection', was known to Thucydides, *FGrHist* 323 T8=Thuc. i 97. The lexicon referred to in the text is LSJ⁹. H.D.F. Kitto, *Poiesis*, London 1966, 352 translates *sungrapheus* as 'compiler'; see also Adam Parry, *Logos and Ergon in Thucydides*, New York 1981 (Harvard diss.1957), 94: 'marshalled the sundry facts of the war and composed them into a meaningful whole.' W.R. Connor, 'Thucydides', in *Ancient Writers*, ed. T. Luce, New York, 1982, 278, says *sungrapho* is 'never a word for writing poetry or elevated prose but for technical discussions, manuals, drafts and analyses'.

setting-forth of my *inquiry*.' There is another, often neglected, occurrence of *historia* in Herodotus which is much closer to the modern word 'history'. In Book vii we are told 'the men who served with the fleet and those who served with the army had their own native officers, but I do not mention them for I am not constrained to do so for the *logos* of my *historia*'.[3] Here the word *historia* is, we may say, travelling towards technicality: history, we think, is selective and Herodotus here says just that.

For us, history-writing is only one kind of literary activity among many. But at the time when Thucydides was writing far fewer literary genres existed, and indeed prose of any kind was recent. Most of the formal literary activity before the fifth century had been poetic (a term which admittedly included didactic, informative writing like the works of Hesiod, as well as writing intended for entertainment). It was natural for thinkers of a more self-conscious age, like the fifth and fourth centuries, to approach the problem of literary categorisation by asking in the first place how far non-poetic activity differed from poetic. For Thucydides 'the poets' form a definite group from whom he distances himself by the words 'what the poets have to say [about the Cyclops and the Laestrygonians] must suffice'.[4]

But it was Aristotle who distinguished firmly and for the first time between the specific, technical word 'historian', a coinage of his own, and the word 'poet'. He says that history covers particulars, while poetry, which is more serious and philosophical than history, covers what is generally true: history is what Alcibiades did and suffered. This distinction is odd because it

[3] vii 96. How and Wells in their commentary translate the last words as 'for the purpose of my history', and they comment: 'Here only in H[erodotus] does *historia* bear the meaning history which later became common'. However they refer to another view which would 'avoid this': '... Macan would translate "I am not compelled by the necessity of my argument to give any account of my inquiries on that head".' That gives a better sense to *logos*, which is even more difficult to translate than *historia*. E. Powell, *Lexicon to Herodotus*, s.v. *logos* 5 (f), tentatively takes *es historiês logon* to mean 'to make up the tally, total, of my *historia*', and takes *historia*, in the entry under that word, to mean here 'results of inquiry'. (Note: in this discussion I have always written *historia* rather than the dialect form *historiê*, which is what Herodotus actually used.)

[4] Prose recent: F. Millar, *Sources for Ancient History*, ed. M. Crawford, 1983, 90 points out that 'the Athenian decree relating to Chalkis of (probably) the 440s [ML 52] remains the earliest documentarily attested piece of continuous Attic prose'. Cyclops, etc.: Thuc.vi 2.1. For different attitudes to poetry (entertainment, instruction) see now P. Hardie, *Virgil's Aeneid: Cosmos and Imperium*, 1986, 6-32. The *Frogs* of Aristophanes explores this issue.

implies that the historian does not generalise, which if true would mean that the historian does not select either (because generalisation is by definition selective: it does not seek to do justice to all instances but to extract or select common factors).[5]

Did Aristotle have Thucydides specifically in mind? If so, his criticism is unjust because Thucydides did concern himself with what is 'true for the most part'.[6] Thus it has been said of the siege of Plataea that the events are 'merely what happened, *ha egeneto* as Aristotle would say; but Thucydides' method of narrating them puts the whole story, a historically true story, into the category of "the generally true, what might happen" '.[7] Aristotle was no doubt thinking of the Thucydides who recorded such details as the fact that Teisamenos of Trachis was the name of an ambassador, or that Proxenos son of Kapaton was the commander of the Lokrians.[8] Gomme, the great commentator on Thucydides, calls the latter 'an extreme case of the unimportant note made at the time and now preserved in the narrative'. 'Extreme case' is right, but we need not follow Gomme in thinking that such trivia would have disappeared in some hypothetical finished version; it is better just to accept that the view of Thucydides as a writer who 'ignores everything adventitious' is simply wrong.[9]

The conclusion must be that Thucydides conforms only partly to Aristotle's idea of a 'historian'; other parts of his work look more like 'poetry'. The Aristotelian word 'historian' and the concept behind it were slow to develop, and slow to catch on even after they had been thought of. We saw that by the time

[5] Aristotle, *Poetics* 1451a36ff.

[6] G.E.M. de Ste Croix in *The Ancient Historian and his Materials, Studies in Honour of C.E. Stevens*, ed. B. Levick, London 1975, at 45ff. 'Aristotle on history and poetry ...'. See also K. von Fritz, *Griechische Geschichtsschreibung* i, Berlin 1967, 5f., S. Halliwell, *Aristotle's Poetics*, 1986, 145, n.13, cf.106, n.39 and S. Clark, *Aristotle's Man*, 1975, 130ff.

[7] Gomme on iii 67 at 354f.; id., *The Greek Attitude to Poetry and History*, Berkeley 1954, ch.vi.

[8] iii 92.2;103.3. Thucydides' use of patronymics seems fairly arbitrary (Griffith, *PCPhS* 187, 1961, 21ff). His avoidance of demotics by contrast is surely studied: see below, p.97 n.98.

[9] Gomme on iii 103; adventitious: J. de Romilly, *Histoire et Raison chez Thucydide*, Paris 1956, 47. Kitto, *Poiesis*, uses vi 95, a passage rich in apparently inconsequential detail, to show what Aristotle meant, and to demonstrate that he may indeed have had Thucydides in particular in mind, for all that nobody could be more serious and philosophical than Thucydides. (Kitto's 'v.95' is a misprint.)

Herodotus wrote his Book vii the word had travelled some way towards its modern sense, but Thucydides did nothing to advance it. Nor did his successors, Xenophon and the other fourth-century writers, including the authors of monographs on Alexander the Great.[10] The first cast-iron use, after Aristotle, of *historiai*, 'histories', in the technical sense is in *OGIS* 13, an inscription in the Ashmolean Museum in Oxford. It is a letter of Lysimachus, one of the Successors of Alexander the Great, to the citizens of Samos, about some territory disputed between Samos and Priene. The date is perhaps the 280s BC. At line 12, Lysimachus writes that the people of Priene have shown 'from the histories and other evidence and documents ...' that Batinetis belongs to them.[11] There are references from the late fourth and early third centuries to 'Histories' as part of the titles of works by 'fragmentary' historians – that is, historians whose works survive only in quotations by later writers (for example, 'as so-and-so says in the eighth book of his histories'), but often it is difficult to be sure whether the word 'history' or 'histories' was part of the title given by the original writer, or has been foisted on him by the writer quoting him. Only with Phylarchus in the late third century do we reach certainty.[12] The remarkable

[10] Xenophon wrote a *Hellenica* ('Greek Affairs'); Theopompus' *Philippika* was the first book to centre on an individual, Philip of Macedon, but it was a general history not a biography. Kallisthenes wrote a *Hellenika*, then a *Deeds of Alexander*. Anaximenes, *FGrHist* 72 F2 and 9, wrote 'first histories', whatever *that* means, and perhaps 'histories of Philip'. But he may be later than, and perhaps influenced by, Aristotle. The authors of monographs about Alexander tend to speak of their writings as 'about Alexander' or as 'deeds' of Alexander (though Kleitarchos may have written 'histories about Alexander', *FGrHist* 137 F1). See L. Pearson, *Lost Histories of Alexander the Great*, 1960, with discussions of titles of Alexander-monographs, and for Anaximenes see J. Hornblower, *Hieronymus of Cardia*, Oxford 1981, 79.

[11] =Welles, *Royal Correspondence of the Hellenistic Period*, Yale 1934, no.7. On citation of historians in such disputes, see M.N. Tod, *International Arbitration amongst the Greeks*, Oxford 1913, 134ff., pointing out the long tradition behind such arguments, which goes back to Solon's appeal to Homer, *Iliad* ii, in support of Athens' claim to Salamis. The only thing which is new about *OGIS* 13 is that such appeals are *called* appeals to 'history'. Solon would probably have said he was basing himself on 'history' had the word been available to him.

[12] Duris of Samos, in the early third century BC, is sometimes (*FGrHist* 76 F1, 10, 12) quoted by the book-numbers of his 'histories', but sometimes (e.g. F11) by the book-numbers of his 'Macedonian affairs' – but they are the same work. It is uncertain whether the great early Hellenistic historian Hieronymus of Cardia included the word 'histories' in his title: J. Hornblower, op.cit., 76. Other writers

conclusion must be that it is not until then that *historia* and *historikos* become the absolutely standard words for what we call 'history' and 'historian', and that Aristotle was indeed coining a term, not describing established usage. We should not be surprised to find Thucydides hard to categorise.

---

soon after Aristotle to whom 'Histories' are attributed are Eumelos (*FGrHist* 77 F1), Eudoxus of Rhodes (79 F1) and Pythermos of Ephesus (80 F1); all these writers are third-century, but we know very little about them. Phylarchus is a more considerable figure, a source for Polybius and Plutarch. His 'fragments' are far more numerous than any of the writers so far mentioned except Duris, whose title, as we saw, is doubtful; there is less doubt about Phylarchus, since of the 85 fragments (46 of them with book-numbers or attributable with confidence to particular books) all those (24) which do mention a title give it as 'Histories' (cf. e.g. *FGrHist* 81 F3); others just say, for instance, 'Phylarchus in his 28th book says'; cf. F46. Polybius in the second century, the first major Hellenistic historian to survive in bulk, uses the word 'history' in the Aristotelian sense at i 1 and i 57.

CHAPTER ONE

Thucydides and Herodotus

In the Introduction, we saw that it is impossible to put a simple literary label on Thucydides' work which he himself would have understood and accepted and say 'This is what he thought he was'. *We* call him a historian, but he did not call himself one. Rather than put a label on him, it may be more profitable to examine his relation to his only fully surviving predecessor, Herodotus. That, in a way, merely pushes the problem a stage further back, because Herodotus' own aims, and the question whether he was in our sense a historian, have recently been the subject of dispute.[1] But first we must try briefly to characterise Herodotus and his work.

Herodotus was a native of Halikarnassos in South-West Asia Minor, who travelled extensively in the Mediterranean area and visited parts of the Persian empire, including Egypt, in the middle of the fifth century BC. He spent some time in Athens and emigrated to the Athenian colony of Thurii in Italy, which had been founded by Athens in 443. We do not know exactly when he died but his work shows knowledge of events of the 420s. Herodotus described what he had seen and learnt in a long and chatty prose narrative, which leads up to an account in three 'books' (i.e. subdivisions) of the Persian king Xerxes' invasion of Greece in 480-79, preceded by nearly two books about the revolt of the Ionian Greeks from Persia in the 490s and the Marathon campaign of 490 in Greece proper. The theme of his first four books is the build-up of Persian power; this theme is developed by means of lengthy and sometimes self-contained treatments (*logoi*) of particular states, countries or races such as Lydia, Egypt, Scythia or Cyrene. This technique of ethnographic digression is most noticeable in these four books, but even the

---

[1] See esp. D. Fehling, *Die Quellenangaben bei Herodot*, Berlin 1971.

later books contain such material, folded into the narrative. So for instance a section of Book vi describes the peculiarities and prerogatives of Spartan kingship, and Book viii has mythical material about early Macedonia. Clearly, then, Herodotus included much that is only distantly relevant to the short period of actual military collision between Greece and Persia, a striking difference from Thucydides, whose narrative is more strictly linear. Another striking difference is the kind of human action which Herodotus likes to describe. In particular, *women* play a much larger part in Herodotus than in the single-sex world of Thucydides. This – since women in ancient Greece were mostly non-combatants (as they still are nowadays) and rarely exercised direct political power or influence (as they do now) – means that Herodotus' handling of war and politics is less austere than Thucydides' since it takes in more of the personal and emotional background. It is also relevant that Herodotus, as we have seen, has more to say than Thucydides about barbarian places, where women's role was less circumscribed. For instance, the queen of Herodotus' own city of Halikarnassos was Artemisia, whose energy at the battle of Salamis made Xerxes exclaim, 'My men have become women and my women men'.[2] Since the dates of Herodotus and Thucydides are so close, the difference of handling must be due to differences of outlook and subject-matter, rather than to a difference in the periods in which the two men lived. Indeed there are hints even in Herodotus that women belonged in the home, where Thucydides and Thucydidean speakers were to put them. Here is a passage from Book iv which illustrates these two features of Herodotus: it gives the more personal and more female flavour of his writing, but it also betrays awareness that behaviour of the Artemisia type was by Greek standards highly abnormal. It concerns Pheretima the mother of the sixth-century king Arkesilas II of Cyrene. (The detailed context is not important for my present purpose).

> Pheretima went to the court of Euelthon [ruler of the Cypriot town of Salamis] and asked for an army to put the party she represented back in power at Cyrene; but, as it happened, an army was the one thing Euelthon was unwilling to give her. Other things he gave her generously enough, and each time she accepted a present she said it was a fine one, but not so fine as to give her

[2] viii 88.3.

what she really wanted – an army. As she continued on every occasion to make the same remark, Euelthon ended by sending her a golden spindle and distaff, with wool on it. Pheretima repeated the same words as before, which drew from Euelthon the reply that he had sent her a present which, unlike an army, he thought suitable to her sex.

It would be hard to find a parallel passage in Thucydides. True, neither Cyrene nor Cyprus were wholly Greek (they contained strong Berber and Semitic infusions respectively). Nor was Halikarnassos, or therefore Herodotus, wholly Greek: there was a Karian element, to which his father Lyxes belonged – to judge from his name which, unlike his mother's, Rhoio ('pomegranate'), was un-Greek. It is true also that the point of this part of the story is that Pheretima is being rebuked for unwomanly aspirations – but Herodotus goes on to tell how she ran Cyrene on her son's behalf, and in his absence, after his return to power; how she fled to Egypt on his death; and how she eventually got an army from the Persian satrap of Egypt, who was glad of the pretext because he wanted to subdue Libya anyway.[3] In Thucydides we could point to a passage in the excursus about Themistocles' flight in Book i: Themistocles was taken in by the wife of Admetus, king of the Molossians, who told him to take her child and sit by the hearth (a symbolic act of supplication) until her husband returned.[4] But that whole section is unique in Thucydides for its 'Herodotean' character and was probably written early (see below, p.26). The whole texture of the Pheretima episode is different: if Thucydides had decided that the Persians had really always wished to subdue Libya, he would have dispensed with the 'pretext' which Pheretima represented, just as he dispensed with the popular story which explained the Peloponnesian War in terms of Pericles' mistress Aspasia, once he had decided that the true cause of that war was Athenian expansionism.

These differences are obvious on the most superficial reading of the two writers. My main purpose in this chapter is to explore

---

[3] iv 162ff. At ix 109.3 an army is said to be a thoroughly Persian present (Xerxes there offers one to a girl to whom he has taken a fancy).

[4] Thuc. i 136-7. The similarity with the *Telephus* was remarked on by Wilamowitz-Moellendorff, *Griechisches Lesebuch*, Berlin 1902, 1 (ii), 31 – rightly, although Gomme, who noted the parallel independently, was more struck by the differences (Admetus' son is not a hostage).

other and subtler debts and divergences. Yet these elementary differences of approach – of attitudes to ethnography, barbarians and women – are too important to be taken for granted. (Incidentally no facile *explanation* of the difference is possible. That Herodotus was only partially Greek is true; but Thucydides, as we have seen, probably had royal Thracian blood. That at least is the obvious inference from his father's name Olorus).

One of my objects in this book (see especially Chapter Five) is to discuss the relation between the thought of Thucydides and that of his contemporaries, the 'pre-Socratic' thinkers, understanding 'thinkers' in the broadest sense (i.e. doctors and orators as well as philosophers). Herodotus deserves a place in any such assessment. He has been called the only fully surviving pre-Socratic, and there are frequent signs that he was alert to the intellectual movements of the third quarter of the fifth century, in particular to the habit of dialectical arguing and of treating debate as a 'contest like a political or a legal *agon*' or duel. The most obvious passage in Herodotus that illustrates this tendency to proceed 'dialectically' is the 'debate on the constitutions', which is set in the late sixth century and purports to be a debate, held in Persia, on the merits of monarchy, oligarchy and democracy. It is obviously influenced by the professional techniques of speaking which are basic to the meaning of the word 'sophist'. We do not however have to deny that Persian informants of Herodotus could have told him that something of the kind happened: in a later book he is emphatic that some such concept as 'democracy' was known in Persian circles (he is specifically replying to those who scoffed at the idea that such a debate could have taken place), and fifth-century hellenised Anatolian Persians may indeed have known something of Greek political language. But his debt here to the sophists remains certain.[5]

[5] Dialectical contests: see G.E.R. Lloyd, *Magic, Reason and Experience*, Cambridge 1978. The quotation is from his p.267. (See also his *Polarity and Analogy*, 1966.) The debate on the constitutions: (iii 80ff.; cf. vi 43): Lloyd, 244; see also M. Ostwald, *Nomos and the Beginnings of Athenian Democracy*, Oxford 1969, 179; G.E.M. de Ste Croix, *Greece and Rome* xxiv, 1977, 130ff. 'Herodotus' at 134. 'Sophist': Edward Hussey, *The Presocratics*, London 1972, 115 and generally G.B. Kerferd, *The Sophistic Movement*, Cambridge 1981. Hellenised Persians: A. Momigliano, 'Persian empire and Greek freedom' in *The Idea of Freedom, Essays in Honour of Sir Isaiah Berlin*, Oxford 1979, 139ff.

Assessing Thucydides' debt to Herodotus is not easy, not least because we must distinguish between different parts of Herodotus. The earlier books are much richer in elements of folk-lore. In Book i, for instance, the boyhood of Cyrus the Great is pure fairy-tale: the baby is saved from execution because a shepherd's wife takes pity on him and substitutes him for her own dead infant, but as he grows up the boy reveals his kingly nature by his masterful behaviour at playtime. Or there is the tale of Arion, who jumped overboard to escape some murderous sailors and was rescued on the back of a dolphin. These stories continue through the earlier books: in Book iii Polykrates tries to get rid of some of his good luck by throwing his ring into the sea, but it is returned to him in the belly of a fish – a story also found in *Sinbad the Sailor*. Most obviously akin to folk-lore is the story of the infant Cypselus, the future tyrant of Corinth, who as a baby was concealed in a chest, not unlike the infant Moses in the bull-rushes in the second chapter of Exodus.[6] Comparable 'foundling' or child-concealment stories were told of Perseus, Romulus and Remus, and Sargon of Akkad.[7] This kind of thing is undoubtedly part of what Thucydides had in mind when he said, 'My own work may seem less enjoyable because of the absence of any element of romance' (*muthôdes*, from the word for 'myth'). It has led some modern scholars to regard Herodotus as nothing more than a Baron Münchhausen or Gulliver, telling mendacious stories of distant travel and of elaborate interrogation of native informants. Of course it is disturbing, because it makes us question his veracity, to find Herodotus echoing the Bible, or *Sinbad the Sailor* (which goes back a long way).[8]

Herodotus also seems to have adopted peculiar rules when acknowledging his sources of information: his attributions get more roundabout the further he is from the Mediterranean,[9] and we should (it is said) be correspondingly and progressively on our

[6] Hdt.i 114ff., 23ff.; iii 41ff.; v 92;

[7] O. Murray, *Early Greece*, London 1980, 143.

[8] Thuc. i 22. Mendacity: Fehling, op.cit.; see also O.K. Armayor, *HSCP* lxxxii, 1978, 45ff. 'Did Herodotus ever go to the Black Sea?'. Bible echoed: in a paper delivered to the Oxford Philological Society in 1981, A.H. Griffiths drew attention to some biblical parallels to stories in Herodotus (e.g. Abimelech and Arkesilas of Cyrene are both barricaded in houses and burnt to death). See already W. Aly, *Volksmärchen, Sage und Novelle bei Herodot und seine Zeitgenossen*, Göttingen 1921.

[9] See Fehling, pp.74ff.

guard. Other scholars have noticed that there is 'ring composition' in Herodotus. For instance, the story of Kandaules' wife near the beginning of Book i balances the story of Masistes' near the end of Book ix: both are stories of adulterous sexual attraction, and both end with the violent death of the husband.[10] Again, there is the problem of recurring formulae: thematic repetition of this sort does not prove the stories false, but it arouses suspicion. Nevertheless there are reasons for refusing to go all the way with Herodotus' more extreme recent critics. First, and most important, the difficulty about the view of Herodotus as a man who was unconcerned with truth as opposed to myth, and who did not attach special importance to knowledge as opposed to untested belief, is that it ignores the definite 'change of gear' after the first four chapters of Book i. In those chapters Herodotus reports the mythical abductions of Io (by some Phoenician sailors), Europa and Medea (by Greeks) and Helen of Sparta (by the Trojan Paris). He then says that that is what the Persians and Phoenicians say but *he* is not going to say whether that is how it was or not, but will 'speak what [he] know[s]' about the first acts of aggression committed against the Greeks. This sentence, it has been justly said, marks the creation of a historical work in our sense, in that it limits the historical narrative to historical time.[11]

To this, two objections can be made. First, it can be said that Herodotus' own practice makes it impossible to see him as making a break with the technique of myth: does he not continue a moment later in Book i to describe the fate of Croesus' son Atys, a story with strong folk-lore elements? (Croesus dreams that his son will be killed with an iron spear, but decides that it is safe to send him out on a boar-hunt; the son is killed, not by the boar but by an inaccurate spear-cast. The unwilling killer is a polluted murderer to whom Croesus had given refuge).[12] Second, it can be said that

---

[10] Hdt.i 8ff.; ix 108ff., discussed by Griffiths, op.cit.

[11] Hdt.i 5, emphasised by F. Jacoby in the greatest modern treatment of Herodotus, the long article in Pauly-Wissowa; the view of Herodotus I accept is that of Jacoby. On i 5 see *RE* supp.ii, col.335. Contrast A. Momigliano, *Studies in Historiography*, London 1966, 130 who comes close to making the same claim for *Thucydides*: 'With Herodotus history became primarily political history and was confined to contemporary events.' The first half of this sentence seems to me truer than the second. On Hdt.i 5 see now M. Lloyd, *Liverpool Classical Monthly* ix, 1984, 11.

[12] Hdt.i 34ff. Cf. How and Wells i, 71: 'The interest of the story, from the historical point of view, is that H. (or his informants) has introduced a cult-myth [that of the vegetation-god Atys] into history.' How and Wells lean heavily on

Herodotus' statement of method ('speaking what he knows') is not very different from poets who claim that 'my' version of a myth is more reliable than anybody else's. Thus Bacchylides can say that the 'safest' thing to believe about Io is as follows ...; and Pindar's First Olympian similarly prefers one version of a myth to another.[13]

Of these objections, the first is the less serious: that Herodotus does not wholly succeed in eliminating the element of the 'mythical' from his narrative does not reduce the significance of his attempt, and anyway, as we shall see, that mythical element diminishes progressively through the nine books. (And note that even Thucydides is not always as sceptically alert as we might have expected: see below, p.23f.)

The second objection is more interesting, and could be expanded to take in fields of intellectual activity other than poetry. The most obvious parallel to Herodotus' announcement is the famous first fragment of the geographer and mythographer Hecataeus of Miletus, Herodotus' only serious predecessor:[14]

J.G. Frazer here, an unfashionable figure today – but the same precise point is made as recently as the second (1961) edition of Nilsson's *Geschichte der griechischen Religion* ii, 643, discussing the Atys cult, and referring to this Herodotus passage.

[13] I owe the point about the poets to correspondence with the late T.C.W. Stinton. See Bacchylides xix 37ff.; Pindar, *Ol.*i 53ff. Note also Adam Parry, op.cit., 30ff., esp.33, on Pindar, *Nem.* iv, vii, viii, observing that, for Pindar, it is his own superior language and thought which discerns truth from myth. This is a valuable point, even if it be allowed that *alêthes*, 'true', only slowly came to have that meaning as opposed to 'not forgotten' (see Strasburger, p.1074 with references; M. Detienne, *Les maîtres de vérité dans la Grèce archaique*, Paris 1973, 48; P. Veyne, *Les Grecs ont-ils cru à leurs mythes?*, Paris 1983, with review by J. Griffin, *TLS* 22 April 1983). In other words, poetic claims to *alêtheia* may once have meant no more than Herodotus' declared intention, in his opening sentence, not to let great deeds fall into oblivion.

[14] I do not accept the position of R. Drews, *Greek Accounts of Eastern History*, Cambridge Mass. 1973, who seeks to identify 'Herodotuses before Herodotus', as Jacoby put it. Charon of Lampsacus (*FGrHist* 262) probably wrote at the end of the fifth century, as Jacoby showed (*Abh.* 178ff.; von Fritz i, 519ff.): Charon's interest in Sparta and her institutions points to a date after the Spartan victory at the end of the Peloponnesian War. Dionysius of Miletus gives the name of one of the Magi in a less authentically Iranian form than does Herodotus (Panxouthes rather than Herodotus' Patizeithes: *FGrHist* 687 F2), which suggests that Dionysius is parasitical on Herodotus, i.e. trying to improve on him. As for Hellanicus, we are expressly told (*FGrHist* 4 F72) that his 'Barbarian Customs' was a re-hash of Damastes of Sigeum and Herodotus. So it does not look as if the Persian empire had attracted attention in a serious way before Herodotus. See Pritchett, *Dionysius*, comm. on ch. 5, for criticisms of Jacoby.

'Hecataeus of Miletus speaks thus: I write what seems to me to be true; for the accounts of the Greeks are various and foolish, in my opinion.'[15] But the same aggressive claims to knowledge are found in treatises whose contents are in other respects remote indeed from either Herodotus or Hecataeus. Greek science generally, and Greek medicine in particular, was combative and polemical, with many debts and resemblances to rhetoric: 'the Hippocratic doctor' it has been said, 'sometimes found himself in a competitive situation that tested his skills in debate.'[16] The Hippocratic treatise *On the Nature of Man* declares: 'I am not going to assert that man is all air, or fire or water, or earth or anything else that is not a manifest constituent of man. But I leave such matters to those who wish to speak about them ...' (It proceeds to say that if a person knows the truth and sets it forth correctly his views should prevail).[17] The similarity to Herodotus and Hecataeus is clear.

Yet the claims of the doctors to know better than their opponents are ill-founded. Even when those opponents are (not other doctors but) the religious school of thought that held that epilepsy was a 'sacred' disease, the doctors' polemic against charlatanry, etc., is more impressive than their own diagnosis or their positive suggestions for cure.[18]

Should we then interpret the polemical utterances of Hecataeus and Herodotus (not to mention Thucydides: see below, p.205) against this background? That is, do they belong merely with the denunciations of charlatans and rivals which are characteristic of a competitive society, prone to judge by oral, dialectical success? To some extent, yes. But there is more to be said. 'Story-tellers, to be sure, rival one another as story-tellers: but they do not seek to be judged according to whether they produce an account of the subjects they deal with that is better in the sense of having stronger arguments or evidence to support its claims as truth.'[19] That is illuminating, although we may feel that Pindar, Bacchylides and Hecataeus on the one hand and Herodotus on the other are rather joined by a bridge than separated by a chasm, the bridge being precisely the decision to

---

[15] *FGrHist* 1 F1.
[16] Lloyd, *Magic*, 92.
[17] para. 1.
[18] Lloyd, *Magic*, 21.
[19] ib., 233.

submit our material to a testing operation. 'He first pays lip service to the mythologists, relating the old legends to the feud between East and West, the story of rape and counter-rape, the seizure of Io, Helen, and Medea; but he quickly passes on to knowledge that he can personally control'.[20] The poets, in fact, may say 'Don't believe *p*, believe *q*', but Herodotus says, 'I won't say whether the Io and Helen myths are true or not'. Modern philosophers speak of propositions as having 'truth-functions'; we might paraphrase and modernise Herodotus here by saying that for him myths lack a truth-function, in that it is not sensible to try to say if they are true or not: you cannot check or 'control' them, by sight and hearing.[21] The doctors perhaps belong half-way across the bridge between Herodotus and the poets: they have the concept of experimental checking, but they are prone to offer dogmatic and argumentative assertion instead.[22] Herodotus, by contrast, takes as his starting-date roughly 546 BC, the time when Croesus' activities impinged on the 'sight and hearing' of Greeks whom he, Herodotus, could question. 'How old were you when the Mede came?' was a familiar question, according to Xenophanes of Colophon;[23] the 'coming of the Mede' (i.e. the Persian takeover of Asia Minor and the overthrow of Croesus of Lydia by Cyrus the Great) was indeed the point from which a new sort of checkable operation could be performed, the claim being to 'write accurately'.[24] Herodotus' announcement that he would 'say what he knew' did, I conclude, mark an important change of approach.

My second reason for rejecting the view of Herodotus as a teller of fairy-tales is that it draws strength from the more remote and anecdotal, i.e. the earlier, books; in the period from the Ionian Revolt onwards (Books v to ix) there is much less to object to. True, the story of the 'man with the tattooed head' looks fabulous. (This was a slave sent by Histiaeus, the instigator of the revolt, to Aristagoras, the ruler of Miletus. A message was

[20] R. Meiggs, 'Herodotus', *History Today* November 1957, 729ff. (an excellent article), at 738.

[21] Hdt.ii 29.1; 99.1 for sight (*opsis*) and hearing (*akoē*).

[22] Cf. too Holladay and Poole, *CQ* xxix, 1979, 282ff. 'Thucydides and the Plague of Athens' (with *CQ* 1982, 235 and 1984, 483), arguing that the doctors were actually less respectful of empirical data than was Thucydides. But see below, p.134.

[23] DK 21 B 22.

[24] Cf. Hdt. vi 14 for this phrase (*atrekeōs sungrapsai*).

pricked on the slave's scalp, and the slave's instructions were merely to tell Aristagoras to shave his head and look at what was beneath.)[25] And it has been shrewdly noticed that Histiaeus himself has a family resemblance to the Odysseus-like trickster folk-hero. (Themistocles is another.)[26] But the battle of Plataia, say, in Book ix, is hardly in the same category as Polykrates and his ring or the baby Cypselus in his chest.

A third reason for keeping to the traditional picture of Herodotus is that the 'fairy-tale' alternative 'makes Thucydides too much of an innovator'.[27] If Herodotus was engaged on such a mendacious enterprise, where and how did Thucydides get the idea of making truthful statements about the recent past? A related point is that we are in danger of proving too much if we assume that parallels between Herodotus and older literatures like the Bible undermine the truth of Herodotus (because he might be thought to have picked up the stories somehow). Thucydides himself is capable of including stories of the 'roving anecdote' type (see below). Such stories, attributed to different individuals in different versions, are a problem familiar to modern historians of the ancient world.[28] Thus if you are interested in Lysander's unscrupulousness you will want to use the story in Plutarch that he said that dice were for cheating boys and oaths for cheating men. But the usefulness of the story is much reduced when we find the remark attributed also to others.[29] Should we try to decide whether to use it of Lysander or someone else? Or should we avoid using it at all? Similarly, there is the story of the old woman who says to a king who tells her he hasn't time to read her petition, 'then stop being a king'. This story was told of Philip II of Macedon, Antipater, Demetrius Poliorcetes and the Emperor Hadrian.[30] (It is not just an ancient problem: Vasari tells us the famous story of Columbus' egg – but he tells it of Giotto!) Another example: in Thucydides Book vi

[25] Hdt. v 35.
[26] See O. Murray, *CAH* iv² (ch. on Ionian Revolt) for the tattooed slave (cf. too Jacoby, *RE* supp.ii, col.441) and for Histiaeus as trickster.
[27] As K.J. Dover remarked in 1981, commenting on a paper given by Fehling in Oxford.
[28] Livy's echoes of early Greek history are specially awkward: see below.
[29] Plut. *Lys.* viii, used for example by D.M. Lewis, *Sparta and Persia*, Leiden 1977, 152. But see R. Parker, *Miasma*, Oxford 1983, 187, n.237.
[30] See Fergus Millar, *The Emperor in the Roman World*, London 1977, 3 with refs.

we read that the inhabitants of Sicilian Segesta passed expensive dinner-plate from house to house in order to give some visiting Athenian ambassadors the impression that Segestan resources were greater than they really were. This resembles the story in Herodotus about the Persian satrap Oroites who filled up chests with stones, putting only a layer of gold on top, and it is found also in a completely different context in Nepos' *Life of Hannibal*.[31] What should we conclude from Thucydides' use of such a tale? Not, surely, that it was necessarily false, but that if literature imitates life, life can often imitate literature.[32] In other words, perhaps the Segestans did indeed do as Thucydides says, but perhaps they were not the first to do so either.[33] Modern scholars may also employ such stories to symbolise important truths; for instance the angry old woman (above) has been used to introduce a book about Roman emperors – to make the point that reading petitions was seen as an essential part of a ruler's duties in antiquity.[34] Similarly we can use the parallels between the fall of Tarquin the Proud, the last king of Rome, and that of the Pisistratid tyranny at Athens as Livy's way of making a general point about tyranny: at Athens as at Rome, the fall of the tyranny was shortly preceded by a sexual scandal provoking general outrage against the ruler or his family.[35]

So neither in Herodotus nor in Thucydides should the presence

[31] Thuc. vi 46; Hdt. iii 123; Nep. *Hann*. ix.

[32] Otherwise, what was the point of collections of 'stratagems' like those of Aeneas Tacticus, Frontinus or Polyaenus?

[33] John Hart, *Herodotus and Greek History*, London 1982, 60, remarks of the Oroites story that 'the trick for which Polycrates fell was an old one but still a good one: it was good enough in 416 when Athenian envoys were tricked by the Egestaeans.' This is the first time I have seen the parallel noted in print, though I had used it in lectures before 1982. In his footnote Hart says of this item, 'Thucydides had high-grade contemporary information on Sicily', but I would not want to exclude in this way the possibility that Thucydides had his leg pulled.

[34] Millar, op.cit. Note also Colin Wells, *The Roman Empire*, London 1984, 233, on a story in the *Historia Augusta* about Hadrian making senators wear the toga: 'This is plausible, but is it true? It might be invented on the analogy of one of Suetonius' anecdotes of Augustus (Suetonius, *Augustus* 40). But if so, it is nonetheless significant. It shows the sort of thing judged to be in character for Hadrian. The story would not have been told of all emperors.' A more sceptical way of putting this is: 'Dramatic stories get attached with appropriate changes to stereotypes, bad stories to Caligula or Nero or imperial freedmen ... good stories to Trajan or Severus Alexander' (Keith Hopkins, *JRS* lxviii, 1978, 185, reviewing Millar). Cf. now W. Ameling, *Historia* xxxv, 1986, 507f. 'Tyrannen und schwangere Frauen'.

[35] Thuc. vi 56ff.; Livy i 57ff.

of 'roving anecdotes' be regarded as necessarily fatal to their general trustworthiness. Equally we should not treat even Thucydides as infallible: there are some very odd features in Book i about Pausanias and Themistocles, which suggest that Thucydides could be gullible, at least in his early writing.[36]

Certainly, Thucydides goes even further than Herodotus in claiming to have checked his facts by original research: at the beginning, perhaps with Herodotus specifically in mind, he remarks that most people do not take trouble over the search for the truth. But even this remark belongs in a tradition, for Aristophanes uses the same rare word in a similar context. We must not assume that it is Thucydides who is here echoed by Aristophanes (he was not a popular author, crying out for parody like Herodotus). It may have been the other way round – perhaps even a shared echo of someone else.[37] But Thucydides, like Herodotus in *his* programmatic statement about 'speaking of what he knew', may have used conventional language to signal what was really an unconventional plan of work. We must judge by results: Thucydides did take trouble, as we can see, for example, by comparing the epigraphically attested Argive alliance with Thucydides' version.[38]

My fourth and final point in defence of Herodotus concerns the formulaic character of his citations of oral informants. This has made scholars sceptical about his travels and enquiries. This scepticism, it must be said, is least plausible where Herodotus gives versions which differ precisely in the ways we should expect them to differ, as for the foundation of Cyrene.[39] But the case for thinking that Herodotus did genuinely examine oral informants is not based solely on explicit source-citations by Herodotus himself (although it is hard to see a motive for inventing so despairing a 'citation' as Herodotus' words about the battle of Lade: 'It is difficult to find out the truth about which Ionian

[36] G.L. Cawkwell, *Auckland Classical Studies presented to E.M. Blaiklock*, 1971, 39ff. 'The fall of Themistocles'; note esp. p.51: 'Elsewhere [Thucydides] eschews *logoi* and personal anecdotes' so this section is early. I agree; not because it centres on individuals (below, Chapter Six), but because it is anecdotal and 'Herodotean', cf. below, p.26.

[37] Thuc. i 20.3, with Gomme ad loc., citing Aristophanes, *Danaids* F254, where the same word *atalaipôros* is used of not taking enough trouble (about *poiêsis*).

[38] Tod 72; Thuc. v 47.

[39] As remarked by Oswyn Murray in a discussion of a paper by Fehling; cf. above, n.27. See also his *Early Greece*, London 1980, 115.

contingents fought well and which badly, because they all accuse each other').[40] Take the tradition of the Spartan king Kleomenes. Notoriously, Herodotus' judgments are contradictory, favourable in Book iii where he is 'the most just of men', but hostile in Books v and vi, especially where he is said to be 'not in his right mind but off his head'.[41] Whence derives the hostile picture? (There are no explicit citations of sources.) A plausible candidate is the deposed king Demaratus, since both Kleomenes and Leotychidas are said to have come to a bad end 'doing requital to Demaratus'.[42] Now we happen to know, though not from Herodotus but from the fourth-century writer Xenophon, that Demaratus settled in the Troad in Asia Minor, on land given him by the Persian king.[43] (Xenophon met his descendants.) It would have been easy for Herodotus to speak to him there, and why should we doubt that he did? Similar arguments can be used about Herodotus' use of Delphi as a source, which must often be postulated even where there is no explicit statement.

I conclude that Herodotus' credibility as a recorder of facts has not been upset. That there are features like ring composition in his work shows no more (and no less) than that, whatever else he was, he was a literary artist, and we shall have to bear this in mind also for Thucydides. 'Formulaic' does not mean 'false'.

I therefore accept the old-fashioned view of Herodotus as 'father of history' in our sense. That was the ancient view: in the next century Theophrastus believed that Herodotus and Thucydides between them introduced a new kind of historical writing.[44]

A final complication is that a similar kind of literary approach has recently been used on Thucydides:[45] it is argued that his information often derives from no more 'historically' reliable source than his own mind, and that his attributions of motive are particularly suspect, being simply extrapolated by him from the factual situation as he has described it. I postpone discussion of this to Chapter Four.

[40] Hdt. vi 14.
[41] iii 148; v 42.1.
[42] vi 72.1; 84.3.
[43] Xenophon, *Hellenica* iii 1.6.
[44] Cicero, *Orator* 39.
[45] C. Schneider, *Information und Absicht bei Thukydides, Hypomnemata* 41, 1974; Virginia Hunter, *Thucydides the Artful Reporter*, Toronto 1973.

Let us now pass to an examination of Thucydides' relation to Herodotus; I begin with the debts and will then discuss the differences.

Thucydides' first and greatest debt to Herodotus is the decision to record truthfully, and to interpret, the past, confining himself to contemporary or near-contemporary events, i.e. knowledge he could control. (Thucydides actually makes a very surprising claim in his very first sentence, that he sat down at the beginning of the war and started to record an event still in the future, namely the course of the war which he expected would be great). The idea that the historian's job is to interpret and explain the past, as well as record it, is not easily traced in Greek thought. Of Roman historians, a writer of the first century BC, Sempronius Asellio, said, in a famous pronouncement, that it was not enough to say what had been done, one must show why: '*quo consilio quaque ratione gesta essent*', 'with what intention and for what reason things had been done'.[46] In modern times the great German historian Eduard Meyer has said that what distinguishes the keeping of a chronicle from the writing of history in the full sense is the 'stamp of individuality'.[47]

That Thucydides in some way regarded himself as Herodotus' debtor is shown by two of the long digressions in Book i – the *Pentekontaetia*, or account of the fifty years (480-431) which fills in the gap between the Persian Wars recorded by Herodotus and the Peloponnesian War to be recorded by himself, and the excursus on Themistocles and Pausanias, which is in a much chattier style than his usual manner: the scholiast commented, 'Here the lion laughed'.[48] Both stories, those of Pausanias and of Themistocles, are accounts in Herodotean manner of 'curses' which were brought down by the killing of individuals in sacred surroundings. The whole excursus also shows clear traces of the dialect (Ionic Greek) which Herodotus used but which Thucydides usually did not.[49] The reader is arrested by Thucydides' return, immediately after the excursus on Themistocles, to his more normal manner; after the account of Themistocles' epic wanderings, Thucydides characterises his

[46] F1 Peter.

[47] *Geschichte des Altertums* i² 1, Stuttgart and Berlin 1907, 223ff., esp. 225.

[48] Gomme, *HCT* i, 446, quoting Forbes quoting the scholiast on i 126.3, applies the remark to the whole Kylon-Pausanias-Themistocles excursus.

[49] H.D. Westlake, *CQ* xvii, 1977, 106; cf. Dover, *HCT* on vi 2-5.

mental qualities, in a sentence full of abstract concepts piled upon each other (e.g. *phuseôs men dunamei, meletês de brachutêti*, 'force of character and rapidity of action').[50]

Thucydides' second debt to Herodotus is the lack of narrow partisanship for one city (*polis*). The predecessors, such as they were, of Herodotus and Thucydides were mostly local historians, like Antiochus of Syracuse, Lysanias of Mallus, who treated the Persian Wars from a Euboian viewpoint, or Charon of Lampsacus. But neither Herodotus nor Thucydides can be convicted of any such worm's eye view of history, a view which found its most ludicrous expression in the fourth century with Ephorus of Cyme, who when he could not find anything to say about his city as he described other places and their achievements, but did not wish it to go wholly unmentioned, would say 'at this time the citizens of Cyme were at peace'.[51] Herodotus, famously, was free from insularity: he praises Athens at one point in the consciousness that this will be unpopular.[52] As for Thucydides, it is clear from what he says about Spartan obedience to law, and from Archidamus' speech at the beginning of the war, that he understood what was admirable and admired about the Spartan way of life.[53] How did they achieve this detachment? The answer is that, like so many of the great historians of Greece and Rome, they were both exiles, Herodotus from Halikarnassos and Thucydides from Athens; as Sir Ronald Syme remarks, 'exile may be the making of an historian'.[54] Think of Xenophon, Hieronymus, Timaeus and Polybius, all uprooted, by choice or circumstance, from their native place, and of Roman historians like Sallust, disgraced and thus excluded from political life. The remarkable impartiality which Thucydides shares with Herodotus is therefore partly due to similar circumstances of life, but is also partly *derived* from Herodotus' work: Thucydides might go to a local historian for particular facts, or lift the odd geographical item from Hecataeus.[55] But from Herodotus he learnt to interpret those

---

[50] i 138.3. Cf. A. Parry, *Yale French Studies* xlv, 1970, 3ff. 'Thucydides' use of abstract language'.

[51] Antiochus: Dover *HCT* on vi 2-5; Charon: n.14 above; Lysanias: *FGrHist* 426; Ephorus on Cyme: *FGrHist* 70 F236.

[52] vii. 139.

[53] Thuc. i 18; 84-5. The latter however is a speech, not necessarily Thucydides' view. See Chapter Seven, p.162.

[54] *PBA* xlviii, 1962, 40.

[55] Dover, *HCT* iv on Thuc. vi 2-5; N.G.L. Hammond, *Epirus*, 1967, 447ff.

facts according to what was 'humanly probable',[56] without grinding a 'particularist' axe. This is remarkable, because Greek city-state particularism went deep.

The third debt is perhaps not strictly a debt to Herodotus at all, but a shared debt to others, namely the poets. The debt consists in the poetic, specifically epic and tragic, arrangement of material and choice of vocabulary. This is a topic we shall have to return to (Chapter Five), but when asking, as we must, why Thucydides so often seems to echo the techniques of poetry, we should first remember that Herodotus had already done so. In view of what was said above about the Herodotean character of the Pausanias-Themistocles excursus, it is not surprising that poetic reminiscences should be specially common there. For instance 'taking with the spear' is an expression from heroic poetry, and the Greek for 'neither night nor day' is in sing-song iambic rhythm.[57] Again, with Themistocles' use of Admetus' son (above, p.15) we may compare Telephus' use of Agamemnon's infant son Orestes in Euripides' lost play the *Telephus*: Telephus seized the child and threatened to kill him unless the Greeks helped to heal his wound.[58] But the debt to poetry goes far deeper.[59] Above all there is a debt to epic in the very choice of subject, a great war. Just as in Herodotus there is Homeric reminiscence in the phrase 'beginning of evils', used of the Athenian ships sent to the Ionian Revolt (Paris' ships were 'beginners of evil' in Homer), so too Thucydides makes the Spartan herald Melesippus say as he is escorted out of Attica in 431 BC, 'this day will be the beginning of great evils for the Greeks.'[60] We must· be careful not to regard all this as purely literary reminiscence, since all Greeks, Melesippus as well as Thucydides, were dipped in Homer from the earliest possible

[56] i 22.4.

[57] i 128.7; 129.3.

[58] Wilamowitz, op.cit. Note Wilamowitz's remark further up the page: 'that Thucydides reproduces Themistocles' speech, as only the poet can, shows that his own strict renunciation of the Homeric and Ionic technique of narration was theoretical only.'

[59] This will be discussed more fully later; the essential study is now Colin Macleod's paper 'Thucydides and tragedy', ch.13 of his *Collected Essays*, Oxford 1983. Note his closing remarks on the relation between Thucydides and 'another tragic historian', Herodotus. 'Great war': cf. Strasburger, pp. 1057ff. 'Homer und die griechische Geschichtsschreibung', esp. 1067.

[60] Hdt. v 97.3; cf. v 30; Paris' ships 'began the evil' at Homer, *Iliad* v 62; cf. xi 604. Melesippus: Thuc.ii 12.

age.[61] So when, before the battle of Lade, Herodotus makes a speaker use the 'Homeric' phrase 'on the razor's edge',[62] it is difficult to say whether Herodotus is echoing Homer or whether for any speaker at the time of the Persian Wars it would indeed be natural to use Homeric language on any solemn occasion.

I move now from Thucydides' debt to Herodotus to his differences from him – to the way he reacted against him.

The only evidence for a direct link is anecdotal: Thucydides is said to have burst into tears after hearing Herodotus recite,[63] but we do not know whether the tears were because he thought it was very good or very bad. It has even been pointed out recently that if Herodotus' history was completed as late as, say, 414, Thucydides may not have known about it until his own ideas were already formed.[64] The story is a reminder, incidentally, that Herodotus' work was designed to be read out loud to a public audience, no doubt in sections rather than in full; whereas we do not know how, if at all, Thucydides' work was launched on the world in his lifetime. It is possible that some of the more highly-wrought sections, such as the Corcyra revolution in Book iii, were read out at the aristocratic dining and drinking occasions called *sumposia*. Certainly we should not assume too quickly, from Thucydides' contrast between his own work as a 'possession for ever' and 'exhibition pieces for the delight of the moment',[65] that Thucydides never 'tried out' anything on anybody.

The first main difference between Herodotus and Thucydides is in their theology and view of causation. Herodotus is much

---

[61] E.A. Havelock, *Preface to Plato*, Oxford 1966.

[62] Hdt.vi 11; *Iliad* x 173; cf. Simonides 97.

[63] Marcellinus, *Life of Thucydides* 54.

[64] W.R. Connor, art.cit. (1982), 280. For the 414 date see C.W. Fornara, *JHS* xci, 1971, 25ff., 'Evidence for the date of Herodotus' publication'.

[65] i 22.4; Connor, art.cit. (1982), at 277 col. 1 says of Thucydides' history that 'it is designed for a private occasion, for the individual alone in his study or gathered with a few friends who are willing to make the intense intellectual effort needed to deal with original thought expressed in a complex style', but in col. 2 he appears to contrast Thucydides' readership with the world of the symposium and other 'collective occasions'. But Plato's *Symposium* (and Xenophon's) should warn us against treating symposia as necessarily frivolous or philistine affairs: 'Xenophon and Plato would not have chosen symposia as the scene for Socrates' operations unless philosophical discussions were known to take place in symposia' (T.B.L. Webster, *Athenian Culture and Society*, 1973, 55). For the intellectual eclecticism of symposia see S. Goldhill, *Reading Greek Tragedy*, Cambridge 1986, 75, 243.

readier than Thucydides to give a place in his causal scheme to oracles, and to see human fate in terms of *tisis*, divine requital, although this does not exclude causation at the human level.[66] At that level, Herodotus does it is true distinguish by implication between surface and profound cause – for instance the Athenian ships sent to help the Ionian revolt in 499 were an *archê* (the word means cause *and* beginning) of trouble; but the whole economy of his work convinces us that the root cause was late sixth-century Persian expansionism.[67] In Thucydides, by contrast, the religious aspect even of apparently 'religious' episodes is absolutely minimised.[68] Above all, though Thucydides leaves a proper place in *his* scheme for 'the unexpected' or 'chance' (*tuchê*), his greatest single contribution was consciously to develop and formulate an account of political causation in terms of deep cause and superficial, announced, pretext. The deep, or 'truest', cause of the Peloponnesian War, he says early in Book i in a celebrated passage, was Athenian expansion, which terrified the Spartans and forced them to fight, not the particular grievances which occupy most of Book i.[69]

Second, Thucydides' historical method. Thucydides' legacy to later historical writing was in many ways profoundly beneficial, in that he set standards of research and accuracy for all time. But in one way it was also profoundly damaging because as we observed at the beginning of this book it was Thucydides who by his influential practice ordained that history should henceforth be primarily a matter of war and politics. That is true of much of later Greek historiography, although there was a revival of interest in ethnography, and in Herodotus in particular, after the campaigns of Alexander had reawakened desire for such knowledge.[70] The difference in scope between Herodotus and Thucydides can be illustrated by their differing uses of the word *erga*, 'works', which both writers describe as an important part of the subject-matter of their writings. For Herodotus, *erga* means

---

[66] *tisis*: above n.42. De Ste Croix, art.cit. (1977), 138ff. Also J. Hart, op.cit, 183ff.

[67] *archê kakôn*: Hdt.v 97. See Momigliano, *Studies*, 118.

[68] See for instance p.81 below on the Pleistoanax episode.

[69] i 23.6. See further below, Chapter Seven, p.182 for 'the unexpected', etc.

[70] O. Murray, *CQ* xxii, 1972, 200ff. 'Herodotus and Hellenistic culture', and esp. J. Hornblower, 137-53.

concrete artefacts as well as political actions,[71] even the 'cities of men' being included in the *erga* about to be described (this is Homeric reminiscence: Odysseus had 'seen the cities of men').[72] This sense of *ergon* as monument is rejected by Thucydides, for instance where he speaks of the unreliability of using the extant buildings of Athens or Sparta as an index of their relative power:

> Suppose for example that the city of Sparta were to become deserted, and that only the temples and foundations of buildings remained, I think that future generations would, as time passed, find it very difficult to believe that the place had really been as powerful as it was represented to be. Yet the Spartans occupy two-fifths of the Peloponnese and stand at the head not only of the whole Peloponnese itself but also of numerous allies beyond its frontiers. Since, however, the city is not regularly planned and contains no temples or monuments of great magnificence, but is simply a collection of villages, in the ancient Hellenic way, its appearance would not come up to expectation. If, on the other hand, the same thing were to happen to Athens, one would conjecture from what meets the eye that the city had been twice as powerful as in fact it is.[73]

By *erga* Thucydides regularly means political or military action, and with one exception he judges human greatness by these criteria.[74] This rejection of Herodotus' criteria of greatness was a pity: the narrower view has prevailed, as we saw. Only recently has the idea been overthrown, with books like F. Braudel's *Mediterranean World in the Age of Philip II*, which for one and three quarters of its two volumes speaks of the Mediterranean world in its physical aspects, with charts showing for example how long a letter took to be delivered when sent from Venice in different centuries.[75] Braudel's approach is a return to the historical spirit of Herodotus, the spirit of the old ethnographic *logos* or account, with its four ingredients, geography, customs, marvels and political history[76] (Braudel's Venetian letters are a kind of 'marvel'). The digressions about the pyramids etc. in

[71] H. Immerwahr, *AJP* lxxxi, 1960, 261ff. 'History as monument in Herodotus and Thucydides'.

[72] Hdt.i 5: cf. *Odyssey* i 3.

[73] i 10.

[74] See esp. i 22; the exception is ii 100.2 about Archelaus' road-building, where however the word *erga* is not used.

[75] Vol.i, 366-7.

[76] See Jacoby, *Abh.*, 27; cf. *RE* supp.ii, col. 331.

Book ii of Herodotus have a good purpose: in assessing the greatness of Persia, Greece's opponent in Books v to ix, he needs to show the greatness of the places which Persia had already gobbled up. All this is relevant to the greatness of the Persian empire itself. Herodotus says he has 'dwelt at length' on Samos because of its three great *erga* (temple, tunnel, mole); the point being to underline the greatness of Samos and to show that, after conquering Polykrates' Samos, the Persian empire was greater still. Thucydides has a reminiscence of this language, but the substance is in deliberate contrast: Pericles says that he has 'dwelt at length' on the city's affairs, because the achievements of the glorious dead prove the city's greatness: their deeds, *erga*, are equal to their fame. Their memory is of the mind and not of a monument (here, exceptionally, *ergon* does mean 'monument').[77] The actions of individuals amount to a kind of reality or truth which is put in opposition to *logos*. It has been argued that this opposition was central to Thucydides' thought and was no mere antithetical word-play. This is a true and convincing insight.[78]

Thucydides, then, moved a long way from Herodotus' emphasis on the more concrete aspects of *ergon*. He was right to reject buildings and so on as a wholly reliable index of the prosperity and greatness of a state, but such things, though they are a fallible guide, are still a guide. The function of Book ii of Herodotus was to introduce us to the scale of the problem which Cambyses was taking on when he invaded Egypt. Thucydides could at several points have afforded to take a leaf out of Herodotus' book, notably at the beginning of his account of Sicily, which with its dry foundation-dates and names of oikists (leaders of colonists) is a poor way of making the point that the

[77] Hdt.iii 60; Thuc.ii 42.; Macleod, *Essays*, 152f. and n.2. See his p. 152 for other remarks on *erga* in the Funeral Speech. Note also Loraux, *Invention of Athens*, 1986, 78.

[78] Parry, op. cit., 60, 166; see esp. Thuc.ii 41.2. Note however that there is epigraphic evidence, which Parry neglected, that the distinction continued to be popular after 400 BC when Thucydides stopped writing: *IG* i³ 39 (mid-fifth-century Athenian alliance with Eretria) has a nice use of *ergon* contrasted with *epos* ('word'). Cf. also ML 47 (Athens and Colophon, c.446). The distinction is epigraphically long-standing; cf. ML 17 (500 BC; alliance between Eleans and Heraeans) and 30 (Teos curses, c.470). But it goes on into the fourth century and the Hellenistic period; cf. *Syll*³ 331; 547; Welles, *Royal Correspondence of the Hellenistic Period*, Yale, 1934, no. 52, line 49.

Athenians were taking on an enemy of formidable resources.[79] In Book i of Thucydides, the great protagonists, Athens and Sparta, are introduced by sketches of a great citizen of each, Pausanias the Spartan and Themistocles the Athenian;[80] and the importance of the link between naval power and commerce is made in the Thucydidean account of early Greece near the beginning of Book i. But there is, in Thucydides, no systematic treatment of Spartan and Athenian strengths and weaknesses other than those of character. The statement of Athenian financial resources is only a slight corrective.[81]

Thucydides' third departure from, or reaction against, Herodotus, whose manner of presentation is very even, lies in the differing degrees of intensity with which Thucydides treats his material. Any candid reader of Thucydides must notice this when coming to him from Herodotus: much of his narrative is extremely austere and dry, and he includes material which is hard to account for except on the view that he aims to put everything in, like the 'historian' of the Aristotelian definition. But that is too simple, because elsewhere Thucydides can select, abridge and build up themes in a way that Aristotle would call 'poetic' not 'historical'. And this too is a departure from Herodotus, for all that both are certainly 'tragic' historians (above, n.59). Thucydides can achieve emotional effects as well by the dry precision of the Aristotelian 'historian' as by more obviously poetic techniques. The tension between these two aspects of Thucydides will be the subject of the next chapter.

[79] Thuc.vi 2-5. It is true, however, that long Greek settlement was itself thought of as a source of strength.

[80] With this we may compare the Lycurgan and Pisistratid digressions of Herodotus i 59-68.

[81] ii 13. He talks about the level reached by the *eisphora* (a capital levy) at iii 19; and note the remarkably assured comment at vii 28 that, when the Athenians substituted a 5 per cent tax on maritime trade for the tribute, they did so in the belief that this would bring in more revenue. On Thucydides' figures, and the extent to which they inspire trust, see generally Conclusion below, p.203; but note also Chapter Four, p.109: Thucydides capable of 'innumeracy' as hopeless as that of Herodotus. See also Chapter Two, p.35 on Thucydides' hyperbolical use of large, and pathetic use of small, numerals.

Comprehensiveness or Selectivity?

We noted in the last chapter that there is in Thucydides much adventitious and repetitive material.

Some of this, such as the division by campaigning seasons, and the annual invasions of Attica, can be explained by the desire to create pauses, as in an epic, with digressions and repetitions which build up tension. We might compare the elaborate description of Priam's cart in *Iliad* xxiv, which, it has been said, 'is designed as a relief after the pain and rage of Priam's speeches'.[1]

We can also explain some apparently trivial or pointless detail, or some piece of factual precision, by reference to its emotive effect – in other words, the detail is not really trivial or pointless at all. For instance, when we are told of the personal possessions and valuables of the Athenian prisoners in Sicily that they were thrown into upturned shields and four shields were filled in that way, the word 'four' is certainly an example of the *akribeia*, precision, promised near the beginning of Book i.[2] But it is more than precision for its own sake: the precision here makes it easier to visualise, and the enumeration adds pathos. We may compare Priam's enumeration of his sons in *Iliad* xxiv:

> There were fifty when the the Achaean expedition came. Nineteen were borne by one mother and the rest by other ladies in my palace. Most of them have fallen in action, and Hector, the only one I could still count on, has now been killed by you ...

Of this it has been said: 'By numbering and classifying his sons Priam gives more weight to his loss.' This rests on a remark in

---

[1] C.W. Macleod (ed.), Homer, *Iliad xxiv*, Cambridge 1982, on lines 266ff.
[2] vii 82; for *akribeia* see i 22.

Aristotle's *Rhetoric*, that 'a single subject when divided into parts seems more impressive'.[3]

A recent study of the numerals in Thucydides (with particular reference to the way he qualifies them) remarks on his occasional 'tragic' use of hyperbolically large, but imprecise, numbers to evoke strong emotion;[4] his motives for the occasional more restrained use of small, precise figures would also repay study.

'Tragic *akribeia*' may take a chronological form; thus we read at the end of the long account of the siege of Plataea, 'This was the end of Plataea, in the ninety-third year after she became the ally of Athens.' The point here is that Plataea's alliance with Athens was absolutely no use to her; 'ninety-third' has pathetic precision.[5] The bite of Thucydides' comment can be appreciated only if we realise how close the Plataeans had been to Athens: they probably enjoyed citizenship rights at Athens even before 427, and afterwards the refugees were fully integrated into the citizen body.[6] Thucydides does not record this reception of the refugees; perhaps he felt it would have detracted from the starkness of the conclusion to his Plataean narrative.

More generally, the use of the dry or deadpan manner can be as effective as the purple passage: Thucydides has in fact more than one register.[7] Discussing simplicity and brevity in Homer, one scholar has observed that there is a kind of 'noble restraint which allows the event to speak for itself'.[8] Another offers an interesting candidate for a short-list of Thucydides' most vividly descriptive passages, namely an unadorned chapter in the *Pentekontaetia* which tells how some Corinthians were surrounded and killed by some Athenians. Half a page 'for this one afternoon's horrible work' was indeed disproportionately much, given the scale of the *Pentekontaetia*; and that fact, combined with the bareness of the narration, helps to make this episode spring out from its context.[9]

---

[3] *Iliad* xxiv 495ff., with Macleod's commentary, citing Ar. *Rhet.* 1365a 10.

[4] Catherine Reid Rubincam, *AJAH* iv, 1979, 77ff. 'Qualification of numerals in Thucydides', at 86.

[5] iii 68. Colin Macleod calls this a 'dry and devastating comment', *Essays*, 231.

[6] iii 55 with *HCT*; Lys.xxiii; Dem.lix 104.

[7] Dover, *HCT* v, 338.

[8] J. Griffin, *Homer on Life and Death*, Oxford 1980, 121. Cf. Charles Hope, *Titian*, London 1980, 85: 'Economy of means can lead to an increase in expressive power'.

[9] i 106, with Kitto, *Poiesis*, 271.

But, all that said, there remains much in Thucydides which is
inexplicably repetitious and trivial (i.e. not 'historically
important' items, as we should say) and for which it is hard to
find explanations in terms of emotional effectiveness. Why, for
instance, did Thucydides tell us that the Megarian contingent in
the Corinthian fleet in 433 numbered precisely 27, or why did he
record all the proper names with which his text is peppered?[10] If
we answer, 'Because of their possible usefulness to future
inquirers',[11] we are saying that *any* information is historically
important, not just as 'raw material' but worth including in a
final draft. But that had not been Herodotus' view, because he
had said that he would not give the names of all the native
commanders since it was not necessary for the *logos* of his
historia. (I discussed the meaning of those words in the
Introduction.)

In historians like Livy or Arrian, such detail can be explained
as due to a desire to give an 'air of scholarly authenticity' to their
work, by 'mechanically transcribing technical terms', or
inventing 'dry catalogues of the allocation of provinces and
armies to give a false appearance of accuracy'.[12] But such an
explanation is hardly available for Thucydides, because
invention of that kind is not intelligible without a long tradition
of factual historical writing such as did not exist when he wrote:
bogus factual 'accuracy' presupposes real factual accuracy. More
subjectively, it is hard to believe him capable of such mendacity,
although blind trust in Thucydidean figures is also out of place:
for instance, the statement that more than 20,000 slaves deserted
after the Spartan fortification of Decelea[13] is perhaps treated
more solemnly by modern scholars than it deserves to be. How
did he arrive at that figure?

It begins to seem that Thucydides had the idea of recording
comprehensively, and we must ask whether there are any
programmatic statements in his work which support that idea.
The manifesto near the beginning of Book i speaks of laborious
research and of the *erga* of the war, but that is not conclusive: he
may have meant, not *all* the erga, as the phrase was taken in

---

[10] i 46.

[11] Cf. i 22.4.

[12] P.A. Brunt, *Arrian*, Loeb ed., vol.ii, 1983, 484; id., *Italian Manpower, 225
BC – AD 14*, Oxford 1971, 645, though Brunt actually rejects this view of Livy.

[13] vii 27. Cf. viii 40.2, very confident about the density of slaves on Chios.

antiquity, but 'the *erga* which I have chosen to describe'.[14] As for the aim to record with *akribeia*, that need not mean more than 'with conformity to reality'; there is perhaps the added idea of exact or accurate conformity to reality. The word is said to be originally a metaphor from carpentry or joinery.[15] Perhaps more helpful is the opening sentence of Book ii where he says that he has recorded 'in order, how each thing happened, by summer and winter'.[16] This seems to me to come much closer to a statement that he intends to be comprehensive, though here too it would be possible to interpret 'each thing' as 'each of the things which I have decided to write about'.

Approaching the problem from the other end, is there any direct statement that he intends to be (not comprehensive but) selective in his war narrative? (Obviously, the *Archaeology, Pentekontaetia* and *Sikelika*[17] are summaries.) Again there is nothing relevant at or near the beginning of Book i, but there is a passage embedded deep in the narrative in Book iii, where he says that he will record only 'the most noteworthy items' in the Sicilian warfare of 426.[18] But although this statement undoubtedly describes his practice for much of the time, it stands alone. It shows, incidentally, that he could, if he had wanted to, have said in his general introduction that he proposed to write up only the most noteworthy events of the war. For the belief that Thucydides omits events which he knew about, we may prefer to rely on commonsense rather than strict proof, but

---

[14] i 22; Marcellinus *Life of Thucydides*, para. 47. G. Schepens, *REG* lxxxviii, 1975, 81ff., 'L'information complète chez les historiens grecs', at p. 86 seems right on this, against L. Canfora, *Totalità e selezione nella storiografia antica*, Bari 1972, 30.

[15] Conformity to reality: F. Egermann, *Historia* x, 1961, 435ff. D. Kurz, *Akribeia* 1970 (non vidi). That the idea of accuracy, i.e. precision plus truth, is present is suggested by the phrase (including *akribes*) about Hellanicus at i 97: see below. Carpentry: M. Trédé, *Mélanges Delebecque*, 1983, 407ff., 'Akribeia chez Thucydide', at p. 407.

[16] Canfora loc. cit.

[17] For these terms see pp. 4ff.

[18] iii 90. Not discussed by Schepens. Gomme ad loc. is surely right to say that this does not mean that he is going to précis Antiochus of Syracuse, as Dover tentatively suggested (see now Dover in Herter (ed.), p.353, a German translation of an article in *Maia* vi, 1953, 1ff.); though Dover also thought that Thucydides might have meant that he would restrict himself to events in which the Athenian forces were directly involved. Dover is anyway right to say that Thucydides' normal practice is to record [only] noteworthy events, without drawing attention to the fact that that is what he is doing.

LIBRARY ST. MARY'S COLLEGE

proof is easily given. There are two kinds of evidence: statements in his own finished narrative[19] which imply knowledge of events not recorded, and non-Thucydidean evidence which relates to facts which must have been known to Thucydides. As an example of the first kind (passing over controversial items like the 449 Peace of Kallias) there is a passage in Book iv which implies that many embassies had been sent by Sparta to Persia earlier than the one there recorded.[20] Thucydides could surely have told us more about this if he had wanted to. Even if it be countered, 'Perhaps he knew only that there had been many previous embassies, he knew no details', he could have found out, and the fact that he did not do so implies that he was being selective about what he bothered to find out. Or there are comparative statements like the remark in Pericles' obituary notice, that his successors were more prone than he was to use demagogic methods; or statements like 'This was the first x of the war'. For instance, he says of the *eisphora* (capital tax) levied in 428/7 that that was the first time it reached 200 talents. This implies knowledge of others.[21]

As to the second kind of evidence, an example might be an inscription which implies that it may originally have been envisaged that a single general (not three) should be sent to Sicily in 415; Thucydides never mentions this, but he surely knew.[22]

So there are items and statements in Thucydides which seem to imply that his aim in the narrative was to be comprehensive, and other items and statements which imply that he was selective.

It is the first aim, comprehensiveness, which is the problem. It goes with another feature: the dryness and austerity which Thucydides' narrative can sometimes assume. It was perhaps the 'comprehensive' aspect of Thucydides which made Aristotle speak of history as concerned with 'what happened' (that is, *everything* that happened?) rather than with the sort of thing that *might* happen, which implies that what is being looked at is a sample.

[19] I postpone to Chapter Six the question which parts are finished.
[20] iv 50.
[21] ii 65 10; iii 19 with J.G. Griffith, *AJAH* ii, 1977, 3ff., 'A note on the first *eisphora* at Athens'.
[22] ML 78.

LIBRARY ST. MARY'S COLLEGE

We must now ask where Thucydides got the idea of recording events, especially military events, in a dry and comprehensive way, fitting them into a year-by-year narrative constructed round campaigning seasons.

The first candidate for consideration must be Herodotus, whose influence in some other departments we have examined. At first sight Herodotus' narrative is far more complex in structure than Thucydides', but the Ionian Revolt shows traces of an arrangement by years of fighting; but only traces. And Herodotus was explicitly selective.[23] Or there is Hellanicus. Remarkably, Thucydides' stricture on Hellanicus is his only mention of a rival by name: he objects to Hellanicus' account of the *pentêkontaetia* as 'brief and chronologically inaccurate'. Whatever he meant by this notorious phrase,[24] which so well describes his own account of the same period, it is clear that Hellanicus did not enumerate events by summers and winters. We are forced to seek other, more general, influences.

The second possible influence is real-life reports by generals. This, naturally, is a genre of writing we know little about, since only the most celebrated, because unusual, examples have been preserved. For instance, there is the 'laconic' Spartan message after Arginusai: 'Ships lost; Mindarus dead; men starving; don't know what to do'.[25] It is true that the most famous 'literary' example, Nikias' long letter from Sicily asking for reinforcements and his own recall, is felt by Thucydides to need a special explanation: Nikias' motive for writing, rather than relying on an oral messenger, is said to be fear that such a messenger might be untruthful through incompetence, poor memory or eagerness to please. But the same letter refers to 'other previous letters'.[26] And Alcibiades does some letter-writing in Book viii.[27] Now Nikias' letter was a particularly anguished production, but surely in an imperial state like Athens, with constant overseas service in the *pentêkontaetia*, many detailed factual letters must have been sent home by generals, perhaps to their colleagues on the panel of ten generals. Thucydides may have read and written

[23] Jacoby, *RE* supp.ii, col.440 (Ionian Revolt). For vii 96 see above, p.9 (selectivity).
[24] i 97.2, on which see *HCT* v, 381.
[25] Xen. *Hell.* i 1.23.
[26] vii 11.1.
[27] viii 51.2.

such letters himself even before the war started; he will certainly have written them by the mid 420s when he had a command in the north.[28] The occasional chatty inscription gives an idea of the sort of enumeration of facts sent back for the archives: the honours granted in such inscriptions must often have been prompted by accounts sent in by agents in the field.[29] These accounts (we may suppose) formed the basis of the list of 'services rendered' in the inscription. Such accounts, then, are one germ of what we call 'history' in the unpretentious sense of a true statement about the past: whatever was 'true' for poets, it mattered that generals should get things factually right.[30] Thucydides' use of the word 'waterlessness,'[31] in the course of an account of an attack on the Aeolian islands, has prompted the remark that 'showing the military conditions' was the chief purpose of the chronological division by summers and winters.[32] This is on the right realistic lines, but I would go further. I am suggesting that a number of peculiarities of Thucydides' style and presentation (dryness, occasional triviality, would-be comprehensiveness – 'They may make something of this even if I can't') can be explained by reference to a lost genre, the military report. After all, we know that Thucydides was a soldier; we do not know that he was a doctor.

A third possible influence is forensic oratory. The political reforms of 462 enormously increased the work done by the large popular law-courts (*dikastêria*), which now ceased to act merely as courts of appeal and heard cases as 'courts of first instance'. This meant more frequent meetings of the *dikastêria*. It also meant that the jurors had to be paid, an innovation which can be dated to roughly this time. All this must greatly have advanced the art of oratory at Athens.[33] Here too there was an imperial

[28] See above p.3.
[29] Cf. for instance ML 91 (honours, for services listed, to Archelaus of Macedon – he received the Athenian shipwrights and gave them timber and oars, etc.)
[30] Dover, *HCT* v app.2, 403 says that whether Thucydides is a masterly historian 'depends on how often he gets things right'.
[31] iii 88.
[32] See Gomme ad loc.
[33] For Aristotle, the decisive date was the fall of the Deinomenid tyranny at Syracuse in Sicily, c.467, which led to a mass of litigation for the restitution of property: Cicero, *Brutus* 46. Professionalism in speaking was then exported from Sicily to Athens, a visit from Gorgias of Leontini in the 420s being specially remembered, Diod. xiii 53. But Athenian oratory was surely not wholly unsophisticated before that. For instance, Pritchett, *Dionysius*, 87 detects

aspect: subject allies, who wanted their rates of tribute reviewed, had no vote in the Athenian assembly, and needed influential Athenians to plead their cause. Fragments of such speeches by Antiphon survive, on behalf of communities on the islands of Rhodes and Samothrace. Thucydides, with his Thracian influence, was perhaps in demand as an orator in a similar capacity.[34] But there were many other calls on barristers' skills.[35] It is an accident that no relevant speeches happen to survive.

All this has a bearing on Thucydides' factual narrative. In arguing a case, barristers then as now had to tell a story with attention to chronology (though perhaps only with a view to obfuscating it). A simple piece of narrative in a forensic speech is in Demosthenes' speech against Polykles:[36]

> We sailed from Thasos to Stryme, when it was still winter and there were no harbours, and it was not possible to disembark or eat our dinner because the terrain was hostile ...

These skills were not, of course, exclusive: a general under attack in the courts or assembly would need 'forensic' skills to get him out of trouble, just as he would need rudimentary 'historical' skills to send home an accurate report.

All this concerns the Thucydides who recorded 'what happened', rather than the other Thucydides who, in Aristotle's language (see Introduction), treated 'the kind of thing that might happen'. This is the aspect of Thucydides to which we must now turn.

As well as providing trivial detail, recorded in a spare and unemphatic way, Thucydides sometimes operates differently, taking certain 'paradigmatic' episodes or individuals and building them up because they are typical in some way of phenomena which he wants to illustrate. Thus Kleon gets full-dress treatment as a demagogue while Hyperbolus is

---

antithesis, isokôlon and homoioteleuton in the early fifth-century Athenian regulations about the Eleusinian mysteries, IG i³ 6. The relevant phrase is ta men hakosia haplei, ta de hekosia diplei.

[34] Antiphon frags. 40, 50 Sauppe. Thuc. iv 105.1.

[35] For instance, it has been plausibly said (Cawkwell, CQ xix, 1969, 163) that there were no doubt wrangles between trierarchs, i.e. rich men who had to pay for the fitting out of a trireme, in the fifth century as there certainly were in the fourth. The trierarchic system itself existed in the mid-fifth century, Hill, Sources² B 42.

[36] Dem. 50, 22.

virtually ignored,[37] and the civil war (*stasis*) at Corcyra is fully
written up but no later *stasis* is. There is something about Megara
in Book iv,[38] and oligarchic revolution at Athens is amply
described in Book viii, but that is different: the ascendancy of the
oligarchs was achieved without prolonged *stasis*. We saw that the
Plataean siege, which was militarily unimportant, was an
instance of the kind of thing that 'might happen' – in fact, an
illustration of what Sparta the liberator was really like.[39] And the
Pentekontaetia is a highly selective set of *instances* of Athenian
aggression; so for example Naxos was the first to be subdued
'contrary to custom', and so on. It has been said that there is not
one Thucydides but two: one is 'the Thucydides who restricted
Kleon to three appearances; the other is the historian who solemnly put down the names and patronymics of endless obscure
commanders and ship captains': the Thucydides who treated
demagogues and stasis so selectively was exploring general
phenomena and searching for 'general ideas'.[40]

As for omission, we have noticed two kinds of proof of it in the
narrative of Thucydides. We can add here that the things he omits
are often as carefully chosen as the things he chooses to write up.
We have already remarked on the absence of women in Thucydides. It has been said 'there are no women as agents in his
writings and no gods: or rather, perhaps, only one woman, the
priestess at Argos who accidentally set fire to the Temple of Hera
and had to flee. She comes in handy for chronology.'[41] (The
Theban attack on Plataea fell in the forty-eighth year of her
priestess-ship, which was also the year when Ainesias was *ephor* at
Sparta, etc.). And if we limit ourselves to the evidence of Thucydides, nobody got drunk during the whole Peloponnesian War.[42]

[37] Strasburger, p.538 says of the whole of Thucydides' work that he has taken a
slice of history and treated it 'paradigmatisch'. For the Sicilian demagogue
Athenagoras, and the reasons for his treatment, see Andrewes, *Phoenix* 1962, 77
n.31.
[38] iv 74.
[39] Gomme, cited above, p.10.
[40] M.I. Finley, introduction to the Penguin *Portable Greek Historians*, 1977
(originally published by Viking Press, 1959), 13. See also his p.11 on general
ideas: 'one good example was sufficient for his purpose; the rest would be useless
repetition.'
[41] Syme, *PBA* 1962, 41. Cf. ii 2.1; iv 133. Note also i 136.3, the wife of Admetus of
Molossia. Some women (110 of them) stay behind at the siege of Plataea – to do
the cooking (ii 78.3). Note also ii 4.2, iii 74.1: women as city-defenders.
[42] Strasburger, p.788. Cf. below p.190 n.1 on laughter in Thucydides.

There is, then, a tension in Thucydides between a desire to record all the particular *erga* of the war (an impossible aim, of course) and an opposite tendency to go to extremes of selectivity and omission, in the desire to draw out the general implications of events. There is, we may say, Thucydides the tape-recorder and Thucydides the sociologist, more interested in the general patterns to which human society conforms but aware (in a remarkable phrase about the Corcyran *stasis*) that 'symptoms may vary according to the variety of the particular cases'.[43] In an unpublished lecture, Edward Hussey has compared this to the language of modern physics, which speaks of differences in 'boundary conditions' which produce differences in the phenomena observed. The principle is simple but profound, and someone had to state it for the first time. Thucydides was that person.

So the claim to accuracy in Book i, and perhaps to completeness at the beginning of Book ii, and the inconsequential detail in much of the narrative, are at odds with what we find elsewhere: a highly stylised and selective treatment of key incidents and individuals. Commentators have tended to dismiss all the triviality – patronymics of obscure men, etc. – as signs of incompleteness, things which Thucydides would have eliminated had he lived longer. But it is worth asking where such a hypothetical process of elimination would have stopped. Would Thucydides have gone on distilling his narrative further and further until it was nearly all pure spirit like the Melian Dialogue? Surely the annual invasions would have remained (though perhaps for artistic reasons), and much else besides, unless we are to allow no meaning at all to the programme at the beginning of Book ii where he says he will describe 'each of the events, by summer and winter'.

To return to the theme of the first part of Chapter One, it is no use protesting: 'How could Thucydides as a historian be guilty of so incoherent a programme and practice?' We may repeat that he did not *know* that he was what we would call, or rather what Aristotle a century after him would call, a historian. He was a 'gatherer-and-writer-down'.

The fluctuation between massive subjectivity and massive comprehensiveness, or perhaps between extreme subjectivity

---

[43] iii 82.

and extreme objectivity, has been argued for in this chapter with reference only to the narrative. In the next chapter we shall discuss the speeches, and we shall see that the same tension is present even more clearly.

CHAPTER THREE
The Speeches

In the last chapter, I argued that there is an unresolved
contradiction in Thucydides between two separate programmes,
the subjective and the objective, between the desire to select and
'write up' in a paradigmatic way and the desire to record
comprehensively. The speeches offer further evidence that two
hearts beat in Thucydides' breast. In particular, the famous
programmatic statement about the speeches in Book i[1] contains
another unresolved contradiction between the criteria of
subjectivity and objectivity. He says that he has recorded what
he thought appropriate (*ta deonta*, literally 'what was
necessary') for his speakers to say, keeping as close as possible to
the general purport (*xumpasa gnômê*) of what was really said
(*alêthôs lechthenta*). It has been well said, of the two halves of
this sentence, that 'the criterion of the one (*alêthôs lechthenta*)
is quite simply the truth, the criterion of the other is suitability'.[2]
Various efforts have been made to get rid of the contradiction.
One scholar has said of the speeches that true historical
objectivity means representing things as they appear to you to be
true, and he speaks of 'ideal' rather than 'ephemeral' reality.[3]
This is dangerously near to an unhelpful denial of any difference
between the subjective and the objective. And the observation
that if Thucydides puts arguments into his speakers' mouths (*ta
deonta*) he does so in the service of historical truth,[4] requires that
'historical' be understood in a rather special sense.
Historians (rather than students of literature) have tended
instinctively to put more weight on the phrase 'what was really

[1] i 22 1.
[2] F.W. Walbank, *Speeches in Greek Historians*, Third Myres Memorial
Lecture, Oxford 1967, 4 (=p.245 of Walbank's *Selected Papers*, Cambridge 1984).
[3] Ed. Meyer, *Forschungen zur alten Geschichte* ii, Halle, 1899, 387; cf. 385.
[4] Macleod, *Essays*, 88; cf.53.

said', and less on 'what was appropriate'. They claim, for instance, that Thucydides does his best to remain anchored to *ta alêthôs lechthenta*;[5] they can even try to save him by denying that there is a contradiction: 'Outside the central core of a speech, its *xumpasa gnômê*, the criterion of suitability alone rules'.[6] This is surely unacceptable if it implies that *xumpasa gnômê* matters more to Thucydides than suitability, i.e. that the participial clause ('keeping ...') matters more than the main clause. But equally, we cannot say that the main clause matters more than the participial. There is, in fact, a perfect and impossible balance between the two halves of the sentence. So the struggle between objectivity and subjectivity, for which I argued when examining the narrative, is just as sharp when we turn to the speeches. To the objection that Thucydides cannot have been such a fool as to utter such a flagrant contradiction, we can reply that the contradiction is far from flagrant: it requires language like 'objective' and 'subjective', and more important a conscious distinction between the historian as recorder of fact, on the one hand, and the writer of the dramatically plausible on the other, which as we have seen is a distinction not formulated until Aristotle – though Thucydides' own admirable practice may have contributed to its formulation.

But those whose interests are literary more than historical tend to emphasise *ta deonta*, 'what is appropriate', sometimes leaving 'what was really said' out of account altogether. An excellent modern treatment of the Melian Dialogue opens by pointing out that the phrase *ta deonta* puts Thucydides firmly in a rhetorical tradition, and by comparing what Gorgias said about his purpose in the *Helen*: to say rightly what is appropriate (*to deon*).[7] And Isokrates has the phrase too.[8] This rhetorical approach to Thucydides has enormously deepened our understanding of the speeches: parallel after parallel can be produced between what

---

[5] Walbank, *Papers*, 246.

[6] G.E.M. de Ste Croix, *Origins of the Peloponnesian War*, London 1972, 11.

[7] Gorgias, *Helen*, 2; see Macleod, p.52. Note also Connor, 'Thucydides', 273: *ta deonta* are the appropriate responses for any rhetorical situation; the exact phraseology of a speaker was beyond recall, but one could determine the general proposition and the circumstances under which the speech was given. Then, 'from these facts one could derive the rhetorically appropriate strategy and thereby create an approximation of the original speech'. Thus, Connor concludes, 'the influence of the sophists helps explain his otherwise baffling statement about his method'.

[8] Isok. xiii 7-8.

Thucydidean speakers say and what was said by the practitioners and theoreticians of Greek rhetoric – the authors of tragedy, forensic oratory, philosophical dialogues and the rhetorical handbooks of the fourth century. No one can for the future ignore the relation between Thucydides' speeches and productions of these various types.

But some problems remain about the relation between 'what is [rhetorically] appropriate' and 'what was really said'. The kind of difficulty I have in mind is illustrated by two contrasting modern views of the first pair of speeches, the exchange at Athens between the Corcyreans and Corinthians. On one view, this is 'the extreme instance when Thucydides reported the general sense of what was actually said'. The speech is concerned with the city of Epidamnus, a particular offer of arbitration, Corinth's specific claims on Athens' gratitude with her loan of twenty ships earlier in the fifth century, etc. But on another view, the Corinthians 'represent, broadly speaking', what is just, while the Corcyreans represent what is expedient[9] (though we may note the irony that their speech begins with the words 'it is just'). Again, the Corcyrean speech resembles both the Mytilenean speech in Book iii and the rhetorical prescriptions for proposing an alliance to be found in a fourth-century treatise called the *Rhetoric to Alexander*.[10] For instance, in that rhetorical work we read 'show that [the proposed allies'] power is substantial': this matches both the Mytileneans' claim that the Spartans, by helping Mytilene, will acquire a big fleet; and a similar claim by the Corcyreans.[11]

This recent use of rhetorical treatises, in particular the *Rhetoric to Alexander*, is of great interest. We could go on to analyse similarly many more Thucydidean speeches, pointing out the ways in which they tally with the recommendations of

[9] The first view: N.G.L. Hammond, in P. Stadter (ed.), *The Speeches in Thucydides*, Chapel Hill 1973, 49ff. 'The particular and the universal in the speeches in Thucydides, with special reference to that of Hermokrates at Gela', esp. 51f. The second view: Macleod, p.55. 'It is just ...': i 32.1.

[10] This work is sometimes attributed to Anaximenes, but is often printed among the works of Aristotle, e.g. Loeb *Aristotle* vol.xvi. The relevant section is 1424b28ff. It is worth noting that a date no later than the fourth century for the *Rhetoric to Alexander* is now certain: E.G. Turner, *Greek Papyri*[2] Oxford 1980, 99. On the treatise generally, see K. Barwick, *Philologus* cx, 1966, 212ff.; cxi, 47ff.

[11] Op.cit. 1425a36ff.; cf.Thuc.iii 13.7, i 36.3. See also J.H. Finley, *Three Essays on Thucydides*, 12.

such works on rhetoric. Take for instance the Spartan speech at Athens in Book iv: the Spartans, embarrassed by the plight of their troops at Pylos in 425, come to Athens to ask for peace. There are striking parallels with the section in the *Rhetoric to Alexander* on how to give advice to people when you are trying to stop a war which has already begun:[12]

> If those whom we are advising are getting the upper hand, the first thing to say is that sensible people should not wait till they have a fall but should make peace while they have the upper hand, and next that it is the nature of war to ruin many even of those who are successful in it, whereas it is the nature of peace to save the vanquished while allowing the victors to enjoy the prizes for which they went to war; and we must point out how many and how incalculable are the changes of fortune that occur in war.

With this compare the following points made by Thucydides' Spartans:

> It is not reasonable, therefore, for you to think that, because of your present strength and your recent acquisitions, fortune also will always be on your side. True wisdom is shown by those who make careful use of their advantages in the knowledge that things will change ... As for war, they will know that it will go its way directed by chance and can not be restricted to the conditions which one or other of the two sides would like to see fixed. They will be least likely to meet with reverses because not puffed up by success in war; and they will make peace while they are doing well ... Now is the time to be reconciled while the issue is undecided and you can acquire glory and our friendship and we can be relieved from our distress before anything shameful has happened.

The parallels are undeniable, and it is obviously right to use the Aristotelian term 'symbuleutic [i.e. deliberative] rhetoric' about Thucydides' speeches.[13] The only question we might pose is about the implications of saying that 'Thucydides is well-versed in rhetorical theory and practice'[14] as if we could be sure that the

---

[12] Thuc. iv 17-20; cf. *Rhetoric to Alexander* 1425a36ff; J.H. Finley, op. cit., 36 and n.53.

[13] Macleod, p.88. 'Symbuleutic' (as opposed to 'dikanic', i.e. forensic and 'epideictic', i.e. display oratory): Ar.*Rhet.*1358b and Pritchett, *Dionysius*, 82.

[14] Macleod, p.52. I am not of course suggesting that Macleod was unaware of the chronological relation between the two, or that he does not make full use of

Rhetoric to Alexander were representative of what was available to Thucydides. The *Rhetoric* dates from the fourth century, and it is an obvious and stultifying possibility that the influence worked the other way. In other words, it was perhaps not so much that Thucydides was well versed in rhetorical theory as that the rhetorical theorists were well versed in Thucydides. Didactic handbooks in any age presuppose the theory they set out to teach, i.e. practice dictates the theory which in turn dictates practice. No Roman orator, arguing for a big command for a general after 66 BC, could ignore Cicero's speech *pro lege Manilia*.[15] This is not to deny the rhetorical element in Thucydides' speeches, but to suggest that the rules followed him, not he the rules.[16]

There is, perhaps, a risk of over-valuing a fourth-century

---

more nearly contemporary works like Antiphon. On the relation between Thucydides and the *Rhetoric to Alexander* see further P. Moraux, *Les Etudes Classiques* xxii, 1954, 3ff. 'Thucydide et la rhétorique' and O. Luschnat, *RE* supp.xxi, 1970, 'Thukydides', cols. 1147ff.; see further below, p.56, cf. 100.

[15] Fronto in the second century AD sent this speech to Marcus Aurelius: 'You will find in it many chapters aptly suited to your present counsels ...' – and so Lucius Verus, like Pompey, was sent out as supreme commander in the east: A. Birley, *Marcus Aurelius*, London 1966, 170.

[16] There is a similar problem, worth brief discussion since it has aroused more attention than this aspect of Thucydides and may therefore help us, about Horace's panegyrical poetry in relation to (later) works like that of Menander Rhetor, who in the third century AD laid down rules for praising a king. Are Horace's utterances merely rhetorical *topoi* (conventional themes), a contribution to a long-lived genre of writing 'About Kingship'? (See, for example, p.114 of R. Seager's good article '*Neu sinas Medos equitare inultos*: Horace, the Parthians and Augustan foreign policy', *Athenaeum* lviii, 1980, 103ff. For Menander Rhetor see now the edition by D.A. Russell and N.G. Wilson, Oxford 1981.) Or is it not rather possible that when Menander (230) offers 'We do not fear barbarians or enemies' as the kind of thing to say to a king, he is echoing Horace's *nec mori per vim metuam tenente Caesare terras* (*Odes* iii 14) rather than the other way round? Jasper Griffin, in the course of an entertaining attack on the 'generic' approach to ancient literature (the view, that is, that the whole of classical poetry is written according to the rules of the various genres), observes that some of the genres treated by Menander may not have existed at all in the Augustan period: *JRS* lxxi, 1981, 39ff., 'Genre and real life in Latin Poetry', at p. 40 (now reprinted in his *Latin Poets and Roman Life*, London 1985). He remarks (ibid.) of Menander and pseudo-Dionysius: 'These rhetoricians, who hitherto have led quiet lives respectively in the second volume of Usener and Radermacher's Teubner edition of the opuscula of Dionysius and in the third volume of Spengel's *Rhetores Graeci*, thus have sudden greatness thrust upon them; they become the key to the understanding of ancient poetry, Greek and Latin, from beginning to end.' What I am suggesting is that we should be equally careful not to make the *Rhetoric to Alexander* the 'key' to Thucydides.

handbook like the *Rhetoric to Alexander* precisely because of the closeness of the parallels with Thucydides, parallels which may be due more to Thucydides' influence on the treatises than the other way. Certainly there were rudimentary treatises on oratory in the fifth century which Thucydides would have known, and we noted in the preceding chapter the growth of professionalism in Sicily and Athens. But in general it is the fourth century which is the age of the didactic handbook.[17] We shall see later that Thucydides in several areas stands at the frontier between the loose and the technical, the amateur and the professional. He was certainly a connoisseur of oratory – witness his appreciation of Antiphon's speech when on trial for his life, 'the best in my time', or the judgment on Brasidas, 'not bad at speaking – for a Spartan'.[18] But what Thucydides says in the speeches need not have been determined by theory, except in so far as theory could be extracted from the practice of the most accomplished diplomats of his own day: which returns us to the problem of 'what was really said' *vs.* 'what was appropriate'. The real-life Corcyreans and Corinthians, who were nearer, geographically and culturally, to Gorgias' Sicily than the Athenians were, could have had some idea of 'what was appropriate'. And we should not lose sight of the other half of Thucydides' programme, to keep as close as possible to the general purport of what was actually said. The 'trial' of the Plataeans in Book iii, it has been said, is a 'travesty of legality as the Melian Dialogue is of dialectic' ... 'the historian, like the tragedians, here and often uses rhetorical skills in order that they should be seen to fail'.[19] That suggestion ('that they should be seen to fail') will be looked at later; for the moment I wish to notice the assumptions that it was the historian not the real-life Plataeans who used the skills in question. Have we the right to make that assumption? It is a natural one to make. It is surprising that some ordinary Plataeans, on trial for their lives, should follow copybook rhetorical methods (though perhaps not more surprising than the oratory of Sacco and Vanzetti); and it is tempting to treat the

[17] L. Radermacher's *Artium Scriptores, Sber. Öst. Akad. Wiss* 227.3 (1951) gives such evidence as there is for fifth-century rhetorical theory. Handbooks: see my *Greek World 479-323 B. C.*, London 1983, 156.

[18] viii 68.2; iv 84.2.

[19] Macleod, p.109; cf. his p.156 on Eur. *Hec.* 814ff.: 'Here, then, as in the Plataean Debate, is one of those speeches which tragically fail.'

speeches simply as an exercise in 'what was rhetorically appropriate'. Thucydides does, however, *name* the Plataean speakers, something which it is easy to overlook; indeed it is overlooked by the author of a valuable recent book on Thucydides' speeches, who says twice on one page that the Plataeans who plead for their lives are 'unnamed'. They are not: they are called Astymachos son of Asopolaos and Lakon son of Aeimnestos.[20] There is no reason to doubt either that they existed or that they spoke, although it has been sensibly said that, since there are two of them, Thucydides has done some telescoping: the two men did not speak in unison.[21] Lakon, which just means 'Spartan', is an unimpeachable name for a Spartan *proxenos* or honorary consul[22] (as Thucydides tells us he was), just the man to be pushed forward to make the best case before the Spartans. As for Asopolaos, it is a good Boiotian name, derived from the local river Asopos. Names beginning Asop- are far from exclusively Boiotian; for instance, Asopios is found in the family of the famous Athenian general Phormio; but there can be no quarrelling with the generalisation that Asop- names are characteristically Boiotian.[23] Thucydides' man, the son of Asopolaos, is authentic. A Plataean speech, then, was indeed delivered; but (it has been shrewdly asked): 'From what source did Thucydides hear anything of the speech? Was there some honest Spartan or Theban (or Thespian) present who gave him the drift of it? ... If Thucydides asked, what did they say? The answer may have been, "only the usual things – the Persian

---

[20] iii 52.5, oddly overlooked by Mark Cogan, *The Human Thing: The Speeches and Principles of Thucydides' History*, Chicago 1981, 219.

[21] A.W. Gomme, *Essays in Greek History and Literature*, Oxford, 1937, 156ff., 'The speeches in Thucydides', at p. 173. But note his p. 175: 'Thucydides had been at pains to discover the names of the two Plataeans; is it to be supposed he took no trouble to find out what was said?'

[22] *Proxenoi* were citizens of state A looking after the interests of state B in state A.

[23] Cf. e.g. Asopodorus (Theban): Hdt. ix 69, cf. *SEG* xxiii 271 line 12 (Thespiai), and the index to *IG* vii; Asopodotus: P.M. Fraser and T. Rönne, *Boiotian and West Greek Tombstones*, Lund 1957, 11, Thebes no.5; *SEG* xxvi 577; xviii 235 line 23. See also Fraser/Rönne, *Some More Boiotian and West Greek Tombstones*, Stockholm 1971, 55, Thebes no.103; *SEG* xxvi 576; 1041; 583; xxv 504 (Asopotimos, Asopodon, Asopokles, Asopoklidas, Asopokritos, Asopon). Athenian Asopios: Thuc.i 64; iii 7. Cf. too *SEG* xxii 32; 33; xxiv 33, 34; 194 line 26 (Asopodoros, Asopokles); xxix 412 (Achaean). There were other rivers called Asopos, e.g. one between Corinth and Sikyon, and another in Lakonia. But that in Boiotia is the most famous.

wars, the gods and the oaths, the special sanctity of Plataea, the honour of Sparta; but it was very honestly done"; and in that event he clothed it in the language that we have, and made it of such and such a length, because he wanted it for his purpose.'[24]

This approach is surely the only correct one towards the speeches: not to treat them just as *tours de force* of rhetorical appropriateness, nor (naively) as a summary or amplification of a tape-recorded transcript of 'what was really said' (Thucydides' own phrase, 'keeping as close as possible to the actual purport', in fact implies that complete fidelity was impossible), but to look at each speech separately and ask the questions we asked about the Plataean speech.

It may help to review, first, the kind of considerations which have made students of Thucydides' speeches claim to have detected 'what was really said', and after that to review the arguments which have made people think that the speeches were, on the contrary, unauthentic exercises in 'what was appropriate'. I shall end the chapter with an attempt to ask what Thucydides' aim was in including the speeches in the form that he does.

We saw that, at Plataea, something was 'really said', and this suggests one general clue: if Thucydides offers circumstantial detail like the patronymic Asopolaos, this is his way of guaranteeing his information and surely means that the degree of invention was to that extent less. For instance, how would we feel if the Melian Dialogue, instead of being offered as an exchange between 'the Melians' and 'the Athenians', purported to be between a *named* Melian, let us call him Grophon, and Alcibiades (who in antiquity was certainly held responsible for the decision about Melos)?[25] We would, I think, feel more inclined to view the Dialogue as a 'record in the terms laid down in i 22.1'.[26] This argument from the naming of speakers is not meant to imply the converse, viz. that the anonymity of other speakers necessarily proves the unauthenticity of their speeches. Even the Melian Dialogue may be based on reports of what

[24] Gomme, *HCT* ii, 346.

[25] Alcibiades and Melos: Plut.*Alc*.xvi 6. For the Melian name Grophon see *SGDI* 4872 and *LSAG* 320.

[26] For this phrase see Andrewes, *HCT* iv, 182. Dionysius of Halicarnassus (*On Thucydides*, ch.41) was worried about how Thucydides got his information about the Melian Dialogue.

happened: it has been acutely noted that the narrative statement that the Athenians were refused access to the *plêthos* (people) at Melos implies that Thucydides had some account of the proceedings.[27] Of course there are times when the way in which a speaker is introduced actually reduces the chances that he really said what Thucydides puts into his mouth; for instance the statement in Book vii that 'the generals and Gylippos gave encouragement as follows' has been seen as a warning against too rigid a defence of the historical fidelity of all Thucydides' speeches; 'We are not to think of Gylippos as the speaker'. (That is putting it very strongly: compare what was said above about the two Plataeans.) The obscurity or celebrity of the speaker is relevant: our belief in the historicity of the Athenian speaker Diodotus in Book iii, and in the authenticity of what he says, is increased, through a kind of paradox, precisely by the fact that we know nothing else about him.[28] Which is also true of Astymachos the son of Asopolaos.

Other speeches have a claim in virtue of their content to be 'what was really said'. For instance (to start at the bottom) there are 'speeches' like the brief and terse exchange in Book i between the representatives of the Athenians and Peloponnesians after the battle of Sybota – not normally enumerated among Thucydidean speeches at all.[29] Or we might think that some speeches before battles were close to the ideal of 'what was really said', but here[30] the advice is often very general, for instance Brasidas' advice before a battle with Illyrians. Not that such generality is fatal. The short speech of Teutiaplus of Elis in Book iii is uniquely introduced by *tade* ('this') rather than the normal *toiade* (a vaguer demonstrative, 'in some such way as this'), and some scholars have sought to build on the difference.[31] But it is

[27] Andrewes, ibid., referring to Thuc.v 84.3.
[28] But see M. Ostwald, *GRBS* xx 1979, 5ff. Gylippus: vii 65 with Dover, *HCT*, ad loc.
[29] i 53.
[30] As Hammond observes (Stadter (ed.), 1973) at his p.50. Illyrians: iv 126ff.
[31] iii 30. Gomme, *Essays*, 166f. seems to think that the *tade/toiade* difference is significant (he is thinking of Herodotus as well) but does not there mention Teutiaplus. D. Lateiner, *GRBS* xvi, 1975, 175ff., 'The speech of Teutiaplus (Thuc. 3.30), at p. 181, citing Gomme, *HCT* ii, 292f., accepts the historicity of the speech, but does not consider *tade*. On Teutiaplus see also Gomme in *Essays*, 175. Sthenelaidas' short speech at i 86 is prefaced by *hôde*, 'thus', which Jebb thought vaguer than *tade* (R.C. Jebb, 'The speeches in Thucydides' in *Hellenica*, ed. Abbott, London 1898, 244ff. at p. 252 n.2). See also Jebb, ibid., on iv 58 where

not easy to believe that Thucydides, no slave to technical terms (p.99), deliberately 'flagged' one speech, and one only, in this way, namely that of Teutiaplus. Are all the others then invented?

Another line of approach has been to distinguish, within speeches, between parts which are rooted in what is, from the speaker's point of view, the 'here and now', and parts which look characteristically 'Thucydidean'.[32] For instance, it has been thought that the beginning of Pericles' first speech (a section which speaks of the need to show resolution and not rescind the Megarian decree) and the end (the 'solemn' passage where Pericles is made to stress what the Persian War generation of Athenians achieved through determination and boldness uncombined with power, i.e. [?] material resources) cut at the root of the argument of the central part of the speech, which is based on a prudent calculation of, precisely, material resources.[33] From this change of style or mood, and from this illogicality, it has been concluded[34] that the central passage, in which Periclean strategy is outlined, is Thucydidean rather than Periclean, and that it was composed late. We may have reservations about this. For instance, the speech shows awareness that there were people who were grumbling at the war policy, and it would not have been unnatural for the historical Pericles to take this opportunity to answer his critics on this point. As for the change of mood, strange consequences would follow if we applied the same sort of reasoning to Cicero's *pro*

---

dē ('we may presume') may suggest that Thucydides resorted to guesswork in an unusual degree; cf. Gomme ii 521. Against Tarn's use of similar formulae in Arrian, see P. Brunt, Loeb *Arrian* ii, 1983, 530.

[32] That was the approach of F. Jacoby, whose fifteen-volume collection of the 'fragments' of the Greek historians has rightly been called 'the most important modern work on Greek history' (O. Murray, *Early Greece*, 294) but who wrote extremely little about Thucydides. This was partly due to the accident that Thucydides' name begins with a 'T' and not, for instance, with 'H' or 'K' which are in the part of the alphabet which was being covered by the great encylopaedia Pauly-Wissowa around the time that Jacoby was writing for it. This accident means that all the more value attaches to a Kiel dissertation by Rose Zahn on the first speech of Pericles (i 140-44): *Die erste Periklesrede (Thukydides I 140-144), Interpretation und Versuch einer Einordnung in den Zusammenhang des Werkes*, diss. Kiel 1934. This incorporates material by Jacoby.

[33] i 141.2-143.

[34] On the 'solemn' closing section (i 144) see Zahn, p.34; contradiction between beginning/end and middle: pp.26f., 32, 68, 114ff. n.123. Grumbling at war policy: 140.1.

Caelio. But if the argument is not pressed to extremes, we may perhaps accept that the historical Pericles did indeed say a certain amount about the Megarian decree, as the speech makes him do – in defiance of the narrative, which virtually ignores it; and that a 'Thucydidean' speech about Pericles' war plans has been inserted into a Periclean speech about whether the Megarian decree should be lifted or not.

Another, related, kind of detail which may suggest authenticity is the inclusion in a speech of arguments which are so bad that they could not have been regarded by Thucydides as appropriate; it must therefore have been really been delivered (i.e. it is not a Thucydidean invention). One suggested candidate here is the Corinthian plea in Book i that they should be allowed to punish Corcyra because they themselves had allowed Athens to punish Samos.[35]

A difficulty about this approach is its extreme subjectivity; more serious is that it is two-edged: the aggressiveness of the Athenian speakers at Sparta, again in Book i, has been thought to be implausibly tactless, and therefore invented.[36] But we could argue equally well that the inclusion of such ill-judged, i.e. inappropriate, arguments is the best proof that the speech is 'what was really said', rather than 'what was in Thucydides' view appropriate'.

We may turn now to the various arguments for inauthenticity,[37] partial or total.

First, there is the selection, compression and omission to which Thucydides has subjected the speeches. Here, again, is the 'paradigmatic' Thucydides at work, organising his material subjectively. The allocation of speeches to Kleon is instructive. From other evidence[38] we know that Kleon was politically active before Pericles' death; but Thucydides allows him no speech before then. This is surely for artistic reasons: Kleon has been held back and kept out of Book i so that he can be introduced only when Pericles is off stage for ever. (He was perhaps one of

[35] J.B. Salmon, *Wealthy Corinth*, Oxford 1984, 274 and n.17.

[36] i 75ff.

[37] There is a very helpful chapter on this aspect of the speeches in K.J. Dover, *Thucydides; Greece and Rome* New Survey in the Classics no.7, 1973, ch. vi. Good remarks also in J.H. Finley, 'The origins of Thucydides' style', *Three Essays on Thucydides*, 1967, ch.ii.

[38] Plut.*Per*.xxxiii 8; J.K. Davies, *Athenian Propertied Families*, 1971, 145, but note F. Bourriot, *Historia* xxxi, 1982, 404ff.

those who argued[39] that Athens should go to war, but who are not given a speech.) Kleon is given sentiments which deliberately echo Pericles, as Homer's Thersites echoes Achilles;[40] some of the point of this would be lost if the two politicians were treated as rivals rather than as a succession. But a different explanation is needed for Thucydides' denial to Kleon of any reply to the Spartans' speech in Book iv, which we examined earlier in this chapter (p.48). The commentaries do not remark on the omission, but it is surely very odd: Kleon's recommendation, that the Spartan peace offer should be rejected, is successful, but he is not allowed by Thucydides to demolish the sophistry and empty offers of the Spartans. Why not? If Kleon was right to reject the peace offer, and he surely was, despite Thucydides' talk of Athenian greed (the Spartans were really offering very little), it was unfair of Thucydides to deny him a speech. There is the clue: Thucydides' personal malice against Kleon (below, p.166). Kleon, then, has been held back (Book i) and denied a full say (Book iv). With Hermokrates of Syracuse, whom Thucydides admired (below, p.70), the opposite has happened: Thucydides has boldly brought him forward; he is given a powerful speech in Book iv, ten years before his real prominence.[41]

We have already noted some examples of compression – 'Gylippos and the generals', and the two Plataeans; note also the formula 'Knemos, Brasidas and the other Peloponnesian commanders ... spoke *toiade*'.[42]

Second, excessive obedience to the 'rules' of rhetoric. We have already seen that there are correspondences between Thucydides and the prescriptions of the oratorical handbooks. However, we suggested reasons for treating those correspondences with caution; we shall return to the general question of Thucydides' relation to *contemporary* oratory under my seventh heading, namely the (alleged) implausible difficulty of Thucydides' speeches. For the moment we may note a general point: to show

---

[39] i 139.

[40] With ii 63.2. compare iii 37.2 (empire as tyranny; Pericles had merely said it was *like* a tyranny). Kleon as Thersites: F. Cairns, *JHS* cii, 1982, 203f. (cf. already Macleod, p.93).

[41] Spartan speech: iv 17-20. Hermokrates: at vi 38.5 Athenagoras denounces the ambition of 'youthful' politicians – surely a hit at Hermokrates. But if Hermokrates was 'youthful' in 415, he cannot really have been a major figure a decade earlier, as iv 58ff. requires.

[42] ii 86.6.

conformity to general rules does not prove inauthenticity, it merely proves that whoever 'thought' the speech had had a good Greek education. To take a later example, Alexander's speech at Opis, as reported by Arrian, follows rhetorical rules,[43] but the explanation of this may just be that rhetoric was on the syllabus for Alexander's tutorials from Aristotle at Mieza (tutorials which Arrian's source, Ptolemy, shared). This is not to defend the authenticity of the Opis speech, merely to make a general point about the limits of arguments from rhetoric.

Third, there is characterisation, something denied most flatly by Cornford in his *Thucydides Mythistoricus*.[44] Cornford says that Kleon is like a character on a playbill, a character with no past and no future. But there is more characterisation in Thucydides than is sometimes allowed: Sthenelaidas in Book i is laconic (short, few connecting particles); the Sicilian Hermokrates in Book iv shows the influence of his fellow-countryman Gorgias; Alcibiades before the Sicilian expedition in Book vi is given extravagant language like 'quench their pride', and his tinsel phrases and thoughts in this speech are designed[45] to bring out Alcibiades' egoism and misleading optimism: if Kleon in Book iii is a cruder, Alcibiades is here a more lightweight, Pericles (which is not to deny, see below, that both men took Pericles as a model in real life). Herodotus had attempted characterisation of a sort: Croesus, Cypselus, Xerxes and Demaratus, for instance. And he can depict national characteristics: the Spartans replied to a long Samian request for help by saying that they had forgotten the beginning of the speech and could not understand the end. So the Samians produced a bag and said 'Bag needs flour', to which the Spartans replied that the word 'bag' was superfluous.[46] So the laconic Sthenelaidas has a precedent. Let it then be accepted that there is characterisation in Thucydides. But the conclusion is two-edged. Attempted characterisation could represent the extreme of artistic polish, the final proof of artificiality; or it could be held to show that the utterly faithful tape-recorder

[43] For instance, in the final abrupt imperative, cf. Brunt's Loeb note on Arrian *Anab*.vii 10.7.

[44] F.M. Cornford, *Thucydides Mythistoricus*, London 1907, 146f.

[45] i 86; iv 59ff.; vi 15-18, with Macleod, ch.9, 'Rhetoric and history'.

[46] iii 46.

caught nuances of individual character, 'what was really said'.
The only thing that would be significant would be if the speeches
were, as is sometimes claimed, all in Thucydides' uniform style,
which would positively rule out 'what was really said' – just as it
is hard to believe that Tacitus' Calgacus, a highland chieftain,
had read Sallust, Livy, Cicero and Quintus Curtius, all of whom
he echoes.[47] But since most of Thucydides' speakers are neither
barbarians nor uneducated, there are no such glaring pieces of
authorial interference.

There is a further problem, however: what do we mean by
characterisation – individual characterisation, or just type-cast-
ing, i.e. the portrayal of national or ethnic characteristics?
Marcellinus said of Thucydides that he was 'clever at portraying
character', but this could refer to something other than
individual characterisation.[48] The problem resembles that
created by the first attempts at portraiture in visual art; these,
significantly, date from the time when Thucydides was writing.
Thus the coins of the satrap Tissaphernes are perhaps attempts
to realise a hook-nosed Iranian type rather than the individual

---

[47] See R.M. Ogilvie and I. Richmond, *Agricola* commentary, Oxford 1967,
253ff.

[48] There is a problem about Marcellinus' view; at para. 50 he says that
Thucydides is *deinos ethographêsai*, and illustrates this by his representation of
the youth of Alcibiades, the (?) villainy (*ponêria*? the text is corrupt: it has
panta) of Themistocles, etc. Poppo-Stahl comment on this that this
characteristic is achieved 'orationibus praecipue'. Cf. Pritchett p.120. But at
para.57 he says that Thucydides is *anethopoiêtos* in the speeches, a word which
D.A. Russell in his edition of Longinus, *On the Sublime*, Oxford 1964,
commenting on ch.34, translates as 'without sense of character'. (The word
can also mean 'unattractive'; cf. F. Zucker, *Sber.Berl.Acad.* 1952(4),
'Anethopoietos', arguing that Marcellinus took the word from Caecilius of
Caleacte.) Poppo-Stahl have no comment to make on this second passage, which
does not fit their view of para.50. Are we to remove the contradiction by
supposing that (contra Poppo-Stahl) Marcellinus is thinking of the narrative in
para.50, but that he is thinking (as he certainly is) of the speeches in para.57? In
favour of this view, Themistocles has no speeches; but there is not much direct
characterisation of Pericles or Alcibiades (cf. I. Bruns, *Das literarische Porträt
der Griechen*, Berlin 1896, 8). Perhaps Marcellinus is just confused. But the
contradiction is worth noticing; some modern scholars cite him for the view that
Thucydides' speeches do contain characterisation (so Poppo-Stahl), others, like
Pritchett, for the view that the speeches contain *no* characterisation. I have not
found a discussion which tries to explain *both* passages. For an attempt to show
that there is characterisation of Nikias and Alcibiades in their speeches, see D.
Tompkins, *YCS* xxii, 1972, 181ff.

Tissaphernes.[49] It has been said that 'the truth of the portraiture of classical Athenian sculpture is that of the speeches in Thucydides' history'.[50] The comparison between portraiture in the different art-forms is worth thinking about (though the remark just quoted may be thought to err by suggesting an analogy with idealistic not realistic sculpture): the technical difficulties in expressing individuality were only just being overcome in other areas of artistic expression. Before Thucydides, the technical problem with literary portraiture was how to get information precise enough to avoid conventional characterisation.[51]

Fourth, responsions, that is, the way in which speakers, especially those who do not actually hear each other, 'answer' each others' points exactly. An example from Book i is the answer of Pericles to a suggestion of the Corinthians about *epiteichisis*, that is, fortifying a post in enemy territory.[52] This is not hard to stomach: security in ancient Greece was bad and confidentiality low. Nor is it impossible that Pericles' political heirs should echo him;[53] this does not have to be a historian's artifice, it could be the speakers themselves, like Mrs Thatcher or Ronald Reagan echoing Churchill. It is more implausible that Phormio should so neatly meet the points made by the Peloponnesian commanders, although separated by several miles of sea.[54] But the most impressive set of responsions are in the 'tetralogy' of speeches delivered at Sparta half way through Book i. One analysis of the four speeches goes like this:[55] the first speech (by the Corinthians) is answered by the third (Archidamus), while the second (by the Athenians), which

[49] W. Schwabacher, in *Essays in Greek Coinage presented to Stanley Robinson*, edd. C. Kraay and G. Jenkins, Oxford 1968, 111ff., 'Lycian coin-portraits'. On the beginnings of portraiture see generally M. Robertson, *A History of Greek Art*, Cambridge 1975, 504ff.

[50] U. von Wilamowitz-Moellendorff, *Antigonos von Karystos*, Phil. Untersuch. iv, 1881, 148.

[51] L. Pearson, *Journal of the History of Ideas* xv, 1954, 136ff., 'Real and conventional personalities in Greek history'=*Selected Papers of Lionel Pearson*, edd. D. Lateiner and S. Stephens, Berkeley, Cal. 1983, 110ff.

[52] i 122; cf.142.2. Cf. also the reference to taking money from Olympia or Delphi and paying for a mercenary fleet with it: i 121.3, cf. 142.1.

[53] For this point, Dover, *Thucydides*, New Survey, 26. But see above, p.56 and n.40 and below, p.69: such echoes perhaps Homeric.

[54] ii 87ff.

[55] Ed. Schwartz, *Das Geschichtswerk des Thukydides²*, Bonn 1929, esp. 102ff.

moves on to the broader question of the legitimacy of the Athenian Empire), is answered by the fourth (Sthenelaidas). Moreover, it is said, each speech ignores the immediately preceding speech: this is unlike the course of a real debate. A refinement of this view[56] takes the Athenians and Sthenelaidas to represent Thucydides' second thoughts on the causes of the war. The most striking responsions are: 'prudence' is picked up by 'sensible prudence'; 'insensitive' by 'insensitively'; and the word 'accusation' is repeated. All these words are thrown back at the Corinthians by Archidamus.[57] The correspondences between the Athenians and Sthenelaidas are substantive rather than verbal, though 'worthy' is a verbal echo of a key word.[58] But how true is it that each speech ignores the preceding one? Actually the Athenians (speech 2) address themselves to Spartan slowness in decision-making (which is the main theme of the Corinthian speech, speech 1): note the Athenian advice – or taunt – 'You should deliberate slowly'. And the 'ships and horses' of Sthenelaidas (speech 4) precisely echo Archidamus in speech 3.[59] Again, the Corinthians in speech 2 touch on the 'truest cause' of the war, namely Athenian expansion, when they refer to Athenian 'acquisitiveness'.[60] So this theme is not just confined to speeches 2 and 4, the Athenians and Sthenelaidas; and the tissue of the four speeches is more complex than first appears. Nor is it necessary to see speeches 2 and 4 as evidence of a later stage of Thucydides' thinking, because in the Corcyrean speech earlier in the book, a speech which ought to be 'early' on any view, we find a reference to Spartan fear of Athens as something which is likely to produce war.[61] In other words, we have here the 'truest cause'. But the 'truest cause' is supposed, on the theory under discussion, to be the result of Thucydides' second thoughts.

Fifth, antilogy, that is, the arrangement of speeches in pairs. This was a technique characteristic of the age of the sophists and as such is brilliantly parodied in Aristophanes' *Clouds* (see p.185). It is certainly reasonable to stigmatise this as unnatural – provided we are prepared to do the same for 'antilogy' when it

[56] A. Andrewes, *CQ* ix, 1959, 223ff., 'Thucydides and the causes of the war'. Contrast Dover, *HCT* v app.2, 415ff.
[57] i 68.1, cf.84.2; 69.3, cf.82.1; 69.6, cf.84.2.
[58] i 76.2, cf.86.1.
[59] i 78.1; 86.3, cf.80.3.
[60] i 70.8.
[61] i 33.

occurs in Herodotus; not just the debate on the constitutions in Book iii, at which offence has indeed often been taken (above, p.16), but the dispute before the battle of Plataea between the Athenians and Tegeans, a mention of which finds a place in a factual modern history of Greece.[62] A degree of literary artifice need not be denied; but Homer – one thinks of exchanges like that between Zeus and Hera in *Iliad* iv – is as much of an influence on both Herodotus and Thucydides as are the sophists. Political debate was not an invention of the classical period: 'Only consider the remarkable debates described in the Homeric poems. Ancient critics noted that the speakers in them employ many of the devices later documented by rhetoricians to excellent effect'.[63]

Something similar can be said about the sixth objection sometimes made to Thucydides' speeches, on the score of the anonymity of his speakers. 'How grey and dreary,' one scholar exclaims, '*Wie grau und trüb*', is Thucydides in contrast to Herodotus, because in Thucydides we get collectives standing for whole peoples – the Athenians, the Corinthians and so on. But the implied contrast is misleading: in Herodotus we find similarly anonymous speakers. Thus it is 'the Spartans' who say that the word 'bag' is superfluous, the Therans and Cyrenaeans who hold this or that belief about Battus and the founding of Cyrene, the Argives who demand half the command against Persia, the Thessalians who urge the Greeks to defend Mount Olympus.[64] And so on.

In any case, Thucydides' views on this subject developed, if it is right to think that Thucydides moved away from thinking in terms of 'grey' collective nouns and towards the view that individuals like Alcibiades did make an increasing difference to the course of history.[65] Thus the oligarchic revolution of 411 is seen very much in personal terms (see further below, Chapter Six).

[62] ix 26ff.; G. Busolt, *Griechische Geschichte*, Gotha 1895, ii,[2] 728. See Limentani on Plutarch, *Aristides* xii for other views.

[63] H. Lloyd-Jones, *Justice of Zeus*[2], 1983, 181. See J.H. Finley, 'The origins of Thucydides' style', *Three Essays on Thucydides*, 1967, 79, who however thinks that Homer's debates are less abstract than those of fifth-century literature. But this must now be judged in the light of Griffin, cited below n.73.

[64] Strasburger, p.541 (=Herter, ed., *Thukydides*, 426); see already Bruns, p.1; Hdt.iv 150ff.; vii 148.4; ix 12; vii 172.

[65] See H.D. Westlake, *Individuals in Thucydides*, Cambridge 1968; below p.146.

The seventh argument is from the difficulty of the speeches. It has been observed, in an illuminating study of 'Thucydides and the Athenians' depiction of themselves' that the Funeral Oration of Pericles in Thucydides Book ii is a far cry from surviving fourth-century examples of the genre, such as Lysias' *Epitaphios* or the *Panegyric* of Isokrates.[66] Thucydides' speeches, as well as following the rules of rhetoric in the way we have noted, sometimes turn conventional rhetorical themes inside out; thus the Melian Dialogue can be seen as a 'travesty of dialectic'. But the unconventionality of Thucydides' speeches should not be exaggerated. The Funeral Oration may indeed be an untypical specimen of the genre; but other speeches are more recognisable as types. For example, Alcibiades' speech in the Sicilian Debate in Book vi, for all its speciousness (above, p.57) and florid expression, has affinities with a speech like Lysias' *On a Charge of Taking Bribes*, in which the young, anonymous speaker lists his expenditure and services to the state. 'You ought also,' he says, 'to consider that it is far more fitting for you to give me of what is yours than to dispute my claim to what is mine.'[67] With this compare the Thucydidean Alcibiades' claim to be given the Sicilian command because of the splendid splash he has made at the Olympic Games. There were ways of dealing with such an argument (and it is perhaps surprising that Thucydides does not allow Nikias to subvert it): Antiphon pointed out that 'contributions to the war tax and the furnishing of choruses are a proof of opulence but not of innocence'.[68] Isaeus' use of this kind

---

[66] Strasburger, pp.676ff., 'Thukydides und die politische Selbstdarstellung der Athener'; Lys.ii; Isok.iv. John E. Ziolkowski, *Thucydides and the Tradition of Funeral Speeches at Athens*, Salem, New Hampshire 1981 (originally a Carolina dissertation of 1963), esp. 17ff. sees Pericles' Funeral Speech as fairly conventional, except that praise is heaped on *contemporary* Athens. Loraux, *Invention of Athens*, 1986, 246, criticises Ziolkowski for his mechanical listing and counting of *topoi*, but agrees (123) that Thucydides' *epitaphios* 'confirms the glorious present' (cf. 290, Thucydides 'challenges the *topoi* of the oration'). Loraux's work has been influential already (see e.g. Goldhill). But its value for the student of Thucydides would have been greater if she had faced more squarely the issue, whether the *epitaphios* represents the thinking of Pericles (as she usually assumes) or of Thucydides (pp. 10, 192 are unsatisfactory). P. 247 speaks mysteriously of Pericles' 'subtlety, doubled by that of Thucydides'. But see above-cited passages for her view that it is *Thucydides* who challenges the *topoi*.

[67] Thuc.vi 16; Lys.xxi 15. Davies, *Athenian Propertied Families*, xvii-xviii compares Alcibiades' boasts with Lysias xxv.

[68] Antiphon, *Tetr.*i 8.

of irrelevance in the fourth century drew from his modern
commentator the reflection that 'old men, who earned their
living by attendance in the courts, must have been familiar with
every move in the game'.[69] We must, as before, allow for the
possibility that Thucydides' Alcibiades influenced the development of the genre, but in this instance the thought that wealth
and athletic success gave a man a right to political power is
traditionally aristocratic. 'Wide is the power of wealth,' says
Pindar frankly, and Alcibiades is in many respects a throwback
to Pindar's world.[70]

Again, the Theban argument in Book iii against the Plataeans'
plea of previously good behaviour, namely that it was only
dissimulation, belongs in a long tradition of law-court oratory.[71]

So it is probable that Thucydides here makes use in a
conventional way of conventional themes. But even if we grant
that his speeches are idiosyncratic, we make it too easy for
ourselves if we compare them to the fourth-century productions
of Lysias and Isokrates, whose prose is more 'periodic' and who
avoid the abruptness and concentration of a Thucydidean
speaker. The true difference may be between the fifth century
and the fourth, rather than between Thucydides and the oratory
of his own day. The only fair comparison should be between him
and the relevant fragments of, for instance, Antiphon who, as we
saw above, composed speeches on the tributes of Rhodian Lindos
and of Samothrace. These speeches may have treated 'imperial
themes' in an astringent, Thucydidean way (see above, p.41, for
the suggestion that Thucydides himself was in demand for this
kind of oratory). The fragment on Samothrace has the sentence,
'They would not have taken thought for the misery of the other
citizens without considering their own safety.' Who are 'they'?
Perhaps disgruntled oligarchs, prepared to forget their

[69] W. Wyse, *The Speeches of Isaeus*, Cambridge 1904, 396.
[70] Pindar *Pyth.* v.1; C.M. Bowra, *Historia* ix, 1960, 68ff. (= *On Greek Margins*,
Oxford 1970, ch.xii), 'Euripides' epinician for Alcibiades'. (But see Kyle 130, n.27.)
[71] iii 64.4; see A.R. Hands, *CQ* xxiv, 1974, 312ff., 'Postremo suo tantum ingenio
utebatur' (a very interesting article). He cites Sthenelaidas' different view that
previous good behaviour should increase the punishment because it implies a
change in character (i 86). Actually the Thebans say something similar at iii 67,
so Hands' suggestion that Sthenelaidas is the better psychologist does not quite
work: it would be better to say that the Thebans have it both ways. Thucydides is
not above this: cf. the contradictory arguments of the Mytileneans at Olympia,
Macleod, p.89, and see below, p.76. See also C. Gill, *CQ* xxxiii, 1983, 469ff., 'The
question of character-development: Plutarch and Tacitus'.

differences with the popular party if they could get free of Athens? If so, we might compare Phrynichus' remark in Thucydides Book viii:

> They [the subject allies now in revolt] were more interested in being free under whatever kind of government they happened to have than in being slaves, whether under an oligarchy or a democracy.[72]

Or there is an Antiphontic speech significantly called 'On Enslavement', which talks of getting away from a *cleruchy* (an imperial institution: *cleruchs* were Athenians who were given allotments of land in imperial territory). Again, the speech about Lindos mentions Amphipolis. There is no city called Amphipolis on Rhodes, the island on which Lindos is situated; but a famous and important Amphipolis, in the North, was lost to Athens in 424. Perhaps Antiphon's speech, like Thucydides' speeches about Mytilene in Book iii, took in broader aspects of imperial policy: don't let Lindos go the way of Amphipolis. Or there is Andokides' oligarchic speech 'To his political associates [*hetairoi*]', which, if it survived, and if we could be sure that it was genuinely his, might have thrown light on the intrigues and lobbying in Thucydides Book viii: note Thucydides' brief but revealing statement that Pisander 'approached the clubs which already existed at Athens for the purpose of winning lawsuits and elections'. But all these speeches are just fragments, or titles, to us. Nevertheless, the general point stands, that if we had more of this kind of thing Thucydides' speeches might seem a little less peculiar. Finally, it is relevant that (as a recent study brilliantly shows) Homer had already used far more abstract innovative and ethically analytic language in the speeches than in the narrative. If Thucydides' speeches make exceptional demands, there was an old and impeccable precedent.[73]

Eighth, some have seen impossible foreknowledge in the speeches to Thucydides, but very few of the examples suggested are compelling – certainly not the mentions of *epiteichisis* in Book i (see above, p.59), because although this was not carried

---

[72] Thuc.viii 48.
[73] On Andokides' speech see Dover *HCT* iv, 286 n.1 (sceptical); Thuc.viii 54.4. (Pisander). On the lack of proper comparative evidence note the sound remarks of J. Finley, 'The origins of Thucydides' style', *Three Essays*, 115. Homer: J. Griffin, *JHS* cvi (1986), 36ff.

out until Pylos halfway through the Archidamian War (425), the idea was nothing new.[74] Nor is Archidamus' fear, that the Spartans might bequeath the war to the next generation, of inconceivable sagacity. Hermokrates in Book iv seems to predict the great Sicilian Expedition, but if so the lapse on Thucydides' part is slight. That Pericles calmly envisages the end of the Athenian Empire has seemed more worrying, but perhaps this sentence should be seen less as a 'prediction' than as 'Homeric': Homer's Achilles foresaw his own death.[75] Scipio Aemilianus, following a line of Hellenistic kings which perhaps goes back to Antigonus Gonatas, wept at the fate of Carthage, quoting Homer – and expressing fears for Rome's future.[76] We do not speak of his 'prediction' of Rome's fall because any such prediction was false. To return to Pericles. It may indeed be Thucydides, not Pericles, who is here speaking, although a Homeric attitude on the part of the historical Pericles can hardly be ruled out.

Ninth and last, there is the question of sources. How did Thucydides get his reports of his speeches? We have seen that Thucydides knew specific detail about Melos and Plataea, and it is impossible to point to a speech of which he could not have heard a detailed version (the two just mentioned are perhaps the hardest to account for). Even the private deliberations of the three generals in Sicily could have been leaked by staff, or disclosed to Thucydides by Alcibiades himself.[77] We shall return to this topic later.

To sum up, none of the arguments for artificiality are so strong that we are forced to think wholly in terms of 'what was appropriate' rather than 'what was really said'. When Thucydides' speakers use formally perfect patterns of argument, that may indeed show that he tidied things up, just as he tidied Kleon out of the way in Book i; but we should not assume that there were not real-life skilful speakers in the fifth century BC. This has been a long discussion, but necessary: there would be no problem at all if Thucydides, unlike all other writers in

[74] G.L. Cawkwell, *YCS* xxiv, 1975, 67.

[75] i 81.6; iv 60.2; ii 64.3; Macleod, p. 157; see also A. Parry, *Logos and Ergon in Thucydides*, 179.

[76] A. Astin, *Scipio Aemilianus*, Oxford 1967, app.4. Gonatas: J. Hornblower, *Hieronymus of Cardia*, Oxford 1981, 105f. citing inter alia Xerxes' tears at Hdt.vii 45.

[77] vi 47ff.

antiquity, had not pledged himself to give in some sense a truthful version of his speeches.

We may turn to the function of the speeches in the narrative. To the question, why are they there at all, one good and even sufficient answer is implied by the conclusion of Chapter One: Thucydides includes speeches because Homer and Herodotus included speeches, and individual 'warners' like Herodotus' Artabanus and Thucydides' Nikias, who in Book vi tries to dissuade the Athenians from sending the expedition against Sicily, have Homeric antecedents. Again, Thucydides can sometimes use his speeches as 'pause points' in the narrative.[78] Pericles' first war speech, at the end of Book i, comes at a lull before the war proper starts in Book ii. We may compare the exchange between Xerxes and Artabanus at the beginning of Herodotus Book vii, which is the prelude to the Persian War proper; or the debate on the constitutions in Book iii, which is at a pause between the stories of the establishment of the Persian Empire and of its clash with Greece. But in other respects Thucydides' speeches are used differently.

We lose much of the point of the speeches if we forget that they are part of a larger structure, and that Thucydides' full intention can be seen only by looking at speeches and narrative combined.[79] It may indeed be, as is often said,[80] that Thucydides' speeches come at moments of decision. It is obviously true that some speeches are persuasive and effective: Pericles' war strategy is carried out, Alcibiades prevails in the Sicilian debate (the decision to go is not reversed) – and so does Nikias, in a way: he tries to put the Athenians off the whole idea by telling them they need to send a much larger force than they had envisaged, so they vote the larger force;

> In making this speech Nikias thought that either the Athenians would be put off by the scale of the armament required, or, if he were forced to make the expedition, he would in this way sail as

[78] A. Deffner, *Die Rede bei Herodot und ihre Weiterbildung bei Thukydides*, diss. Munich, 1933, 201f. Other examples are the Melian Dialogue and the Funeral Speech.

[79] W. Schadewaldt, *Die Geschichtsschreibung des Thukydides*², 1971, 25 n.2; H.-P. Stahl, *Thukydides, Die Stellung des Menschen im geschichtlichen Prozess*, Zetemata 40, 1966, is remarkable for giving proper weight to this.

[80] For example by Macleod, p.52 n.7, citing with approval de Ste Croix, *OPW*, app. iv.

safely as possible. The Athenians, however, far from losing their appetite for the voyage because of the difficulties in preparing for it, became more enthusiastic about it than ever, and just the opposite of what Nikias had imagined took place. His advice was regarded as excellent ... The result of this excessive enthusiasm of the majority was that the few who actually were opposed to the expedition were afraid of being thought unpatriotic if they voted against it, and therefore kept quiet.

Thucydides has here hit off exactly the psychology of military adventurism: in a similar way, it is said that General Westmoreland told President Johnson that the Vietnam War could be won only by a massive stepping-up of the military commitment and, when asked how many troops were needed, named what he thought was an impossibly large total and was told, 'You've got them.'[81] So Nikias' oratory was effective – and disastrous. Again, Diodotus prevails in the debate about Mytilene. And it is worth asking whether his opponent Kleon really 'lost' the argument: by urging severity he got a reputation as a strong man, and that may have been all he wanted for the moment.

But we should not exaggerate the effectiveness of the speeches, which, as Thucydides frequently goes out of his way to stress, have little effect on the action or none at all. We have already noticed that the Spartan speech early in Book iv, asking for peace, is unsuccessful in its object, and that Thucydides gives no speech to Kleon, whose policy actually prevails. There are other examples. In Book i the Spartans vote that the Thirty Years Peace has been broken 'not so much because they were persuaded by the arguments of their allies as because they were afraid that the power of the Athenians might grow even greater'. In Book iv the Akanthians let the Spartans in 'partly because they were persuaded by the seductive arguments of Brasidas, partly because they were afraid for their grape-vintage' which Brasidas had threatened to destroy (the second motive, we may feel, makes the first redundant, but Thucydides is drily impartial).[82] In Book viii, which contains no formal speeches, we are told that the reason for the overthrow of the Samian democracy was partly the persuasiveness of Alcibiades, but more

[81] vi 24.1; 4.
[82] i 88; iv 88.

important (*to de pleon*) was the fact that the impulse to overthrow it had already taken hold. Sometimes a similar conclusion must be inferred from the narrative; thus it has been acutely noted, about the great Camarina debate in Book vi, that the news of the capture of Plemmyrion by the Syracusans, which made Camarina give positive help to Syracuse, 'achieved what persuasive arguments could not'.[83] But the most remarkable failure of the spoken word is in Book iii, where the arguments of both the Plataeans and the Thebans are ignored in the end by the Spartans, who put a simple question to each Plataean: 'Have you done anything to help the Spartans and their allies in the war?' As each man replied 'No', he was taken away and put to death. Two hundred Plataeans were done away with in this way.[84] The rest, who had escaped, took advantage of the general citizenship grant mentioned above (p.35, where we suggested a reason why Thucydides suppressed their friendly reception by Athens).

Even the most innocuous or creditable sentiments may be undercut by the narrative. 'Look what happens to those characters in [Thucydides'] History who make appeal to the gods – the unfortunate Plataeans, the people of Melos, or the Athenian general Nikias, in the retreat from Syracuse.'[85] That is, speakers may be made to say things which are in themselves unexceptionable, but which turn out to be 'ironies, plausible arguments which are belied by events'.[86] Thus the word 'patriotism', rare in Thucydides, is put into the mouth of Alcibiades at Sparta, a man to whom the word meant less than to virtually any other Greek.[87] And it may say something for Thucydides' view of democracy that the best theoretical defence

---

[83] viii 47; Dover, *HCT* iv on vii 33. H.D. Westlake, *Essays on the Greek Historians and Greek History*, Manchester 1969, 188 takes a more positive view of the outcome of the Camarina debate. Note his pp.163, 165 on i 88.

[84] The futility of the whole 'trial' is a main theme of Macleod, ch.11. For Tacitus' use of an eloquent and elegant, but deliberately ineffective, speech see R. Martin, *Tacitus*, London 1981, 231 (on Curtius Montanus).

[85] So Syme, *PBA* 1962, 52.

[86] Macleod, p.92. Note Tacitus' use of the same device, e.g. Galba's speech in *Histories* i 15f. about adoption: 'noble and fine-sounding', but 'his claims are at odds with the facts': Martin, op.cit. (1981), 251; cf.77 on Otho and his 'Senate' speech.

[87] W. Nestle, *Neue Jahrb.f.kl.Alt.u.Päd.* xxxiii, Jg.17, 1914, 649ff. 'Thukydides und die Sophistik' (reprinted in his *Griechische Studien*, Stuttgart, 1948) at p.682 of the original publication; *contra*, N. Pusey, *HSCP* 51, 1940, 213ff. See vi 92.

of it is put into the mouth, not of Pericles, but of the far from admirable Syracusan demagogue Athenagoras.[88] It is correct, but too simple, to say that the speeches give us the motives of the speakers.[89] Sometimes it would be better to say that it is through speeches that people (like Alcibiades at Sparta) *give themselves away*. In any case, the speeches often have a subversive effect; and they may even illustrate the uselessness of making speeches at all. If we are interested in Thucydides' relation to the sophists, to whose profession speaking was crucial (below, p.120), this difference must be set against the debts and similarities. But even here there are literary precedents, if it is right (above, n.40) that Kleon's echoes of Pericles are meant to suggest Thersites' echoes of Achilles, and we are meant to judge Kleon, like Thersites, by *who he is* not *what he says*.

A final question: how far do the speeches support the view that things got progressively worse as the war went on? Or, if we see them as Thucydides' own composition, how far is he trying to make that point through the speeches? It has been said that if Thucydides wants his readers to draw any one moral from his work, it is that 'war is a violent teacher' (the Thucydidean phrase comes in the description of the Corcyrean *stasis*).[90] Certainly, the Mytilene and Plataea debates 'reveal how conventional morality is undermined in war';[91] the problem is, are we meant to conclude that the deterioration went on? It has been held that the Athenians of Book i stand at a more idealistic level than their successors, but the motives for Athenian imperialism given in Book i (in the debate at Sparta in the middle of the book) are not noticeably elevated: honour, fear, advantage.[92] And the view that 'intelligence' *gnômê*, gradually gives way to chance, *tuchê*, is right but can be pressed too far.[93]

---

[88] vi 39-40, with Andrewes *HCT* v, 336.

[89] So Gomme, *Encyclopaedia Britannica*, 1963 ed., s.v. Thucydides.

[90] iii 82.2, with Gomme's note on i 1 in *HCT* i. Below, p.156.

[91] Macleod, p.119.

[92] J. de Romilly, *The Rise and Fall of States According to Greek Authors*, Ann Arbor 1977, ch.3, with my review in *TLS*, 5 viii 1977.

[93] L. Edmunds, *Chance and Intelligence in Thucydides*, Cambridge, Mass. 1975, with my *TLS* review, 12 iii 1976. Note that at v 75 the Spartans showed the world by their victory at Mantinea that they had been hitherto worsted only by 'chance'; their *gnômê*, resolution, was as great as ever. This is against Edmunds' thesis: Mantinea is far on in the war. I am not disputing the general and important truth that for Thucydides success is 'fragile' or 'vulnerable' to *tuchê*, to

It is not certain anyway that Thucydides thought that decline was progressive: 'not everything was better in the past', as Tacitus was to say.[94] For instance, it is only in Book viii that Thucydides specifically praises a political regime; perhaps a finished version of that book would have contained a speech showing what was praiseworthy about it.[95] And we should not forget that the unwritten books, which would have treated the years 411-404, would have contained speeches to balance those in the surviving books (although that balance should not be interpreted too literally:[96] the idea that a hypothetical 'Book x' would have contained an 'Athenian Dialogue' about the fate of Athens at the end of the war, to mirror the Melian Dialogue of Book v, is an entertaining guess, but only a guess). However, Hermokrates of Syracuse, whom Thucydides admired, not least for his belief in Sicilian unity,[97] would certainly have been prominent in 'Book ix', just as he is in Xenophon and Diodorus: even in the books which Thucydides did write, Hermokrates gets three full-length speeches, which is more than any other non-Athenian, including Brasidas and Archidamus.[98] And an 'Arginusai Debate' from Thucydides need not have been wholly

---

use the language of Martha Nussbaum, *The Fragility of Goodness*, Cambridge, 1986 (who cites Edmunds with approval).

[94] *Annals* iii 55.

[95] viii 97.

[96] As by H. Rawlings, *The Structure of Thucydides' History*, Princeton 1981, with my *TLS* review, 12 ii 1982.

[97] G.F. Bender, *Der Begriff des Staatsmannes bei Thukydides*, Würzburg 1938, chs.4 and 5; Westlake, op.cit. (1969), ch.12, esp. p.198: 'Hermokrates is one of Thucydides' few heroes.' Unity: G.P. Landmann, *Interpretation einer Rede des Thukydides: Die Friedensmahnung des Hermokrates*, diss. Basel, 1932. Diodorus records the Syracusan fear that Hermokrates aimed at a tyranny, xiii 75, but we do not know if this fear was well grounded, or, if it were, whether Thucydides would have held that against him: he admired Pericles, and Pericles' position was after all quasi-monarchical (ii 65.9: 'was', not 'became' or 'was on the way to becoming' one-man rule: see Macleod, p. 149 on *egigneto* here, citing inter alia Andrewes on viii 20. Note however W. Thompson, *CQ* xxxiii, 1983, 293, showing, though without reference to the problems of ii 65.9, that the argument from viii 20 is not quite compelling). Pericles' enemies no doubt muttered about tyranny just as did the enemies of Alcibiades; cf. R. Seager, *Historia* xvi, 1967, 6ff., 'Alcibiades and the charge of aiming at tyranny', for what this really meant. For Thucydides' admiration for the tyrant Pisistratus see below, p.171.

The idea that demagogy tends to monarchy is not peculiarly sophistic, despite Hdt. iii 82.4 (*prostas tou dêmou* becomes a monarch): see Stroheker, *Historia* iii, 1953/4, 389-90 n.1, citing *inter alia* Solon F9 West.

[98] As pointed out by F.T. Hinrichs, *Hermes* cix, 1981, 46ff., 'Hermokrates bei Thukydides'.

pessimistic: it could have contained a magnificent but
ineffective speech from Socrates denouncing the Assembly's
arbitrary behaviour, and upholding the rights of individuals. So
although it is true that, for instance, the question of the
Plataeans' guilt in executing the Theban prisoners is left open by
Thucydides, whereas such topics are positively excluded in the
Melian Dialogue, so that to that extent the moral element is
reduced between Books iii and v,[99] we cannot be sure that
Thucydides would have continued to use the speeches to show
that things got worse – if he ever did so use them.

In conclusion, Thucydides' aim in speeches, as in narrative,
was to record truthfully – to give 'what was really said'; but again
there was present an opposite and inconsistent aim, to omit
select and concentrate, giving instead 'what was appropriate'.
We also suggested that Thucydides wished, by bringing out the
actual ineffectiveness of speeches, to suggest that there are clear
limits to the power of rational debate. To this extent it is right to
compare him with the Euripidean chorus which exclaims:

> I do not grudge wisdom, I rejoice to pursue it. But other things are
> great and shine brighter.

It has been said that 'both Thucydides and Euripides lost faith
in debate, although both, it must be added, were molded
intellectually by it'.[100] But Euripides' own views are not
necessarily those of his choruses (p.169); and we have suggested
that this picture of progressive disenchantment may not be
entirely fair to Thucydides, and that the latter (and by him
unrecorded) phases of the war could have given reason for
optimism.

One feature of the speeches has been reserved for treatment in
the next chapter, the question how far Thucydides makes his
speakers avoid technical, and even merely concrete, terminology,
such as he does use in the narrative. This is an additional
argument for the unauthenticity of the speeches.[101]

---

[99] As Christopher Pelling points out to me. For a similar argument, J.H. Finley,
Three Essays, 387. Cf. Andrewes, *Phoenix* xvi, 1962, p.72, n.20.

[100] Eur.*Ba*.1005-7 (perhaps corrupt: C.W. Willink, *CQ* xvi, 1966, 236); J.H.
Finley, 'Euripides and Thucydides', *Three Essays*, 24. Cf. Macleod, p. 156 for
Hecuba's complaints about the limits of Persuasion.

[101] Antiphon speaks of cleruchies, as does Thucydides in the narrative (iii 50),
but no Thucydidean speaker ever does. However, it may be that in the Assembly,

Finally, a point that will be relevant to a later chapter still (Chapter Seven). Whether Thucydides reported or invented his speeches, or did something in between, the sentiments contained in those speeches can never be used as evidence for his own opinions. Nor can the successful identification of intellectual influences on his speakers tell us that he endorsed, rather than that he was merely prepared to give currency to, the idea, fashion or attitude in question.

---

as opposed to the Council, which was the place for technical discussions, technical language was conventionally avoided by real-life speakers.

CHAPTER FOUR

Use of Evidence

(i) Authority

The earliest poets claimed that their words came from the Muses. The Muses instructed Hesiod on Mt Helicon and this is the guarantee of his truthfulness. Pindar in the fifth century, as we saw in Chapter One, appeals to his own superior knowledge; but the poem he offers to Diagoras of Rhodes is the gift of the Muses. Pindar is thus halfway between appealing to derivative, and claiming independent, authority.[1]

Clio, subsequently the Muse of History, landed the job only in late Hellenistic times: in the fifth century she was a goddess of song, with *kithara* (lyre), and appears so equipped on the sixth-century François vase in Florence.[2] There could not be a Muse of History before there was History; but that is not the most important reason why such writers as Hecataeus, Herodotus and Thucydides do not invoke her. Their information was guaranteed, not by supernatural powers, but by their own exertions. The appeal to authority is there, but the authority is entirely the author's own. A 'muse' of personally conducted 'inquiry' is a nonsense, and Clio had no place in the prefaces of Hecataeus, Herodotus or Thucydides.

A recent study seeks to explain Thucydides' attitude to his subject as part of a more general 'breaking down of traditional forms of authority'. Before the fifth century, it is claimed, Athenian decisions were based on oracles and 'unwritten law' expounded by the members of a few distinguished families: 'the patriarchal sources of authority – exegete, priest, clan leader, or elder'. During that century these traditional sources of authority

---

[1] Hesiod, *Theogony* 22ff.; Pindar, *Ol.* vii 7.
[2] See M. Robertson, *History of Greek Art*, Cambridge 1975, 127; *Kleine Pauly*, s.v. 'Kleio'. The nine 'Muses' (=books) of Herodotus are a late conceit.

had been weakened or bypassed; instead we get calculations and arguments, an analysis of power and its sources.[3]

This is a simple and attractive account which contains some truth (the arrival of democracy in the fifth century is a fact) but it needs qualifying. Above all, we should not exaggerate the political power conferred at any period by rights of religious exegesis. After all, 'the [Athenian] exegetai did not come forward either in 480 or in 415 BC when oracles and *sêmeia* [signs, portents] had a great share in very weighty decisions'.[4] The intellectual advances made in archaic Ionia (which affected Athens in turn) would not have been possible had the Greeks there been 'priest-ridden'; and several scholars have, from very different viewpoints, stressed the relative openness of archaic and even Homeric society.[5]

It is also relevant that Athenians never quite lost their deferential habits towards their 'betters': Alcibiades' claim to the Sicilian command (p.62) was an appeal to the 'irrational' admiration which aristocracy always excites even when it has no automatic claim on political authority. Alcibiades' approach in 415, if correctly reported, is very traditional, and poses difficulties for the view that 'new' politicians with new techniques came in during the 420s.[6] It is true that the loss of traditional power by the Areopagus in 462 (p.118) was a crucial episode in the 'democratisation' of leadership and prestige.[7] But here too the process of democratisation was never quite complete: it is startling that an inscription of 337 BC, found in the early 1950s, seems to envisage the Areopagus (which has never been mentioned in all Thucydides) as a real threat to democracy.[8] Nor should we forget Thucydides' own reference to the 'political associations which had

[3] W.R. Connor, 'Thucydides', in *Ancient Writers*, 1982, 271f., 276.

[4] F. Jacoby, *Atthis*, Oxford 1949, 48, cf. 32. R. Garland, *BSA* lxxix, 1984, 75ff.

[5] Ionia not priest-ridden: E. Schrödinger, *Nature and the Greeks*, Cambridge 1954, 54. This book does not feature in Lloyd's *Magic Reason and Experience*, though he reaches similar conclusions. Openness: Lloyd-Jones, cited above, p.61; M. Detienne, *Maîtres de vérité*, 92; 'Speech is no longer [in the Iliad] the privilege of an exceptional man, endowed with religious powers'. And O. Murray, *Early Greece*, 1980, 302 protests, against some extreme theories of the Toronto School about the consequences of Greek literacy, that they 'make much use of the concept of "restricted literacy", for which there is no evidence in Greece'; in other words, there was no priestly caste monopolising knowledge and access to it.

[6] For this view see W.R. Connor, *The New Politicians of Fifth-Century Athens*, Princeton 1971.

[7] So Connor, 'Thucydides', 272.

[8] *SEG* xii 87.

existed even before this time [411] for the purpose of winning lawsuits and elections'.[9] This is not very democratic, given that most 'elections' were actually supposed to be settled by the operation of the lot.

We have already remarked that Thucydides' intended audience may not after all have been so very different from that of the poets and the authors of 'encomiastic oratory heard at festivals', if he tried out set pieces at symposia; the description of the Corcyra stasis could, we suggested, have been designed for the applause of such a circle: there is something of the 'prize entry' about this section of Thucydides, which has justly been said to contain some 'reckless paradox'.[10]

So the 'patriarchal', religiously-based sources of authority of pre-462 Athens were not so influential as all that. Nor need tough prose and intellectual combativeness have been altogether a novelty in Thucydides' circle.[11] And yet one feels that it is right to detect a new rigour of method in Thucydides' prose; it also gives the appearance of greater *technicality* in its use of evidence. It is one object of this chapter to test that impression: is Thucydides' language about evidence systematic and technical? But first, I shall ask, how 'scientific' is his attitude to his sources? In this section we shall include oral sources, myths, written sources (Homer, the poets), inscriptions, archaeology and so on.

(ii) Evidence

First let us look at Thucydides' use of evidence, as opposed to his terminology.

In the speeches, there is one central kind of evidence, the way in which 'character', i.e. good or bad behaviour in the past, is adduced. Thucydides' usage here is thoroughly forensic. For instance, we have already noticed (p.63 n.71) that the Athenians' claim to have been worthy of the position of leadership which they enjoyed in 479 is countered by Sthenelaidas' retort that

---

[9] viii 54.4.

[10] Encomiastic oratory: Connor, 'Thucydides', 277 with p.29 above; prize entry: Thuc.i 22.4; reckless paradox: Andrewes, *Phoenix*, xvi, 1962, 74 n.25 and his remark in the text at p.74: 'Diodotus [at iii 43.3] has brought paradox dangerously close to the border of nonsense'. Dionysius of Halicarnassus had trouble with the Corcyra stasis section: Macleod, ch.12.

[11] Hecataeus of Miletus was not a product of Periclean Athens, but his preface is already highly polemical: p.20.

their subsequent bad behaviour therefore deserves double penalty. And the Thebans make a similar reply to the Plataeans: 'a good record should double the penalty for those who have behaved badly'. Thucydides' use of this argument in the mouths of the Thebans and Sthenelaidas is comparable to the treatment of character by Tacitus, who can argue that bad behaviour is proof of underlying bad character. But equally Tacitus can make Arruntius imply that Tiberius' character was changed by the experience of power, and that alone of the Roman emperors Vespasian changed for the better. There was available an obvious reply, namely to invert this use of evidence from character: in one of Lysias' speeches the defending counsel admits the offences but argues that in other respects the defendant has proved himself a good man. Or again Euripides makes Hippolytus plead, 'Being pure, I would not have laid hands on your wife.' This is the kind of evidence which a modern court would admit only in mitigation of sentence.[12]

So Thucydides can make his speakers use 'character evidence' either way. We may compare[13] Gorgias in the *Palamedes*; or Antiphon, who can vary such arguments. For instance, Antiphon turns the argument from likelihood on its head: a speaker argues, 'I was known to be an enemy of the dead man; therefore I would not have killed him, because I would have been an obvious suspect for his murder.'[14]

But what of Thucydides' own view of character, expressed outside the speeches: that is, of human character as it affects the course of events? The generalisations in the narrative about human nature or the human condition[15] – like those, in the speeches, about the compulsion to rule over others[16] – imply that although human behaviour changes according to changes in attendant circumstances, the 'nature of men' can be made the

[12] Thuc.i 75.1; 86.1; iii 67.2; Tac.*Ann*.vi 51, *postremo suo tantum ingenio utebatur*, cf.Thuc.iii 64.4 'the true tendency of your character is now revealed'. Arruntius: *Ann*.vi 48, cf. *Hist*.i 50 on Vespasian, *solusque ante se principum in melius mutatus est.* See A. Hands, *CQ* xxiv, 1974, 312ff. and C. Gill, xxxiii, 1983, 469ff.; cf. above, p.63. Lysias xiv 23; Eur.*Hipp*.993ff.

[13] Chr. Schneider, *Information und Absicht bei Thukydides*, Hypomnemata xli, Göttingen, 1974, 161.

[14] Antiphon, *First Tetralogy*, iiB 3.

[15] For a useful collection of references to human nature as a constant, see de Ste Croix, *OPW*, 29. (Only some, however, are authorial.)

[16] i 76.3; v 105.2; but speeches, like these, are not evidence for Thucydides' own view.

basis for predictions.[17] The assumption behind all this is that people are rational and act according to their own interests – a Socratic view – so that outsiders can infer motive from action. (See below, p.128.)

We may pass to Thucydides' general use of evidence.

First, oral sources. Naturally Thucydides cross-questioned oral informants, despite his hard words, in the Introduction to his work, about information derived from chance sources, and about his own avoidance of it when writing his narrative of the *erga* of the war.[18] But it is unusual for Thucydides explicitly to claim the authority of an oral informant. There is an exceptional claim to such authority in the Pisistratid excursus in Book vi: 'I know that Hippias was the elder son of Pisistratus; I am particularly positive about this because of oral information supplied to me'. This is emphatic, and possibly to be explained by Thucydides' blood relationship with the Pisistratid tyrants.[19] But there are many passages where oral information can be assumed. An example is a passage in the narrative of the Sicilian expedition, where we can be very sure that Thucydides' information was both reliable and obtained from an oral source. Demosthenes and Eurymedon, *en route* to and from Sicily respectively, are told by Konon, in command at Naupaktos, that the enemy look threatening and he has only eighteen ships against their twenty-five. By 413 Demosthenes and Eurymedon were dead; but Konon went on to serve in the North Aegean between 410 and 407. Clearly, Thucydides, who had property in Thrace, i.e. the North Aegean, got the account of this episode from Konon himself, on a visit to the commander's flagship. But there is absolutely no specific attribution of source.

Similarly, he could have got an account of the debate about Sicily in 415, between Nicias and Alcibiades, from Andokides, who went into exile in the north.[20]

---

[17] iii 82.2. There are good remarks on this in Schneider, pp.87, 119ff., citing medical theory about causation and behaviour. Schneider generally (p.110) makes Thucydides' descriptions of actions as well as his speeches conform to the principle of *ta deonta*, 'what is appropriate', because nobody willingly acts against their own interests (a Socratic principle; see Plato, *Protag.* 358). For *ta deonta* applied to actions as well as speeches see Schneider, p.136.

[18] i 22.2.

[19] vi 55.1; see above, p.1. But for the more promising possibility that Thucydides spoke to members of Pisistratus' family on Chios see below, p.84.

[20] vii 31; iv 105 (above, p.3). On Andokides and Thucydides see, however, A. Raubitschek, 'Andokides and Thucydides' *Classical Contributions*, McGregor

These are two instances where we can be confident that his information was good. At the other extreme are statements like that in the account of the Corcyrean *stasis*, that the cleverer people were less able to defend themselves against attack than the stupid. It is hard to imagine what sort of particular evidence Thucydides could have had for this, or what sort of informant – hardly clever Corcyreans, because *ex hypothesi* they were dead. But, to judge from the sophistication of the remark, hardly stupid ones either. It is easy enough, by contrast, to see what information lies behind 'Debtors killed their creditors' – particular instances would be easy for Thucydides' informant to spot. But the first generalisation seems to be just an example of what has been called the 'reckless paradox' of these chapters (see above, p.75). Thucydides has been led on from specific remarks about debtors and creditors to think about *stasis* paradigmatically and without reference to particular bits of Corcyrean evidence.[21]

There are other more straightforward points where we can say with assurance that he has surely no evidence for his judgment. For instance, commentators have noticed the frequency with which, in the Pylos debate, knowledge and motives are attributed to Kleon which go far beyond what Thucydides could have known, since he is not likely to have been in Kleon's confidence. ('Knowing that ...' is used no less than three times of Kleon in two chapters of Book iv).[22]

This sort of consideration has prompted a general theory:[23] namely, that Thucydides' statements about the motives and intentions of his agents are without serious exception invented. This theory, one might say, is to Thucydides as the theories discussed above in Chapter One are to Herodotus. The differences are, first, that the Thucydides theory is more convincing as an account of Thucydides *as a whole* than those theories are convincing about Herodotus as a whole; and second, that since Thucydides, unlike Herodotus, very rarely gives a

Studies, 1981, 121ff. at p.121; C. Fornara, *Panhellenica*, T.S. Brown Studies, Lawrence, Kansas 1980, 43ff.

[21] iii 83.3; 81.4. Macleod, however, p.130, calls ch. 83 'striking and thoughtful'; perhaps more fairly.

[22] iv 27.3; 27.4; 28.2; Schneider, p.51.

[23] Formulated by, above all, Schneider, though the conclusions of V. Hunter, *Thucydides the Artful Reporter*, Toronto 1973 are similar (but independent). See too M.I. Finley, *Tria Corda*, Momigliano Studies 1983, 206.

source-attribution, an attack on his credibility must take the form of an attack on his attribution of motives. Over Kleon, such an attack is easy – perhaps too easy, because we must, exceptionally, allow for sheer bias and anger on Thucydides' part (see Chapter Seven). But the attribution of motive or knowledge to Themistocles, to Aristogeiton, and to Nikias and Pausanias the Regent just before their deaths,[24] must really be Thucydides' own inference: in the last example he uses the phrase 'it is said that ...' of Pausanias' behaviour and thoughts, which 'he normally uses to indicate that he has misgivings about the trustworthiness of his evidence'.[25] We can add that some passages which attribute *collective* motives or knowledge are probably the result of guesswork: an example is the statement that the Athenians at Ithome knew that they were being sent away by the Spartans for discreditable reasons.[26]

But can we really doubt[27] that Thucydides talked to Brasidas, whom he handles sympathetically and with every appearance of possessing inside information? Thucydides' northern exile gave him the opportunity to talk to him. This does not apply absolutely everywhere – not, for instance, to knowledge attributed to Brasidas just before his death. To explain this we do not have to fall back on the supposition that Thucydides consulted Brasidas' subordinate Klearidas.[28] It is just as likely to be guesswork on Thucydides' part. True, there is literary art in the way in which the aims of Brasidas and those of Thucydides the general are made to balance each other in the Amphipolis narrative towards the end of Book iv. But this literary handling hardly *excludes* knowledge by Thucydides of Brasidas' intention. And the *reductio ad absurdum* would be to say that Thucydides *qua* historian guessed, rather than knew, about the motives of Thucydides *qua* general, i.e. himself. With Thucydides, as with Herodotus, it is a mistake to suppose that a literary device is somehow inconsistent with a truthful account; it may rather be a stylised way of presenting what is true.

Again, the Athenian ambassadors to Persia in Book iv came

[24] For these examples Schneider, p. 129.
[25] i 134.1; H.D. Westlake, *CQ* xxvii, 1977, 104.
[26] i 102.4.
[27] With Schneider, p.20.
[28] As does Westlake, *GRBS* xxi, 1980, 333ff. 'Thucydides, Brasidas and Clearidas'.

home because they heard that Artaxerxes was dead. Surely these envoys explained themselves at Athens; contrast the collective 'knowledge' of the troops at Ithome, all four thousand of them. (The number is from the *Lysistrata* of Aristophanes.)[29]

Mimêsis is the name given to this presentation of events as seen through the eyes of protagonists, rather than as direct narration. At best, the concept of *mimêsis* does not account for more than the routine wartime narrative and a few other narrative sections (for example, the Pausanias excursus[30]); the *Archaeology*, by contrast, is there to illustrate Thucydides' own beliefs about naval power and the importance of the Peloponnesian War. *Mimêsis* works slightly better with the *Pentekontaetia*, which can be seen as illustrating Spartan belief in the dangers of Athenian dynamism. The *Sikelika* at the beginning of Book vi is designed as a gloss, not on the state of Athenian knowledge about Sicily, but on Athenian ignorance about it.[31]

But *mimêsis* is as much Herodotean as Thucydidean. 'Pausanias', says Herodotus in his account of the battle of Plataea in 479,[32] 'thinking – quite rightly as the event proved – that Amompharetos would not stay behind if the other Lacedaemonian troops withdrew ...' gave the order for retreat. Then 'Amompharetos did not at first believe that Pausanias would actually go so far as to leave him behind ...'. Again, the battle of Salamis is described largely in terms of people's reaction to news (cf. the *Persai* of Aeschylus). And as for authorial digressions which like Thucydides' *Pentekontaetia* take the form of realisation by X of such-and-such, note Herodotus' digressions in Book i about Pisistratid Athens and about early Sparta. They are there because Croesus *hears* that these are the two major states of Greece, one Ionian, the other Dorian. Pisistratid Athens indeed is there by a transparent story-teller's device: mid-sixth-century Athens was not really on a par with Sparta, which was already the leading power in the Peloponnese. Herodotus simply wishes to introduce us early on to Persia's chief antagonists among the Greek powers.[33]

[29] iv 50; Aristophanes, *Lysistrata* 1143.
[30] i 128-34.
[31] See below, p.147.
[32] Hdt. ix 56.
[33] i 59ff.

Finally, the *mimêsis* theory does not do justice to such highly sophisticated narrative as the fusing of the Boiotian- and Athenian-inspired lines of narrative about the battle of Delium.[34]

In conclusion, we can accept that Thucydides often guessed at the motives behind actions. All modern historians do the same. The only difference is that Thucydides usually offers his descriptions of motives with as much confidence as his statements about numbers of ships and so on: not 'Kleon must have known *x*', but 'Kleon knew *x*'. Nevertheless, we should not doubt that where possible, as with Brasidas, Thucydides did make oral inquiries. Neither of the extreme views is plausible – whether that he always invents motive, or that he never invents motive but always mechanically works from concrete information of some kind.

Second is a class of evidence (and action thereby motivated) which is midway between oral and written evidence, the evidence of oracles. Thucydides' treatment is certainly sparing. For instance, an eclipse led Nikias to wait in Sicily 'thrice nine days'; but we know, not from Thucydides but from Plutarch, that a different interpretation, favourable to a retreat, was current at the time.

Let us take a single detailed example. It concerns the exiled Spartan king Pleistoanax. Thucydides says that Pleistoanax and his brother Aristocles had induced the priestess at Delphi to repeat constantly, to any Spartan envoys who came to inquire of the oracle, the answer that 'Pleistoanax must be recalled'. Eventually he was recalled. It is instructive to compare this with Herodotus' account of the bribing of the priestess at Delphi by the Alcmaeonid family to tell the Spartans to expel the Pisistratid tyrants from Athens.[35] In Thucydides' account the influence of Delphi is minimised (it is Pleistoanax himself who 'induced the Spartans to recall him'; that is, he made representations at Sparta, exploiting the oracle). And yet that is not likely to be historically right, given Spartan superstition: Thucydides himself tells us that they interpreted their failure in the Archidamian War as due to the impiety of the original

[34] Thuc.iv 96.3-5 and 101 contain material from different sources within the same chapters.
[35] Sicily: Thuc.vi 50; Plut.*Nic.*xxiii=*FGrHist* 328 Philochorus F 135. Pleistoanax: Thuc.v 16; cf. Hdt.v 63.1. Note also Thuc. v 11.1, cynically 'political' about Brasidas' hero-cult at Amphipolis.

Theban attack on Plataea in time of truce.[36] Thucydides
provides a detailed paraphrase of the oracle: the Spartans 'will
plough with a silver ploughshare' unless they bring Pleistoanax
back. (The scholiast explains this as a threat of starvation which
would make food very expensive.) But this strictly oracular
evidence, which need not emanate from Delphi but could be
from Pleistoanax or any Spartan, has surely been supplemented
by evidence from Pleistoanax himself. Thus it is significant that
we are told exactly where he lived in exile (on Mt Lykeion);
Thucydides perhaps visited him there. Certainly Thucydides
treats the accusations against Pleistoanax about the Delphic
bribery in a way sympathetic to Pleistoanax.

It may seem obvious that Thucydides should have ignored
Delphi as being anyway unimportant; thus it has been said with
justice that Delphi took no political initiatives after 479.[37] But
one can put that another way:[38] the impression that Delphi took
no fifth-century initiative may be due in part to the different
ways in which Herodotus and Thucydides chose to handle their
evidence.[39] In any case there are moments even in the period
after 479 when Delphi's advice was politically important: first, in
431, Apollo at Delphi, consulted by Sparta about whether to
fight, sticks his neck out and says that he will help the Spartans
whether they ask him to or not, provided they fight with all their
might. Second, Xenophon's appeal to Delphi in the *Anabasis*
about joining Cyrus' expedition should not be misrepresented, as
Xenophon himself seeks to do, as a private affair: it was (as we
learn from the same author's *Hellenica*) an official and
provocative action involving the Spartan state, which wanted to
help Cyrus while seeming not to do so. This action resulted
ultimately in the battle of Cunaxa between Persia and the Ten
Thousand, and great diplomatic difficulties between Persia and
Sparta in the 390s.[40] Thucydides' attitude to the evidence
obtainable from Delphi is, I suggest, in danger of misleading us
about the oracle's true importance. It was a kind of evidence

[36] vii 18.
[37] By W.G. Forrest in an unpublished talk.
[38] As pointed out to me by my pupil Ashley Beck.
[39] Note for comparison that the best modern book on Sparta, W.G. Forrest, *A History of Sparta*[2], London 1980, 113, describing the Pleistoanax incident, leaves out Delphi altogether, thus going even further than Thucydides in seeing Pleistoanax's recall in purely factional terms.
[40] Thuc.i 118.3; Xen.*Anab*.iii 1.4ff., cf.*Hell*.iii 1.1.

which he not only minimised; he may not even have troubled to check it at source, since nowhere in Thucydides do we have the feeling we have when reading Herodotus Book i, that Delphi stands behind much of the narrative.[41] (See also below under poets and myths.)

Third, there is the evidence of written sources. There are two kinds: first, the unacknowledged (Herodotus, Antiochus of Syracuse, the fifth-century compilers of thalassocracy lists, and perhaps Hecataeus of Miletus);[42] and second, the acknowledged – Hellanicus and the poets, especially Homer. We have already said something about his use of Herodotus, in Chapter One. Thucydides used Herodotus freely for facts: for instance, he must be drawing on Herodotus when he refers to Xerxes' cutting through the rock of Mt Athos.[43]

In the two relevant excursuses, the great *Archaeology* at the beginning of Book i, and the Athenian material early in Book ii, there is free use of poetic written sources. We shall discuss this presently.

But first something must be said about Hellanicus, a writer whose works survive only in fragments. As we saw (above, p.39), they included a history of Athens which Thucydides certainly knew: his disparaging reference to it in Book i is his only mention of any prose writer, Herodotus included. How much did Thucydides take from Hellanicus without acknowledgment? The picture of King Theseus the synoikiser (the primeval unifier of Attica) in Thucydides Book ii, is similar to that implied by the fragments of Hellanicus.[44] But this kind of thing shows agreement, not use; and in any case most of Thucydides' own work was detailed contemporary narrative which did not compete with Hellanicus, most of the fragments of whose *Atthis* do not deal with contemporary events at all. More significant is disagreement, at least where it seems that Thucydides has gone out of his way to controvert a view which we know to have been held, perhaps eccentrically, by Hellanicus. What Thucydides

---

[41] I am not here specifically concerned with Thucydides' own belief in oracles; see further below, p.182.

[42] See N.G.L. Hammond, *Epirus*, 1967, 459, 461; cf. Westlake, *CQ* xxvii, 1977, p.97 and n.18. Westlake in that article (pp.95ff.) argues that a written source lies behind the Pausanias-Themistocles excursuses. *Antiochus*: above, p.27 and n.55.

[43] i 97.

[44] Thuc.ii 15; *FGrHist* 323a, esp.F15; Jacoby, introductory commentary on FF 14-19.

had said about Hellanicus' *Pentekontaetia* was that it was 'brief and chronologically inaccurate', and it has been suggested that this was more than a mere abusive aside: Thucydides' arrangement of the war proper, by campaigning seasons, was specifically directed against Hellanicus.[45] We know that Hellanicus wrote a treatise on the Priestesses of Argos; Thucydides opens Book ii solemnly by dating the attack on Plataea in various ways, including (as we saw in Chapter Two) the forty-eighth year of the priestess-ship of Chrysis at Argos. But in Book v, Thucydides explains that his own way of dating by campaigning seasons is preferable to the system of dating by annual magistracies.[46] Putting the Book ii and Book v passages together, it is hard to avoid the conclusion that this, too, is a specific criticism of Hellanicus' chronology.

There are also, it seems, more substantial historical issues on which Thucydides parted company with Hellanicus. The Pisistratid excursus in Thucydides Book vi is probably polemic against Hellanicus: Thucydides' arguments are directed against the view that Hipparchus, not his brother Hippias, was the actual tyrant, a view which would have made Hipparchus' murder in 514 more important than it really was. If this was Hellanicus' view, he stands at the head of a tradition which sought to rewrite the past to the greater glory of the tyrannicides Harmodius and Aristogeiton. It should not surprise us that these issues were still live in the late fifth century: after all, there were, when Thucydides was writing, living members of families which had been active in the events of 514, most notably Pericles and Alcibiades. And it now seems possible that the descendants of Pisistratus settled in Chios, where Thucydides could have spoken to them.[47]

Hellanicus, if all this is right, was party to the rewriting of history, and Thucydides crossly put the record straight. Is there any other issue where we can see the same thing happening? Here is another candidate: Hellanicus treated the myth of Orestes as Aeschylus had in the *Eumenides*. They both departed

---

[45] J.D. Smart, 'Thucydides and Hellanicus', in *Past Perspectives, Studies in Greek and Roman Historical Writing*, edd. I.S. Moxon, J.D. Smart, A.J. Woodman, Cambridge 1986, 19ff.

[46] *FGrHist* 4 FF 74-7; Thuc.ii 2.1; v 20.2.

[47] Thuc.vi 54ff.; Dover, *HCT* iv, 321, 325 (but note Raubitschek, p.123). Chios: W.G. Forrest, 'A lost Peisistratid name', *JHS* ci, 1981, 134.

from the traditional story by representing Orestes, the son and killer of Agamemnon, as having been brought to trial before the Athenian court of the Areopagus. This was a politically significant change of literary emphasis, because the powers of the real-life Areopagus were curtailed in 462/1, shortly before the production of the *Eumenides*: thereafter the formal competence of the Areopagus was restricted to the decision of certain homicide cases. It is open to dispute whether Aeschylus' motive in so focussing on the Areopagus was conservative or not, but there is surely no doubt that he had a political motive of some sort. By following him, Hellanicus was taking a trendy new line about a very old myth.[48] Thucydides' bad-tempered approach in Book vi and elsewhere is, I suggest, prompted by overtly partisan use, by such writers as Hellanicus, of antiquarian material. Thucydides' own method is nearer to being 'free from anger or bias'.[49] Thus he implicitly denies that the Athenians had been deprived of their weapons by the year 514; this is to their discredit because it means that they could have resisted the tyrants and attacked the bodyguard.[50] Thucydides evidently did not mind risking unpopularity in the interests of truth. We may contrast Herodotus' method, which is to juxtapose favourable and unfavourable material: for instance, in the Cypselus digression a basically hostile speech includes a Delphic oracle which speaks of Cypselus bringing justice to Corinth. Again, Book v praises democracy as an 'excellent thing not in one respect only but in all respects'; but fewer than twenty chapters later Herodotus remarks that it is easier to fool thirty thousand people than one man (the Athenian Assembly voted to accept the appeal of Aristagoras of Miletus, and to help the Ionian Revolt; King Kleomenes of Sparta more prudently said 'No').[51]

[48] *FGrHist* 4 F 169a=323a F 22. The traditional story derived the name 'Areopagus' from a trial of Ares. Jacoby in his commentary on 323a F1, cf. comm. on F 22 at p. 43 with n. 7, argued that Aeschylus was the first to connect Orestes with the Areopagus, but that Hellanicus and the other Atthidographers (authors of local histories of Athens and Attica) differed from Aeschylus in not denying the earlier trials of Ares and others. For the problem of Aeschylus' view, see Macleod, ch.3.

[49] Tacitus, *Annals* i 1.

[50] Thuc. vi 58.1-2. See Dover's excellent note on para. 2, which makes it strange that he can say in the final volume of the commentary (v, 424) that Thucydides wanted the critical approval of his fellow-countrymen more than other people's. Thucydides goes strongly against flattering traditions when he wants to.

[51] Hdt. v 92; v 78 and 97.2.

Thucydides, as we shall see in Chapter Seven, usually reconciles his own evidence with his own judgments (this is not true of the unfinished Book viii).[52] Herodotus had said that the Pisistratids ruled well, and he ranks them (see above) alongside Sparta in terms of external power. But he also says that under the Pisistratid tyranny Athens achieved nothing in war and, as we have just seen, praises in general terms the democracy which after a few years replaced the tyrants. Thucydides' account of the Pisistratids contains no such inconsistencies and his attitude to the democracy is wary.[53] Similarly the *Archaeology* is remarkable[54] for the neutral way in which it draws on the evidence of the poets. For instance, Thucydides makes a point about archaic Greece by referring to 'wealthy' Corinth, which is so called by the 'ancient poets'.[55]

This leads to Thucydides' use of the evidence of the poets, and of myth. At the end of Book iii Thucydides cites, and quotes at surprising length, the Homeric Hymn to Apollo, in order to show the character and antiquity of the Delian festival.[56] This kind of thing makes nonsense of any idea that Thucydides' rejection of the 'mythical element', i.e. romantic motivation, meant rejection of the poets or of myth *as evidence*. The most startling passage relevant to this point is at the end of Book ii, where Thucydides describes the formation of the Echinades islands opposite Oiniadai. They were settled by Alkmaion, 'as they say', after he was told by the oracle of Apollo [at Delphi] to find a place in which to settle that did not exist when he killed his mother, because the rest of the earth was polluted for him. The islands matched the description, because they had been formed only recently, by the alluvial deposit of the Achelous River. We are reminded of Herodotus' story of the beginnings of the Macedonian kingdom: the boy Perdikkas, claiming wages for farm-work done, was told that the shafts of sunlight through the

---

[52] Below, p.141.

[53] Hdt.i 59.6, v 78; see further below, p.166. for Thucydides' attitude to democracy. The young Thucydides was perhaps less good at avoiding inconsistency: on his treatment of Spartan acquiescence in Athenian leadership in 479 see my *Greek World 479-323 B.C.*, 1983, 22; below, p.175 n.80.

[54] See Virginia Hunter, *Past and Process in Herodotus and Thucydides*, Princeton, 1982, ch.i (a version of an article in *Klio* 1980), esp. 32.

[55] i 13.5.

[56] iii 104, with S. Hornblower, 'Thucydides, the Panionian Festival, and the Ephesia (III 104)', *Historia* xxxi, 1982, 241ff.

roof are the only wages he will get. Perdikkas gathered up the sunlight into the folds of his garment and said he accepted the gift. The striking feature of Thucydides' narrative is how what we would call a 'mythical' story is introduced into a very plain slice of writing; but it is no more surprising than Polybius' account of the origins of the Achaean League, which begins with the calm statement that Tisamenos son of Orestes was the first king of the Achaeans.[57] What was really the attitude, to such mythical and poetic evidence, of Greeks like Thucydides and Polybius, in other respects so sophisticated?[58] Did they 'believe' them? One approach is to say that 'belief' is an unhelpful word here: myths were 'a *tertium quid*, neither true nor false'.[59] In the language of modern philosophy, they lacked a truth-function. That certainly describes Thucydides' attitude to the Cyclops and Laestrygonians: 'I cannot say what kind of people these were or where they came from or where they went in the end. On these points we must be content with what the poets have said and what anyone else may happen to know.'[60]

But the information that Corinth was regarded by Homer as 'wealthy' does not fall into this twilight metaphysical category of 'neither true nor false'. It is, obviously, meant to be treated as *true*. Similarly, the poetic and mythical material in the *Archaeology* is taken seriously. Thucydides presents a coherent picture of the past by a structure of analogies. His language for this resembles at several points the language of another great fifth-century treatment of the same theme, namely a step-by-step intellectual reconstruction of past events by present signs: the *Oedipus Tyrannus* of Sophocles. Key verbs found in both the *Oedipus Tyrannus* and Thucydides' *Archaeology* are *tekmairesthai*, to infer, and *skopein*, to calculate; so Jocasta says at one point that the prudent man infers, *tekmairetai*, the new

[57] Thuc.i 22.4 (*to muthôdes*); ii 102 (Echinades); Hdt.viii 137ff., with N.G.L. Hammond in Hammond and Griffith, *History of Macedonia* ii, 1979, 6f. (Perdikkas). Polybius ii 41 (Tisamenos).

[58] See P. Veyne, *Les Grecs ont-ils cru à leurs mythes?* Paris 1983 (cf. above, p.19 n.13).

[59] So Veyne, p.40. On myth in Thucydides see also Brian Vickers, *Towards Greek Tragedy*, London 1973, 172 and M.I. Finley, 'Myth, memory and history', *History and Theory* iv, 1965, 281ff. (*The Use and Abuse of History*[2], London 1986, ch.1). Cf. Loraux, *Invention of Athens*, 1986, *passim*.

[60] vi 2.1. On Thucydides' 'downgrading' of Homer see Loraux, 70.

by reference to the old.[61] But most of the play is an inquiry into the past, starting from present or recent evidence. This is exactly Thucydides' method. Thus Minos ruled an island empire through his sons because, surely, the Cypselids and Pisistratids in more recent times had ruled, for example, Corcyra and Sigeum through cadet branches of the tyrant house. And the greatest analogy of all is between early 'thalassocracy', i.e. control of the sea, by a figure like King Minos, and the thalassocracy of Thucydides' own day, namely the Athenian Empire. Here, however, written sources may have influenced Thucydides: the so-called thalassocracy lists, which were first compiled in the fifth century and versions of which are preserved in, for instance, Diodorus of Sicily's *Universal History*.[62]

A fourth and related topic is Thucydides' use of inscriptions, which is midway between our third category, written evidence, and the fifth, archaeology.[63] Thucydides' citation of inscriptions impresses us in a way which Thucydides himself might have found surprising. *We* are impressed because inscriptions are what we ourselves use to reconstruct fifth-century history. The reason for *his* surprise, I suggest, would be that the evidence, oral and written, which was available to him was so much more copious than what is available to us, that the historical use of an inscribed decree was, in all but one type of situation, to be discussed shortly, likely to be less fruitful than personal oral inquiry about the circumstances in which a decision was taken. We must agree that the Mytilene debate and settlement in Book iii is more interesting than the inscription recording the detailed consequences that Thucydides does *not* give. For Thucydides, information about Attic resources and the financing of the empire could be obtained no doubt in simpler ways – for instance, by a visit to the office of the *hellēnotamiai*, the imperial treasurers – than by the methods which modern inquirers have to

[61] Soph. *OT* 916. See generally Bernard Knox, *Oedipus at Thebes*, Yale 1957, 120ff. Cf. also Vickers, pp.500ff. But for a *contrast* between Sophocles' idea of blindness and the optimistic striving for clarity of Thucydides and the Hippocratic writers, see R.G.A. Buxton, *JHS* 1980, 35ff.

[62] Thuc.i 4.1 (Minos). Thalassocracy lists: Forrest, *CQ* xix, 1969, 95ff. at 95, 106; J.L. Myres, xxvi, 1906, 84ff. See Diod. vii 11.

[63] The citation of inscriptions was not quite new: see a good discussion in a rather unexpected place, the introduction by Forbes and Abbott to the 1900 revision of Jowett's Thucydides translation, esp. xxvf. For Herodotus in particular see now S. West, *CQ* xxxv, 1985, 278ff.

follow. *They* have to perform a multiplication sum: the surviving inscribed Athenian Tribute Lists, as we call them, are actually not lists of the full tribute at all, but give the small annual payments of 1/60 which were paid to the goddess Athena. To arrive at the tribute paid by a particular state, it is necessary to multiply by sixty.[64]

The exception, where an inscription *was* as good as or better than an oral informant, is treaty documents. This is an area where Thucydides does record the *erga* of the protagonists in full *akribeia*, not just because a written treaty was the culmination of numerous small acts of diplomacy, but because the *text* of a treaty or agreement was itself an important and influential fact, provoking arguments like those between Sparta and her allies after the peace of 421.[65] The decree about Mytilene was not important in that sense.

Thucydides does sometimes use inscriptions. In particular he uses three in the Pisistratid excursus in Book vi, one to prove that the second Pisistratus, son of Hippias and grandson of the famous Pisistratus, held the archonship and that Hippias was the elder son of the first and famous Pisistratus (an issue which we have already come across more than once in the present chapter); a second to show that Archedike, Hippias' daughter, was married to a pro-Persian tyrant; and a third, which he does not quote but simply mentions, an inscribed slab about the oppressions committed by the Pisistratid tyrants. The only other item that comes close to being a quotation of an inscription is the boastful epigram of the Spartan Pausanias the Regent, which he tells us was later erased.[66]

One feature which all these have in common is that they refer to the more or less distant past.[67] Another is that they are all in

[64] Thuc. iii 50; Tod 63. (Mytilene). See Chapter Seven below, pp.165 and 174 for some major corrections, in the light of epigraphy, to Thucydides' picture of the empire.

[65] See, however, Andrewes' notes on, for example, v 29; 39: it is not always easy to correlate the references, in Thucydides' narrative, to the contents of the various agreements, with the documents he quotes. For discussion of some of the inconsistencies see C. Meyer, *Die Urkunden im Geschichtswerk des Thukydides*[2], Munich 1970, and A. Kirchhoff, *Thukydides und seine Urkundenmaterial*, Berlin 1895.

[66] vi 54.7; 59.3; 55.1; i 134.2.

[67] Note that of Herodotus' twenty or so inscriptions, about half were put up by oriental kings; the others were all verse inscriptions, except perhaps the Samian

verse, being dedications, i.e. personal poetry.[68] For him these
documents were like poetry which, as we have seen, he has no
compunction about quoting. We do *not* find him citing the kind
of raw prose inscriptions about financial and administrative
topics which take up so many pages in a book like Meiggs and
Lewis' *Selection of Greek Historical Inscriptions*. It happens that
we have a much more explicit text, an archon list carved in the
last quarter of the fifth century, which probably confirms his
point about the archonship of the younger Pisistratus.[69]
Assuming that the list was available to him, we might suggest
that the reason he did not cite it was that it was not itself a relic,
but a by-product of the researches in the 420s of his
contemporary, the sophist Hippias of Elis (more on this in the
next chapter). Thucydides is proud of having read the younger
Pisistratus' epigram, although its 'letters were indistinct', which
may mean that the paint was faded, because the letters are, to
us, quite clear.[70] We might be tempted to say that Thucydides
cites inscriptions in the absence of a literary tradition; in this he
would be unlike us, who cite inscriptions not only in the absence
of, but to supplement, the literary tradition. But this will not
quite do, because Thucydides says (see p.77) that he knows from
specially reliable personal, oral, information that Hippias was
the eldest son, a rare claim for Thucydides, comparable only to
his claim to have witnessed and caught the plague himself.[71] He
says that this knowledge about Hippias is evidence additional to
that of the inscription about the oppression of the tyrants.
Perhaps we could formulate the answer more simply:
inscriptions are more appropriate evidence for the past than for

---

inscription (vi 14.3) with the names and parents of those who fought well at Lade.
See S. West, art.cit. (1983) for a very interesting discussion. Note the relevance of
her conclusion (p.304) that 'it seems reasonably clear that Herodotus is reluctant
to cite inscriptions, or any other form of non-poetic record, as the source of
information which might fall within the range of oral tradition'. This closely
resembles my conclusion about Thucydides; see below.

[68] The 'oppression of the tyrants' *stêlê* is obscure. If it resembled ML 43, a text
from Miletus about political expulsions in the mid-fifth century, it was probably
in prose. Which is why Thucydides mentions without quoting it. For
Wilamowitz, verse citations like the Homeric Hymn were no less a sign of an
unfinished text than documents: 'Die Thukydideslegende', *Hermes* xii, 1877,
326ff.=*Kl.Schr*.iii, 1ff. See C. Meyer, op.cit (1970).

[69] ML 6, column c, line 5, Pisi]stratos.

[70] vi 54.7; see Dover, *HCT* ad loc., and ML 6 commentary.

[71] vi 55.1. Plague: ii 48.3.

the present, where personal inquiry and research offer superior guidance. So, for example, the existence of the Athenian alliances with the western Greek states Leontini and Rhegium, which we know about from inscriptions, is simply alluded to by Thucydides in the narrative when need arises.[72] We can, if we like, complain that Thucydides does not tell us what we know from inscriptions – for instance, that Athens was in deep financial trouble in the Archidamian War and was borrowing heavily: it was not the 'farsighted' Pericles but the demagogues who extricated her from this. Again, it is certain from inscriptions, rather than from Thucydides, that the empire profited the upper as well as the lower class at Athens. Or we can complain that it is only from an inscription that we know that it was originally intended to send one general not three to Sicily, and that the huge sum of 3000 talents was segregated exclusively for the Sicilian expedition.[73] Very occasionally we can even correct Thucydides from an inscription on a point of detail: Drakontides, not Andokides, is the name of the general sent to Corcyra in 433.[74] But we should phrase our criticism carefully: what we mean is that we think, not that he should have cited an inscription, but that he should have mentioned the historical fact which the inscription implies.

Fifth, there is archaeology, or rather, material evidence.[75] Here Thucydides' habit is similar to his use of inscriptions. Modern historians, at least since Rostovtzeff, regard material evidence as no less informative about periods for which written history does exist, than about prehistory or 'Dark Age' periods. But Thucydides argues, from material evidence, about the *distant* past – the archaic settlement on the southern slope of the

[72] ML 63 and 64; Thuc. vi 6.2. Note that if J.D. Smart is right, *JHS* xcii, 1972, 128ff., 'Athens and Egesta', that *palaian xummachian* at iii 86 refers, not to an existing alliance – note the absence of the definite article – but to 'ancestral friendship' between Athens and Ionia, this removes one of the few occasions where Thucydides could be held to refer to a particular alliance which still today exists on stone. This consideration, I would suggest, strengthens Smart's already plausible case about iii 86 (but not the implausible main thesis of that article, which does not concern us here).

[73] For the points about Periclean 'foresight' and upper-class gains see Chapter Seven, pp.168, 174; ML 78 (arrangements for Sicily).

[74] ML 61 and Thuc. i 51.4.

[75] There is a sense in which to say that Thucydides uses archaeology for the study of the past is tautological. There is another sense: the use of artefacts, material remains, i.e. non-literary evidence generally.

Athenian acropolis, or the Karians on Delos – because ordinary cross-questioning and autopsy were not appropriate. Thucydides (above, p.31) rejects the idea that Athens' buildings were an index of her fifth-century greatness; we saw that this was perhaps polemic directed against Herodotus. Again, Pericles, although elsewhere he alludes vaguely to Athenian 'love of beauty', is made to say that Athens will be remembered for the number of Greeks she ruled, and for her struggles and losses (rather than for Phidias, Ictinus or Mnesikles, the sculptors and architects of the great buildings on the acropolis). Archaeology, then, is a kind of evidence we use when oral proof or witnesses are lacking. This is only part of the way archaeologists work now.[76] Only rarely[77] does Thucydides treat buildings, and what would now be called settlement-patterns, as relevant to his present-day narrative about the civilised, literate parts of the Greek world. The qualification ('civilised, literate') is important: the Thracian and Persian gift-giving, the alleged eating of raw flesh by the Aitolians, and the road-building of King Archelaus of Macedon,[78] are appropriate categories of description where the races in question are, in the modern word, under-developed, or, like Persia, have no native historiography. Athens, Sparta, Corinth and Thebes are, by contrast, defined by their *erga* in the sense of political actions performed in what for Thucydides was the present day.

We may return to archaeology proper. The interesting suggestion has been made[79] that the reason why Thucydides did not find Bronze Age Mycenae impressive, as we do, was that the Treasury of Atreus would have seemed to him a primitive and inferior version of what he was used to. It has further been claimed that what Thucydides took to be Karian remains on

[76] ii 15.4; i 8.1; i 10; ii 40.1; 64.3.

[77] For instance, at i 93.2 he uses archaeological evidence – the different kinds of stone, sculpture, etc. used in the building of Athens' city walls in 478 – to show that work on the walls was hurried. This is rightly cited by Lloyd, *Polarity and Analogy*, 427 and n.3, as showing that Thucydides 'sometimes makes telling use of archaeological evidence' in his attempts to reconstruct the past. But Lloyd does not distinguish between remote and near past: the year 478, although it was before Thucydides' own birth, was within the memory of his oral informants. (Lloyd confuses the city walls with the Long Walls, which were not built until about twenty years later; cf.Thuc.i 107-8).

[78] ii 97; iii 94; ii 100.

[79] By R.M. Cook, 'Thucydides as archaeologist', *BSA* 50, 1955, 266ff. and Finley art.cit. (1965).

Delos were just Geometric remains with armour included, as was normal at that date.[80] The implications of these mistakes are serious – they imply gross ignorance of Mycenaean civilisation and the way it ended – but that is not my concern now. What is interesting for the present purpose is the kind of occasion for which Thucydides found it appropriate to cite archaeological or rather material evidence. Incidentally the Mycenae item underlines, what his silences suggest, that he did not have much aesthetic sense. Of the public funeral in Book ii he says parenthetically that it happened in the 'most beautiful suburb' of Athens. This is surprising, and unique, unless we count what he says in the *Archaeology* about the wearing of expensive and elegant jewellery and dress; or his stress on the visual brilliance of the fleet bound for Sicily in 415 (which he never saw!). 'Beautiful gardens' appear only in a speech (ii 62.3).

This concludes the kinds of evidence used by Thucydides. But we may end with two types which he does *not* use. First is a kind which his predecessors, not to mention his junior Plato (in the *Cratylus*) had used extensively, namely arguments from names and etymology, usually bogus. Even his contemporary Hellanicus argued in this way.[81] Thucydides avoids this kind of argument, unless it is really true that the proper name 'Aeimnestos' is intended to suggest 'long memory' (above, p.51). I doubt this. In the *Sikelika* he says that Sicily was called 'Trinakria' originally, but took the name 'Sikania' from the Sikans who lived there. But this is innocuous.[82] In contrast, note the very intelligent point near the beginning of the *Archaeology*: there was no common Greek enterprise at that early date (the Trojan War), as is shown by the fact that Greeks in Homer are called Danaans, Argives, Achaeans, etc., and not by the general name 'Hellenes'. This is curiously like the argument used in a

[80] Ibid. See, however, C.R. Long, 'Greeks, Carians and the purification of Delos', *AJA* lxii, 1958, 279ff., who thinks that the graves which Thucydides saw were Mycenaean not Geometric, and were confused by him with Karian multiple chamber tombs. This is not so satisfying a view as Cook's – it does not explain the armour – but it is endorsed by M. Giuffrida, 'I Cari e Minosse nelle tradizioni di Erodoto e Tucidide', *Studi di storia antica ... a E. Manni*, Rome 1976, 133ff., esp. 147ff.

[81] *FGrHist* 1 F71a, discussing the foundation of Chios, derives Sinties from *sinesthai*, 'to plunder', and F 89 derives the Idaian Daktyloi from the fingers of Rhea. Word-play in (hellenistic) Timaeus: *FGr Hist* 566 F 102.

[82] Thuc. iii 52. 'Long memory': Connor, *Thucydides*, 1984, 97 n.42. Trinakria: vi 2.

recent book on archaic Greece to prove a point about the antiquity of the Greek tribal structure.[83]

Thucydides was fascinated by certain aspects of language. For instance, there is his comment on the changes in verbal evaluation which were produced by the Corcyra *stasis*. And there are the oscillations between technical, prosaic and elevated vocabulary, as in Book ii where we have highly technical 'plague' language followed by some prosaic military narrative and then some solemn words by Pericles.[84] This is possible, as we have seen, because Thucydides has more than one emotional 'register'; but the effect is partly achieved by shrewd varying of types of vocabulary. We might compare the sudden switches into conversational language used by the modern Greek poet Cavafy, after some particularly elevated passage.[85] Again, there are in Thucydides definitions in the manner of Prodikos, and assonances of thought and phraseology, like *phronêma/ kataphronêma* (put into Pericles' mouth: 'Face your enemies not just with confidence, *phronêma*, but with a sense of superiority, *kataphronêma*').[86] But *names* as such seem to have left him cold, unlike many of his contemporaries. Herodotus often makes play with puns, such as Hegesistratus, 'leader of the host', and 'Krios', the 'Ram', of Aegina, who is told by Kleomenes to get his horns sheathed in metal because trouble is coming.[87] And Euripides has the line: 'Pentheus, may he not bring grief (*penthos*) to the house.' By contrast, the few alleged puns in Thucydides are in my view accidental.[88]

A related characteristic of Thucydides is, however, *shared* with Herodotus: a lack of interest in foreign languages.'[89] 'Assyrian (i.e. Aramaic) letters' are mentioned, as is

[83] A.M. Snodgrass, *Archaic Greece*, London 1980, ch.i, criticising D. Roussel, *Tribu et cité*, 1976.

[84] iii 82.4 with J. Wilson, *CQ* xxxii, 1982, 18ff. and independently I. Worthington *LCM* vii, 1982, 124; prosaic military narrative: ii 58.

[85] C.M. Bowra, *The Creative Experiment*, London 1948, 43.

[86] ii 62.3. See below, p.120.

[87] Hdt.ix 91; vi 50.

[88] Eur, *Ba*.367 with Dodds' note. Sophocles makes play with Oedipus' name: Knox, *Oedipus at Thebes*, 184 and passim. This kind of thing goes back to Homer, see now R. Rutherford, *JHS* cvi, 1986, 157 n.63a. *Puns in Thucydides*: E. Powell, *CR* li, 1937, 103 alleges vii 39.2 (Ariston), iii 70.6 (Peithias), i 110.2 (*helos*; see Gomme on this one). The absence of Herodotean puns in Thucydides is an aspect of his general humourlessness, on which see below, p.191 n.1.

[89] See A. Momigliano, *Alien Wisdom*, Cambridge 1975.

Themistocles' learning of Persian 'as much as he was able', and Gaulites the 'bilingual' Karian.[90] (Actually he was presumably trilingual, in Karian, Greek and Persian or Aramaic.) Thucydides also mentions the hellenisation of the language of Amphilochian Argos. This is the first, and a very interesting, use of the word *hellênizô* in this sense.[91] But Thucydides' lack of oriental knowledge means, for instance, that the *Archaeology* is very lopsided: the great land powers of earlier times, Assyria and early Achaemenid Persia, are quite neglected. Perhaps Thucydides would have partially put this right in a finished version[92] – he is notoriously thin on Persian involvement in the great Peloponnesian War – and there is the occasional flash of awareness of events in Persia, as when he says that the plague affected 'large parts of the Great King's territories'.[93] But his perspective is Aegeocentric, and sheer linguistic ignorance is part of the explanation, as it is of many of the mistakes of Herodotus.

Second there is a type of evidence used by moderns but not by Thucydides, viz. coinage. It may be objected: what sort of argument *could* Thucydides have used coinage to prove, since most modern numismatic argument is different in character (in particular, so technical) from anything Thucydides tries to say? But in fact the Greeks were capable of using coinage as evidence in a fairly modern way. For instance, compare Polybius on the way the members of the Achaean League had, among other things, the same coinage. This is a use of numismatic evidence very like our own, namely to make a political point. Between Thucydides' time and Polybius' there is not much that we can adduce – only, perhaps, the discussion about Solon's coinage conducted by the author of the *Constitution of the Athenians*, and by fourth-century historians like Androtion. Wrongheaded though the conclusions and implications of this debate may now seem to us, the *form* of the discussion is sophisticated enough. Then, after Polybius' time, there is the point made by Jesus Christ about Caesar's image on the tribute money ('Render ... unto Caesar the things which be Caesar's and unto God the things which be God's'), which is, if you like, 'numismatic' in a

[90] iv 50; i 138.1; viii 85.2.
[91] ii 68.3 with N.G.L. Hammond, *Epirus*, Oxford 1967, 419 and my comments on the Thucydides passage in *CR* xxxiv, 1984, 246.
[92] See below, p.140.
[93] ii 48.1.

modern sense; we find a similar use in First Maccabees, a good
historical source, where the Seleucid king Demetrius II concedes
to the Jews the right to mint stamped coinage.[94] Herodotus and
Thucydides certainly make mention of money as such –
Herodotus rightly says that the Lydians invented coinage, and
he mentions Aryandes' pure coinage, and Polykrates' gilding of
lead money.[95] But neither of them uses arguments from coinage
in a modern way: for instance, as evidence of political control or
policy. Where then, given the Polybian analogy, might
Thucydides have drawn on coin evidence? One answer is that for
one so interested in who colonised whom,[96] coinage would have
been useful as a way of stressing the close ties between Corinth
and her daughter cities. Not to mention Athens' coinage decree
of the 440s, which enforced the use of Athenian coins, weights
and measures. This was an expression of imperial power, even if
it was not an outrage against the political sovereignty of her
allies.[97] But it does not seem to have occurred to Thucydides to
use this sort of evidence.

(iii) Technical terms

Thucydides' use of technical terms in general, what lawyers call
'terms of art', deserves attention before we look at his vocabulary
of evidence in particular. His attitude fluctuates. We would
expect a man writing a 'possession for ever' not to use technical
terms without explanation. Did Thucydides ever envisage a time
when civilised human beings would not speak what we call
ancient Greek? Or a time when – for instance – ships powered by
oars would not be a standard weapon of war?

But in fact there *are* technical terms, casually introduced
without even the apology of a phrase like 'the so-called' which he
often uses for place names, even for well-known ones like the

[94] Polybius ii 37.10-11; *Ath.Pol.*x with Rhodes' note for Androtion (*FGrHist* 324
F34) and the whole problem. Tribute money: Luke 20.25. 1 Maccabees xv.

[95] Hdt. i 94.1; iv 166.2; iii 56.2.

[96] See, for example, i 28.2-3; iv 88.2; vii 57.

[97] ML 45; the view of that decree which I have given in the text is that of
Thomas R. Martin, *Sovereignty and Coinage in Classical Greece*, Princeton 1985,
196ff. Thucydides' silence about the decree could be taken as further evidence for
Martin's view (that the purpose of the decree was chiefly financial), though
Martin himself is more impressed (p.206) by the silence of Isokrates and
strangely does not mention Thucydides at all.

Paralia, a large district of Attica:[98] for instance, the *epidêmiourgoi*,[99] Corinthian magistrates sent to Potidaia in the 430s. Thucydides tells us no more than that they were sent annually. In the same category is the mention of the *Kythêrodikês*, an annual Spartan official sent to the island of Kythera.[100] The reproduction, verbatim, of inscriptions involves Thucydides in some technical language. But the most famous, as well as the densest, collocation of one set of technical terms comes in the description of the plague, where medical and anatomical language is freely used, though there is a kind of apology at the point where he speaks of 'all the discharges of bile to which physicians have ever given names'. This is a way of saying, 'I could have been *even more technical* if I had chosen.'[101]

Contrast with this the treatment of Athenian imperialism, which is very 'untechnical' (though inscriptions show that a rich vocabulary was developed for imperial institutions – *epiphora, aparchê, episkopoi*, and so on).[102] This is largely, it seems, because the topic is explored *via* the speeches rather than *via* the narrative (contrast the plague and the *stasis*); and in speeches Thucydides seems generally to avoid technical language. We have seen, at the end of Chapter Three, that the word 'cleruchy', a correct or precise rather than a technical expression, is found in the narrative but not in speeches, although a speech of Antiphon uses it: Herodotus had used it in his narrative.[103] Crucial words like 'autonomous' are used very imprecisely.[104] The word 'metic' (resident alien at Athens), although not strictly part of the vocabulary of imperialism, is illuminating: it occurs seven times

---

[98] ii 55.1. It is, I suppose, anti-parochialism that makes Thucydides avoid giving demotics (for demes see above, p.1) for Athenians; his own is known from Marcellinus. Xen. *Hell* (i 4; v 1) distinguishes the Thrasybuloi by demotics, and Herodotus gives a few demotics (e.g. viii 93: was this copied from an inscription?). Thucydides refers to only one deme as such, ii 19, Acharnai, cf.23 'other demes'. Elsewhere where he refers to what are in fact demes he avoids the word, cf. viii 95 (Thorikos). Even Acharnai is 'one of the *so-called* demes' (Herodotus does not mind the word, e.g. v.74 and (?) i 60. 4; and of course v 69 on Kleisthenes). Whitehead (above, p.2; his p.48) curiously says that Xen. *Hell.* has no demotics (v.sup.) and cites only *Mem.*ii 7.6.

[99] i 56.2.

[100] iv 53.2.

[101] Plague: ii 49ff.; bile: ii 49 with Parry, *BICS* xvi, 1969, 113.

[102] For these terms see Meiggs, *The Athenian Empire*, 1972, chs.11 and 13.

[103] Thuc.iii 50; Hdt. v 77.

[104] For example at Thuc.iii 10.5.

in Thucydides, but every time in the narrative, never in a
speech. The only indirect reference to metics in a speech is in
Nikias' address shortly before the final catastrophe in Sicily. He
speaks of people who, though not Athenians, have shared in the
benefits of Athenian rule, since it makes them objects of fear to
the subject allies, and they enjoy greater freedom from injustice
(?) even than the Athenians themselves. This seems to refer to
metics.[105] Perhaps Nikias avoids the word because it was
opprobrious,[106] in which case this is not straightforward
avoidance of 'technicality' (the word was anyway surely too
common to count as truly technical). However, by describing
metics in this periphrastic way, Nikias is able to make some
flowery points about the benefits of Athenian rule.

Generally, the speeches are vague even when the arguments
could have been reinforced by rather more technical language.
The Athenians reply to allegations of abuse of legal process; the
word *xumbolimaiai* [*dikai*] is used of the lawsuits in question,
and this technical term can be elucidated with the help of
inscriptions.[107] So here is one technical term at least; but the
Greek which follows is not only hard to translate (is there one
grievance or are there two?) but, on any translation, imprecise
and heavily compressed. In what respect are the laws established
for the allies 'equal' as the Athenians allege? Does the phrase 'in
our own courts' conceal a reference to the transfer of cases to
Athens? If the Athenians have a point here, it has been blunted
by imprecision, and we are left with a mere assertion. Again, the
Athenian pretexts for intervention against their allies (listed in
Book vi: desertion, fighting among themselves, other specious
pretexts),[108] are very economically put. It is perhaps relevant

---

[105] vii 63.3, which the scholiast takes to refer to metics. See A. Amit, *Athens
and the Sea, Collection Latomus* lxxiv, 1965, 38; D. Whitehead, *The Ideology of
the Athenian Metic, PCPhS* supp.vol.4, 1977, 43, cf. 85. The group addressed
seem to be something less than citizens, but something more than just subject
allies from whom they are explicitly distinguished. 'Freedom from injustice': does
this refer to, for example, privileged rights of access to the polemarch's court; cf.
ML 31? But this hardly puts them in a *better* position than actual Athenians.
The text may not be wholly sound; cf. *HCT* ad loc. J.H. Finley, *Three Essays*, 45
compares Jason's words addressed to another famous 'metic', Medea:
Eur.*Med*.536ff.

[106] Whitehead, op.cit., 43; G. Steiner, *Antigones*, Oxford 1984, 279.

[107] Above all ML 31. The Thucydides passage is i 77.1. See my note on no.172 of
the *Athenian Empire* LACTOR sourcebook, ed.3, 1984, at 142f.

[108] vi 76.3.

that most of our Thucydidean speeches are delivered before large gatherings, the Melian Dialogue being an exception. We suggested above[109] that greater technicality was customary before the Athenian Council, a probouleutic body with a maximum attendance of 500, than before the Assembly, which might be made up of as many as 6000; similarly, today's criminal barrister adopts a different manner before a jury from that of a chancery barrister arguing a point of construction before a judge.

If we turn to the narrative, the language used of imperial and related institutions is a little more precise: Thucydides mentions the *eisphora* (capital levy), and 'tribute-collecting ships'; there is an *etheloproxenos* in Book iii. This technical word, which probably means a voluntary *proxenos* (see p.22), is found nowhere else in extant Greek.[110] But the use of, for example, 'autonomous', 'subject but/and tribute-paying' at vii 57 is hopelessly ill-defined, causing historical difficulties which can here be passed over. In this passage there was no stylistic reason for the vagueness: here was no speaker trying to simplify complex issues. For the political historian it is perhaps the most unsatisfactory feature of Thucydides that he addresses his central problem, that of Athenian imperialism, at such a high level of generality and abstraction. Or rather, as has been said (of the Archidamian War), Thucydides' narrative is 'a compromise between the methods of tragedy and of a laboratory notebook'.[111]

Our general conclusion so far must be that Thucydides stands on the frontier between un-technicality and technicality. This frontier should not be confused with the line delimiting prose from poetry: there is 'technical' description in Homer, for instance Odysseus' building of a raft. (Tragedy is *more* free from technical language, though, for instance, Euripides speaks of the annual rotation of political office at Athens.)[112] And technicality is singularly absent in the *prose* writer Herodotus.[113] For example, note the vague 'council' which Herodotus says resisted Kleomenes of Sparta when he attacked Athens. Is it the Areopagus (though he was certainly capable of using the correct

[109] p.71 n.101.

[110] *Eisphora* and tribute-collecting ships: both at iii 19; the *etheloproxenos*: iii 70.3.

[111] By Wade-Gery, *OCD²*, s.v. 'Thucydides', 1068; but see below, p.197.

[112] *Suppl.*267.

[113] This is surely part of the point of Thucydides' viciously put objection, i 20.3, about the 'Pitanate *lochos*', which he says never existed. See Hdt.ix 53.

expression for this body)? Or is it Solon's council of 400, or Kleisthenes' new council of 500?[114]

But Thucydides *is* at an important frontier: a 'monograph' like that on the plague has close affinities to other kinds of technical literature (see above, p. 50 and n.17); on the other hand, there is tragedy but no technicality, though there is precision and concreteness, about the end of the Sicilian expedition. And we have seen that the speeches tend to avoid technicality. A final point: there was, by the fourth century, a technical language to describe the figures of rhetoric; is it detectable in any of the speeches of Thucydides? It has been ingeniously suggested that the word *epideixis*, which occurs in the Mytilene Debate, is a giveaway, technical, term of art in rhetoric.[115] But usually the scaffolding is kept well out of sight. On the whole, the speeches prefer the general to the particular, the normal to the technical. The narrative is different: here Thucydides *sometimes* permits himself technicality.

(iv) Vocabulary of evidence

With these general points in mind, we must pass now to the vocabulary of evidence, and ask whether Thucydides uses technical language about one particular and crucial area: namely, his own methods of inquiry. Here the reader of the first two books in particular is struck by the comparative richness of the relevant language, compared with the later books, in which terms like *sêmeion* (sign), *tekmêrion* (evidence), *marturion* (testimony) appear much less frequently. This is due partly to the unbalancing presence of the *Archaeology* early in Book i, but only partly: the methodological statements scattered through the first two dozen chapters of Book i, the Pausanias-Themistocles excursus, and the Athenian topographical and antiquarian digression early in Book ii also account for a large

[114] Kleomenes: v 72.2. Areopagus: viii 52. For this sort of reason – Herodotus' avoidance of technical terms – one may doubt whether at vi 92.2 the ingenious emendation *dekacha* ('by tens', a very technical word, found at ML 94) can be right. The language about the polemarch being appointed by 'the bean' (i.e. the lot) at vi 109 is technical; cf. ML 40 line 9 (but perhaps Herodotus was wrong: the archons were elected, not appointed by lot, until 487, see *Ath.Pol.* xxvi. See, however, Badian, *Antichthon* v, 1971, 1ff; cf. Kelly, ib.xii, 1978, 1ff.).

[115] iii 42.3; Luschnat, *RE* supp.xii, 1970, s.v. 'Thukydides', col. 1147 (but note that some Mss. have *antideixin*).

number. Much of what we can say, therefore, about the relevant language and terminology of Thucydides relates to these books in particular.

Let us then take some key terms and ask how far Thucydides uses them in technical senses. First, the pair of terms *sêmeion* and *tekmêrion*. The rhetorical Aristotelian handbooks distinguish these two as follows:[116] *sêmeion* is a sign, which may be fallible, pointing to a result. A *tekmêrion* is an indication that the result will *necessarily* occur: for example, 'No smoke without fire' could be translated 'Smoke is a *tekmêrion* of fire'.[117] So the distinction is between signs which are certain and signs which are merely probable. How does Thucydides compare? Readers of Books i and ii must notice the frequency of the tag *tekmêrion de*, meaning 'and a proof of this is as follows ...'. It is used, for instance, to explain why Thucydides believes that the Athenian acropolis and the area to the south of it were once the city.[118] He says, 'And the proof, *tekmêrion*, is that there are numerous temples on the southern slope'. He also uses the phrase in his discussion of the plague, to explain why he thinks that animals which normally ate carrion did not at this time eat human flesh, or if they did died of it. The *tekmêrion* is the disappearance of birds of prey.[119] Finally, there is a Periclean speech: the proof, *tekmêrion de*, that although the Athenians live in a relaxed way they are none the less formidable is that they conduct their invasions unaided while the Spartans only go out against them with their whole league.[120]

Does *tekmêrion*, in these examples, make some specially strong claim of the Aristotelian kind? Surely not. Thucydides is not claiming to do more than infer the cause of, for example, the absence of birds of prey, and he would accept that there might be other explanations, alternatively or in addition. Indeed that seems to be proved by his continuing with a contrast between, on the one hand, the behaviour of domestic dogs, which provided the perceivable evidence (*aisthêsis*) of the conclusion, and, on the other, the purely 'negative evidence'[121] of absence of birds of

---

[116] See E.M. Cope, *An Introduction to Aristotle's Rhetoric*, London 1867, 160ff.
[117] Taken from Cope.
[118] ii 15.
[119] ii 50.
[120] ii 39.2.
[121] The phrase is from Gomme, in his commentary on ii 50.

prey. Thucydides seems to be contrasting *tekmêrion*, as a more distant reason for making judgments, with perception, which is nearer at hand. (But the word *sounds* convincingly 'legal'.)

But perhaps we are pressing these arguments from terminology too far. Edward Hussey has suggested to me that Thucydides generally thought more in terms of clarity, *to saphes*, another key term. Thucydides makes a move from 'clear' to 'definite and certain'; this implies the appreciation of things by a mental sense organ.[122] The attitude of Thucydides or his speakers towards the problem of knowledge shows awareness of the two extreme positions.[123] First, there is the view implied in the plague passage, that perception (i.e. the deliverances of the senses) is the closest approximation to knowledge, a position associated with Protagoras. Second, there is the view associated with Parmenides, that reason and sense perception are to be radically contrasted, only the former yielding true knowledge. So, for instance, Thucydides makes Pericles contrast 'confidence of freedom' with 'calculation'. This is a passage with a Platonic character: for Plato, 'guesswork' and 'belief' are subdivisions of 'opinion'; and the objects of opinion, even when it is 'right opinion', hover between being and non-being.[124]

The conclusion must be that Thucydides' use of *tekmêrion* does not correspond to the distinction in Aristotelian logic. Nor does Thucydides seem to use the word in the same way as Aristotle's philosophical predecessors: it is in fact an exceedingly rare word in their work.[125] By contrast, perception, *aisthêsis*, is an extremely common term with the 'pre-Socratic' philosophers. So far, then, it appears that *tekmêrion* in Thucydides is not technical; but for him as for Sophocles (see below) pseudo-technicality was attractive.

[122] This point is very like one made by Schneider, p.131: clarity is, for Thucydides, rational evidence, of which evidence of physical appearance is only a special case. For clear=true see also Knox, *Oedipus*, p.133.

[123] For the 'extreme positions' see G. Lloyd, *Polarity and Analogy*, Cambridge 1966, 122.

[124] ii 40, with Ed. Meyer, *Forschungen zur alten Geschichte* ii, Halle 1899, 388, n.1 to 387, a passage of polemic against seeing Thucydides as a sophist.

[125] *Tekmêrion* occurs only once in Diels and Kranz's collection of the fragments of the pre-Socratic philosophers, namely in Plato's *Phaedrus* (266d=DK 80 Protagoras A 26), where it is ranged between rehearsal of evidence, *marturia*, and arguments from probability, in the account of the way an argument should be drawn up. The verb, *tekmairein*, occurs once in Antiphon the sophist, in a fragmentary passage; and see n.127 below.

But there is still the question, can we press the distinction
between *sêmeion* and *tekmêrion*? Again the answer is 'no'. The
clearest and neatest demonstration of this comes in the
Pausanias excursus in Book i. The setting is explicitly legal. Here
the Spartan ephors (magistrates) are said to have no clear proof
(*sêmeion*) against Pausanias, without which they did not want to
proceed against a man of the royal house. But only four
paragraphs later, they are said not to want to proceed against a
'Spartiate man' (Pausanias again) without clear proofs. This
time the word for proofs is *tekmêria*.[126] I can see no difference in
sense between the two sentences, and hence between *sêmeion*
and *tekmêrion*.

Thucydides' use of the phrase *sêmeion de* ('and a proof of this
is as follows ...') is as untechnical as his use of *tekmêrion de*. It
comes in the *Archaeology*, where Thucydides says that the fact
that the custom of arms-bearing continues in some parts of
Greece shows (*sêmeion de*) that it once prevailed everywhere.
This is a kind of 'part for whole' argument; but is it very different
from saying that the existence in the fifth century of temples on
the southern slope of the acropolis is a *tekmêrion* that there were
once other civic buildings as well? Surely not; here *sêmeion* and
tekmêrion are indistinguishable except to the eye of casuistry.[127]
There is however a passage that does seem to point the other
way: to say that Mycenae must have been insignificant because
it was physically small is to use an inaccurate *sêmeion*. Perhaps

---

[126] i 132.1; 5.

[127] i 6.2; ii 15.3. *sêmeion de* at i 6.2 also seems to rule out – as does the
Pausanias passage in a cruder way – the idea that Thucydides regularly uses the
sêmeion/tekmêrion distinction in the way laid down by Antiphon F72 Blass;
sêmeion is evidence of the past, *tekmêrion* of the future. E. Täubler, *Die
Archäologie des Thukydides*, Leipzig/Berlin 1927, 105, goes too far in asserting
that Thucydides' usage corresponds to Antiphon's theory, though he is right that
the verb used at Thuc.i 1 (*tekmairomenos*) does so correspond, and so does
sêmeion when applied to Mycenae and arms-bearing (i 10; i 6). But *tekmêrion* at
i 3.3 refers to the *past* (Homer is cited for a point about what the early Greeks
called themselves). Täubler is nearer the truth when he says that Thucydides can
also use *tekmêrion* in a general and shifting sense. Like Sophocles (cf. Knox, p.
123 and above, p.87), Thucydides found the technical *connotations* of the word
(which were surely more legal than academic or philosophical) attractive. Note
Knox's discussion of a fragment of the sixth-century Alkmaion of Kroton (DK
B1) which distinguishes clarity, *saphêneia*, from mere inference, *tekmairesthai*.
Here the *tekm-* root is being contrasted with a better sort of knowledge, whereas
tekmêrion was later, as we have seen, contrasted with a worse sort of evidence, a
sêmeion.

Thucydides here uses the word *sêmeion* because it is appropriate
to *fallible* signs, such as the size of Mycenae; we may contrast
the expression 'from the *tekmêria* which I have mentioned',
which, Thucydides says, will *not* lead one astray.[128] So there are
passages which do (Mycenae), and passages which do not
(Pausanias the Regent) fit the distinction made in Aristotelian
handbooks between *sêmeion* and *tekmêrion*. We might conclude
that Thucydides' usage stands at a midway point: he is happy,
as over Pausanias, to vary his terms capriciously, or rather from
purely literary motives; but he may also – as over *tekmêrion* as
opposed to *aisthêsis*, perception, and over *sêmeion* applied to
Mycenae – choose his terms carefully, in a way which has
affinities with later practice. Nor (as one might have hoped) does
he confine technical usage to technical contexts: witness
tekmêrion used of the southern slope of the acropolis. The
Pausanias episode may (p.24) have been written early, which
could be relevant. Finally, to repeat a point made when we
discussed the speeches, Thucydides' own practice may have
affected what found its way into the handbooks, and indeed into
the practice of the Aristotelian school: notice for example that
the author of the Aristotelian *Constitution of the Athenians*[129]
uses *sêmeion* in a very Thucydidean way, for an argument about
what to the author was ancient history. He says that the *sêmeion*
that Solon introduced sortition is the law about the treasurers,
'which remains in use even today'.

Let us turn to another pair, *tekmêrion* and *marturia* (another
word for 'evidence', from a root meaning 'witness'). It has been
said by the greatest modern authority on Thucydides that
'*marturia* is evidence, and *tekmêrion* is inference from the
evidence',[130] a usage said to be forensic. Actually the distinction
made by the orators seems to be slightly different: the basic text
is in Isaeus. The orator says that it is better in inheritance suits
to trust to 'arguments from probability' (*tekmêria*) than to
'testimony' (*martusin*, i.e. witnesses).[131] In the Isaean context,

---

[128] i 10; i 21.1.

[129] See P.J. Rhodes, *Commentary on the Aristotelian Athenaion Politeia*,
Oxford 1981, 27, 59, 147.

[130] Gomme, *HCT* on i 20 (at p. 135, top). Note that Herodotus uses *tekmêrion*
and *marturion* very loosely, e.g. vii 221; 238. He does not seem to use *sêmeion* in a
comparable way.

[131] Isaeus iv 12, with Wyse's note, *The Speeches of Isaeus*, 1904, 384. In my text
I have borrowed from his paraphrase at his p.382. This is not cited by Gomme.

the so-called probability is the mere forensic assertion (frequently found in family cases, and commented on in the *Problems* of Aristotle), that the claims of kinship ought to matter more, and must have weighed more with the testator, than legal instruments.[132] Athenian juries notoriously needed little encouragement to set aside a will and find in favour of the testator's relations.

But the alleged *marturion/tekmêrion* distinction must be tested. We have already looked at some examples of *tekmêrion de*: for instance, the ancient temples on the southern slope of the acropolis are proof, *tekmêrion*, of a southern slope polis in earlier times. But Thucydides' use of *marturion* is indistinguishable from this. Karians, he says,[133] originally inhabited the islands, and the proof (*marturion de*) is that when the Athenians purified Delos half the tombs excavated were found to be Karian. The supposed distinction between inference from evidence, and the evidence itself, here becomes impossible to maintain.[134] In both the Karian and the southern slope examples Thucydides seems to be inferring earlier settlement from existing remains, which in both represent part of the picture from which the whole picture can be reconstructed. Finally, it should be noted that not every use of *marturion*, even in forensic contexts, means 'direct evidence' as opposed to inferences from it. For instance, a clear case, the Mytileneans say[135] that the Athenians need themselves, the Mytileneans, as evidence, *marturion*, that the subjection by Athens of her allies was not wrong; here the 'evidence' is the free acquiescence of Mytilene. Now Jowett translates *marturion* here as 'witness to their character', and indeed the Mytileneans are being described as witnesses, of a kind. But surely there is at best a kind of metaphor here: the Mytileneans were never actually arraigned in any witness-box. The point is rather that the complaisant *behaviour* of the Mytileneans offered grounds, so the Athenians alleged, for inferring that they acquiesced. The use of *marturion* here is, then, hardly more than a variant for

On probability *vs.* truth see G. Lloyd, *Polarity and Analogy*, 121ff. and Schneider, p.164.

[132] Ar. *Prob.* xxix 3.; see Wyse, p. 177, and J.W. Jones, *Law and Legal Theory of the Greeks*, Oxford 1956, 135.

[133] i 8.1.

[134] Gomme does not comment on the word *marturion* here, nor on its use at iii 11.4 (see text, below).

[135] iii 11.4.

tekmêrion; it is more vivid, perhaps, but it does not imply that the stage of inference, between the evidence and the conclusion, has been eliminated. So the supposed *marturia/tekmêrion* distinction does not correspond very closely with the way the terms are used by Thucydides.

Then there is *paradeigma*, proof. This is sometimes used in an antiquarian or archaeological context:[136] the fact that people took refuge in Attica is a *paradeigma* that Attica was more physically secure than the rest of Greece. Here the word does not mean, as in the fourth-century orators, 'example'.[137] *Paradeigmata*, in the normal sense of 'examples', are listed among types of proof by Aristotle in the *Rhetoric* and in the *Rhetoric to Alexander*.[138] But Thucydides here goes further and uses *paradeigma* to mean 'proof' without any sense of 'example'. Again, I suggest that Thucydides' strained use of an ordinary forensic term influenced, rather than was influenced by, rhetorical theory. In favour of this suggestion is a passage in the Melian Dialogue (which must have been a section of Thucydides much studied in antiquity) where it is said that Melian enmity for the Athenians is a *paradeigma* (surely 'proof', not 'example') of Athenian power.[139] So too, for Sophocles, Oedipus is a proof that mortals are not blessed;[140] Sophoclean and Thucydidean language for intellectual inquiry is similar, as we have seen.

Finally, there is *eikos*, 'likely', 'reasonable', 'natural'; in particular the tag *hôs eikos*, 'as is/was reasonable (etc.)'. There is an immediate problem: 'as was natural' does not mean the same as 'as was likely' ('He probably went' is not the same as 'Of course he went'), and a detailed discussion has concluded that on the six occasions that Thucydides uses *hôs eikos*, the phrase means 'as was natural' not 'as was likely'.[141] If this was true, it

[136] For example, i 2.6.
[137] Cf. Lys. xxii 20; Aischin. i 177.
[138] *Rhet.*1356b; *Rhetoric to Alexander* ch.vii.
[139] v 95. Bétant's lexicon erroneously takes both i 2.6 and v 95 as instances of *paradeigma* in the sense of *exemplum*, and neither Gomme nor Andrewes notices the unusual sense of *paradeigma*. Thucydides elsewhere uses the word in its normal sense. On the problems of i 2 see H.W. Stubbs, 'Thucydides i 2.6', *CQ* xxii, 1972, 74ff. and M.H. Marshall, 'Urban settlement in the second chapter of Thucydides', *CQ* xxv, 1975, 26ff. Marshall does not consider the possibility that *paradeigma* may mean no more than 'proof'.
[140] *OT* 1193, with Knox, pp. 48, 138 (contrast 98f., 157).
[141] H.D. Westlake, *Essays on the Greek Historians and Greek History*, Manchester 1969, ch.10 at pp.55ff., '*Hôs eikos* in Thucydides' (=*Hermes* lxxxvi,

would imply that Thucydides used *hôs eikos* more rigorously than the other expressions we have looked at, such as *tekmêrion*, etc. But in fact, *hôs eikos* does *not* mean 'as was natural' in the most interesting of the relevant passages.[142] So it was after all a more flexible formula for Thucydides than has been thought, and his usage does not prove that he had a consistent vocabulary, distinguishing *kata to eikos*, 'as was probable', and *hôs eikos*, 'as was natural'. Thucydides perhaps," here as elsewhere if my arguments are right, stands at an intermediate stage between the loose use of his predecessors and the more systematic language of the fourth century:[143] he is capable of a noticeable degree of precision – so that the conclusion that he uses *hôs eikos* to mean 'as was natural' is *generally* (though as we have seen, not wholly) convincing; but he is equally capable of vernacular lapses.

Incidentally, the close link, in the vocabulary of evidence, between Antiphon and Thucydides, is perhaps most strikingly illustrated by the word *abasanistos*, 'untested', used by Thucydides to describe the methods of careless researchers'. Antiphon uses it of slaves being put to the torture, 'untested', because not tortured.[144]

(v) Conclusion

To sum up, Thucydides' language about his use of evidence does not fit the later oratorical and rhetorical categories, though sometimes the later distinctions (to whose formulation

---

1958) and now in *Mnemosyne* xxxviii, 1985, 103. On *eikos* as a fifth-century rhetorical principle see J.H. Finley 'Euripides and Thucydides', *Three Essays*, 9.

[142] viii 88. Thucydides is talking about Alcibiades' knowledge of Tissaphernes' motives, and says that Alcibiades knew, *hôs eikos*, the intentions of Tissaphernes. Here the phrase surely means 'as was likely' (i.e. he *probably* knew) rather than 'he knew, as was natural', since there are other passages in Book viii where Thucydides puts doubt on the closeness of the relation between Alcibiades and Tissaphernes. (So Andrewes, *HCT* on viii 88, with addendum on p.456, specifically discussing Westlake – Andrewes cites viii 81.2 and 82.3, but not viii 46.5.) A particularly illuminating parallel is the earlier use (viii 46.5) of the linguistically related phrase *hôs eikasai* to *hôs eikos*, to express doubt about the same point, the degree of influence which Alcibiades had over Tissaphernes. Here there is no question that *hôs eikasai* means 'as one may conjecture', which makes it likely that the meaning of *hôs eikos* in the later passage is similar.

[143] Note that Antiphon's *First Tetralogy* (ii 5ff.) uses *eikos* or a cognate seven times in three paragraphs, and here it is much harder to sort out the senses of *eikos*.

[144] Thuc.i 20.1; Antiphon i 13.

Thucydides may have himself unconsciously contributed) seem to be inchoately present. His vocabulary for intellectual inquiry has affinities with that of the Sophocles of the *Oedipus Tyrannus*. As for his *use* of evidence, *erga*, in the sense of human military and political actions, are his prime 'sources': that is, evidence for what he says. Material and other kinds of 'non-speaking' evidence are usually relegated to archaic contexts. In this he departs from Herodotus' idea of *ergon* (above, p.31). An instructive contrast is Herodotus' apology for 'dwelling at length' (*emêkuna*) on Polykrates' Samos, about which there was plenty of poetic evidence. He says that the reason was the three great *erga* (*tria exergasmena*): the tunnel, the mole and the temple. Contrast that with the echo in Thucydides: Pericles says that he has dwelt at length (*emêkuna* again) on Athens' affairs, because of the achievements – *ergon*, in the sense of human political and military action, is thrice repeated in this chapter of Thucydides – of the glorious dead. Those achievements prove (they are *sêmeia*, again without any implication of *withheld* belief) the city's fame, its *eulogia*.[145]

Finally, how successful is Thucydides in his use of, and attitude to, evidence? We have seen, here and in Chapter One, that the narrowing of the scope of *ergon* involved the loss of the discursive richness which characterised Herodotus, although it undoubtedly enabled Thucydides to maintain a tighter story-line than his predecessor. And Thucydides' vocabulary has a new sophistication, even if it is not technical. We cannot, however, claim that greater sophistication of manner always meant greater sophistication in handling evidence. David Lewis has observed one striking respect in which Thucydides missed an opportunity to improve methodologically on Herodotus. In the *Archaeology*, Thucydides belittles the Persian Wars by saying that they were settled in two land- and two sea-battles. It would have been a far more telling objection to Herodotus (who is the real target here) if Thucydides had argued that his *numbers* for the Persian land and sea forces were wildly exaggerated, as

---

[145] Hdt.iii 60; Thuc.ii 42. The poetic evidence for Polykrates' Samos is exploited in Mary Renault's novel *The Praise Singer*, 1978. The poets include Ibycus, Anacreon and Simonides. Cf. also J.P. Barron, *CQ* xiv, 1964, 210ff. and M.L. West, *CQ* xx, 1970, 205ff.

modern scholars believe they are.[146] On this point Thucydides is, to use Lewis's word, as 'innumerate' as Herodotus, perhaps because he too subscribed unconsciously to the myth of Persia as a cumbersome giant. In our final chapter, however, we shall return to this issue, and we shall see that the charge is unjust if applied to Thucydides' own war narrative, where figures are not implausibly inflated so far as we can gauge. It would be surprising if Colonel Thucydides[147] gave reckless military totals in his routine narrative: this was a kind of evidence which he was used to handling when sending home military reports (see Chapter Two).

---

[146] i 23.1. Lewis's remark was made in a seminar given by G.L. Cawkwell on 'Greece and Persia', summer 1986. Loraux, *Invention of Athens*, 1986, 157, accuses Thucydides himself of exaggerating on this topic (i 74.1, the Athenian contribution to the victorious fleet at Salamis). But as usual she confuses Thucydides with his speakers.

[147] As Oswyn Murray calls him: *Oxford History of the Classical World*, 1986, 195 – but the phrase is really Momigliano's, see his *Alien Wisdom*, Cambridge 1975, 27 for Colonel Polybius.

CHAPTER FIVE

Intellectual Affinities

Intellectual influences on an author of Thucydides' linguistic richness are easy to posit but exceptionally hard to identify precisely. Two areas in which large claims were made earlier this century are tragedy and medical writing. A famous literary study, *Thucydides Mythistoricus* (1907), was written round such ideas as that 'Thucydides seems to me to have learnt from Aeschylus'.[1] Similarly the author of a book called *Thucydides and the Science of History* could write confidently in 1929 that Thucydides was attempting to 'do for history what Hippocrates was at the same time trying to do for medicine'.[2] Contrast with these two statements two more recent ones on the same topics. In an already classic paper, 'Thucydides and tragedy', delivered in 1981, we were warned: 'I doubt if tragedy should be numbered among the literary influences on Thucydides'.[3] And an important article in 1979, 'Thucydides and the plague of Athens', concluded that Thucydides' ideas (on the crucial issues of contagion and acquired immunity) 'certainly owed nothing to contemporary medical thinking'.[4]

[1] F.M. Cornford, *Thucydides Mythistoricus*, preface, p.x. J.H. Finley's essay 'Euripides and Thucydides' was first published in 1938 (reprinted as ch.1 of his *Three Essays*, 1967). This very valuable collection of parallels leaves open the question 'what those resemblances mean' (p.1).

[2] C. Cochrane, *Thucydides and the Science of History*, Oxford, 26; see also D.L. Page, *CQ* iii, 1953, 97ff. 'Thucydides and the Great Plague at Athens'; K. Weidauer, *Thukydides und die hippokratische Schriften*, Heidelberg 1953.

[3] Macleod, *Essays*, 157. Note also H. Lloyd-Jones, *The Justice of Zeus*[2], 1983, 144: 'Thucydides sees the history of the empire in tragic terms not necessarily because he has been influenced by tragedy', but – like Herodotus and the tragedians themselves – by the epic. Cf. also Dover in n.5 below.

[4] A.J. Holladay and J.C.F. Poole, *CQ* xxix, 1979, 299ff (cf. xxxii, 1982, 235; xxxiv, 1984, 483). But see p.134 below. See too A. Parry, *BICS* xvi, 1969, 106ff., 'The language of Thucydides' description of the plague': he was 'medical' neither in objectives nor terminology.

This move towards scepticism may be just a swing of fashion,[5] or it may be the result of more sophisticated techniques of analysis (though, logically, still greater sophistication in the future might lead to the reversal of the judgments of the 1980s). But I suspect that the more recent views are in fact preferable, because they accept the similarities on which the older scholars insisted but ask more rigorous questions about what is meant by an intellectual 'debt'. We need to ask, not just whether *a* resembles *b* (as earlier critics tended to do, and left it at that: they assumed always that Thucydides was the debtor), but whether *a* actually influenced *b* or the influence was the other way. Alternatively did *a* and *b* arrive at similar views independently? Or is there a shared debt to *c*? Or are the similarities merely superficial? Shared debt to epic is one modern explanation of the features which Thucydides has in common with tragedy[6] (though we should not forget Thucydides' debt to Herodotus, that 'most Homeric'[7] of writers). And modern experts regard the similarities between Thucydides and the Hippocratic medical writings as less important than the differences.[8] The extent of these differences is not agreed upon and we shall return to the question at the end of this chapter. We shall see that he was at the least an autonomous, if not a superior, figure. In other areas too we must accept that we can go no further than establishing a similarity of position, and

[5] Recent fashions in Thucydides studies are interestingly discussed by K.J. Dover, 'Thucydides "as history" and "as literature" ', *History and Theory* xxii, 1983, 54ff., who points out (p.55) that there are elementary differences between Thucydides and tragedy: 'If in discussing a tragedy we ask "Did Creon do that?" the question is answerable through familiarity with the text [sc. of Sophocles]. If we ask, "Did Cleon do that?" there are circumstances in which we expect an answer founded solely on familiarity with the text of Thucydides, but that is not as a rule the point of the question. "Would Creon have done that?" means, "Is the action consistent with the character of the kind of person the playwright, up to that point, has constructed?". "Would Cleon have done that?" however hard the question may be to answer, is rarely if ever reducible to such terms.' Dover, in his general discussion of recent approaches, surprisingly ignores the work of Colin Macleod. W.R. Connor, in 'A post-modernist Thucydides?', *Classical Journal* lxii, 1977, 289ff., discusses the recent tendency in Thucydides scholarship to concentrate on Thucydides' emotional power rather than his supposed objectivity or detachment.

[6] Macleod, p.157.

[7] Macleod, ibid.; 'most Homeric': Longinus, *On the Sublime* xiii.3, with D.A. Russell's note, giving some Homeric echoes in Herodotus.

[8] n. 4 above.

accepting that the two similar positions may have been independently reached. This should not surprise us in an age such as that of the sophists, which was characterised by intellectual curiosity on all fronts at once and by a remarkable readiness to apply the techniques of one discipline to another[9] in a way and at a speed which makes the direction of any 'borrowing' impossible to trace.

Medical writings and tragedy are two possible influences, to which we shall return shortly. A third influence is rhetoric. (In Chapters One and Three we discussed some of the issues which rhetoric raises, and there is therefore no need for a section on rhetoric here.) There is a special problem about rhetoric. The extant Hippocratic corpus is voluminous and thirty-four Attic tragedies of the fifth century survive more or less complete; so although much has been lost from both categories we have a solid foundation of evidence on which to base our theories. But the fate of oratory in Thucydides' time has been very different. As we saw in Chapter Four, there are virtually no speeches preserved from earlier than the very last years of the fifth century. Theoretical treatises there must also have been, but they too have perished.[10]

There is a comparable problem about Thucydides' debt to a fourth influence: Socratic teaching, the most important contemporary philosophy, which notoriously was not written down. What we have is a 'Socratic literature' transmitted mainly in the dialogues of Plato and Xenophon. The relation of these to Socrates' own doctrines, and to each other, is one of the hardest puzzles in the whole field of classical literature and thought. There is no question about the chronological relation of Thucydides to Plato and Xenophon: he was their senior, and we can speak only of *his* influence on *them*. But Thucydides was the contemporary of Socrates, and there is a serious possibility that Thucydides should be counted as in some sense a 'Socratic' thinker.[11]

---

[9] For this tendency see, above all, G.E.R. Lloyd's *Magic*, discussed above, p.20. Discussing the relation between tragedy and philosophy, S. Goldhill, *Reading Greek Tragedy*, 229 (with 243) sensibly rejects talk of 'influences' and prefers to speak of 'shared response' to problems like the relation between man and the city. On N. Loraux's influential *Invention of Athens*, 1986, see my remarks above, p.62 n.66.

[10] Radermacher's *Artium Scriptores*, 1951, collects what fragments there are.

[11] The relation of Thucydides to contemporary sophistic, and the Socratic corpus, has not been much studied since the writings of Nestle in the early part of

A further, and general, difficulty is that Thucydides' explicit
mentions of the names of his intellectual creditors and
contemporaries are extremely few (see further below, p.142).

Let us return to Thucydides' literary and emotional relation to
poetry, specifically to tragedy and epic. (Thucydides' dismissal
of the *factual* testimony of Homer was dealt with in Chapter
Four.) It is surely right to insist that the poetic streak in
Thucydides was nothing new, nor directly borrowed from
tragedy, but that 'Herodotus, another tragic historian, was a
much more direct influence' on him [sc., than tragedy itself].[12]
We looked at some of the shared echoes of Homer, and noted that
Herodotus' choice of theme – a great war – is itself Homeric, and
that this is no less true of Thucydides' theme.[13] Can we go
further? It has been said, for instance, that Thucydides, in his
detailed attitudes to that theme, the theme of war, death and
suffering, draws on Homer, or rather on the values which Homer
exemplifies. (The qualification is important, and reduces the
significance of the borrowing; see below.) In Thucydides, as in
Homer (it is said),[14] no mercy is shown on the battlefield, and
every attempt is made to deny burial to the enemy dead. I am
not sure what Thucydidean passages are meant: perhaps the
squalid argument about the corpses after the battle of Delium,
though even there we find, in the mouth of the Athenian herald,
the protest that Greek custom requires the return of the dead for
burial.[15] This is the normal situation, the background against
which the particular argument develops.[16] Actually, the
attitudes to burial of the dead in Thucydides seem to be different
from those in Homer; and those in tragedy are even harder to
categorise. In Sophocles' *Antigone* the heroine asserts the
family's right to bury its dead, and the poet makes it clear that

this century. I am much indebted to papers by Richard Rutherford and Edward
Hussey, delivered in their Oxford seminar on 'Literature and philosophy in the
age of the sophists', summer 1985.

[12] Macleod, ibid.

[13] Above, p.28.

[14] Macleod, ibid., and p. 158. For the desire to deprive the dead of a grave see
also J. Griffin, *Homer on Life and Death*, Oxford 1980, 46f.

[15] iv 97ff; herald's protest: 97.2. See also n. 18 below.

[16] There are no other passages I can think of; and no obviously relevant
Thucydidean items in W.K. Pritchett's *The Greek State at War* iv, 1985, which
assembles literary passages about burial or non-burial of war dead. I hope I have
interpreted Macleod rightly (he seems to be speaking of both Homer and
Thucydides in this section).

the state, in the person of Kreon, is wrong to interfere with that right. But in the real-life Athens of Thucydides' time, the *polis* (at least after 465 BC) invaded family privacy to the astonishing extent that it assumed responsibility for transporting the war dead home, and seeing to their public burial.[17] This is different from the very personal treatment of corpses in Homer; of which Achilles' unique act of renunciation, the return to Priam of Hector's corpse at the end of the *Iliad*, is the supreme example. Euripides is different again. In the *Supplices*, Evadne prefers to immolate herself on her husband's pyre than participate in a burial organised by the *polis*.[18]

(We shall return to Thucydides' attitude to war in Chapter Seven.)

In general, though, we may agree that the human agents in both Thucydides and Homer inhabit a world of 'suffering on the grand scale', in which 'fortune and pride often lead to a fall'.[19] But Greek education made extensive use of Homer, and to say that Thucydides (or Sophocles, or Euripides, or the readership, or the audience, of any of them) reflects Homeric values may be to say little more than that Thucydides and the rest of them were ancient Greeks.

But that is perhaps too facile and negative. Thucydides' debt to Homer may lie not so much in shared values as in the way in which they present their material. This includes, but goes beyond, the verbal borrowings which we have mentioned. The debt is best summed up as *simplicity*. It is characteristic of the greatest poetry and literature that it can produce its effects by the use, in an appropriate context, of quite ordinary language, as was observed by Longinus *On the Sublime*.[20] Quoting Euripides' line, 'I'm full of troubles, there's no room for more', he says: 'This

---

[17] Thuc.ii 34, with F. Jacoby, '*Patrios nomos*: state burial in Athens and the public cemetery in the Kerameikos', *JHS* lxiv, 1944, 27ff. = *Abhandlungen*, 260ff., also Goldhill, op. cit., 145, Pritchett, op.cit. 123 and Loraux 29f. (vague on the dating problem). Note however that the archaeological evidence for family tombs in Attica in the classical period shows that state funerals, so far from excluding private commemoration of the dead, actually encouraged it: S.C. Humphreys, *JHS* c, 1980, 96ff., esp, 123 (= *The Family, Women and Death*, 1983, 79ff.)

[18] As Richard Rutherford points out to me. J.H. Finley, *Three Essays*, 37, discusses the relation between the *Supplices* and Delium in Thucydides. See also Loraux 191f.

[19] Macleod, p.157.

[20] Ch.xx.

is a very ordinary remark, but it has become sublime as the situation demands'.

Some of the most telling Shakespearian effects are achieved by comparable means: it has been noted that any poet of talent could write 'the multitudinous seas incarnadine', but only a master could get away with 'Pray you undo this button' or Lear's quintuple 'never'.[21] Similarly a fine recent study of Homer draws on *King Lear* to illustrate the point that simplicity and brevity convey a sort of understatement:

> she's gone for ever.
> I know when one is dead and when one lives;
> She's dead as earth.[22]

To return to the ancient world, critics earlier even than Longinus were aware of the devastating power of ordinary words in appropriate contexts and in appropriate arrangement: Aristotle's *Rhetoric*, like Longinus, associates this technique specifically with Euripides.[23] But none of the ancient literary critics speaks of *Thucydides* in this connexion. Dionysius of Halicarnassus observes that 'in Homer the most commonplace words can be found'; but he treats Thucydides as an exponent of the 'austere' style. In the treatise which Dionysius devotes to Thucydides specifically, he acknowledges that Thucydides can be poetic, but finds his self-conscious attempts to be 'tragic', and depart from the common meaning of words, merely annoying. He does not examine *how* Thucydides uses ordinary words.[24] Nevertheless I think that some of Thucydides' best effects are the product of this 'Euripidean' device of using ordinary language where the context invests it with special pathos. An example is at the end of Book vii: 'Few out of many returned', a passage neglected by the modern commentaries. It is a quietly terrible way of conveying the ruin of the Sicilian expedition.[25]

[21] Cyril Connolly, *Enemies of Promise*, Penguin ed., p.29.
[22] v iii; J. Griffin, op. cit. (1980), 121. See also L.P. Wilkinson, *CQ* ix, 1959, 182.
[23] I am grateful for help on this question to Jasper Griffin. See Ar.*Rhet*.iii 2; Hor. *AP* 47ff., 240ff. with Brink; Isoc.xii *Panath*. 3 (but this passage, cited by Brink, seems merely to be saying that when you are old and grey, it is more seemly to use ordinary language). And see above all Longinus xl with Russell ad loc. and Dion. Hal., *De comp.*, conveniently translated in Russell and Winterbottom, *Ancient Literary Criticism*, 334.
[24] *De comp.* 12 (Russell/Winterbottom, p.334); 22 (p.339); *Thuc.*, chaps. 24, 28.
[25] vii 87.6. For the Sicily books as tragedy, see further below, p.148.

But it is not a straightforward example. The word for 'returned', *apenostêsan*, is Homeric, but rare in tragedy and prose (except, significantly, in Herodotus).[26] Here what is so effective is the combination of the simple 'few out of many' with the rich Homeric *apenostêsan*, which perhaps suggests the sufferings and *nostoi* or 'Returns' from Troy of wandering Greeks like Odysseus: *nostoi* is the name of a whole literary genre describing such returns, of which the *Odyssey* is just one instance. What some commentators[27] *have* picked up is the recurrence of the phrase 'few out of many' in Books i and iii to describe the Egyptian disaster and a defeat of the Ambraciots (the latter passage is worked up poetically, as we shall see). Like Homer, Thucydides sometimes makes his comparisons by use of similarities of phrasing, rather than explicitly.[28]

We have already discussed a striking example of Thucydidean pathos, achieved through plainness of language: namely, the account in the *Pentekontaetia* of the Corinthian defeat at Megara.[29] We called this an example of 'tragic *akribeia*'. Unlike 'Few out of many returned home', the description of the Corinthian defeat is *not* the culmination of a strongly poetic passage: the surrounding colour is grey rather than purple.[30] As we saw there, the restraint of such a description owes something to Homer. Homeric too is the 'asyndetic' (abrupt) way in which the Corcyra narrative starts: 'Epidamnus is a city' – with which compare Homer's 'Ephyra is a city ...'[31] Compare the simple and tranquil language with which powerful episodes are finished off. After the funeral games for Patroclus, 'The concourse was dissolved, and the people dispersed to their ships'. After the Funeral Oration in Thucydides, Pericles tells the Athenians to depart: 'That is how the burial happened that winter. And so the first year of the war ended.'[32] But we must not exaggerate: the

---

[26] *Iliad* i 60, iii 499, xvii 406; *Odyssey* xiii 6, xxiv 471; see Liddell and Scott[9] s.v.

[27] Classen-Steup, but not Gomme or Dover; see i 110.1; iii 112.8.

[28] See R.B. Rutherford, 'At home and abroad: aspects of the structure of the *Odyssey*', *PCPhS* 211, n.s. 31, 1985, 133ff.

[29] i 106, on which see above, p.35.

[30] For this colour metaphor, see Wilkinson, art. cit (1959), at p. 181: 'neutral [words] are apt to go now grey, now purple, according to their company.'

[31] Thuc.i 24.1; Homer, *Iliad* vi 152, with Lloyd-Jones, *Justice of Zeus*[2], 203 n.53 (Dionysius had compared Hdt.i 6 'Croesus was a Lydian' etc: *De comp*.4, Russell/Winterbottom, 325f.). See generally Strasburger, chs.15, 18, 20.

[32] *Iliad* xxiv 1; Thuc.ii 47.1.

refrain 'And so the *n*th year of the war ended' is also found in
emotionally neutral contexts (for example, the final sentence of
Book iii, where the immediately preceding sentences are
low-key); perhaps the true conclusion is that there is something
reassuring, something of rest after the storm, about the
appearance of a familiar and simple formula after an episode of
heightened tension.

The latest treatment, as we saw, refuses to number tragedy
among Thucydides' literary influences, preferring to trace
similarities to 'the common source, Homer'.[33] This seems to me
essentially right, but too sweeping. Some literary devices in
Thucydides are easier to parallel from tragedy than from epic.
The rapid cross-talk of the Melian Dialogue, for instance,
suggests tragic *stichomuthia* (lines delivered alternately), rather
than the more leisured exchanges of Homer's speakers (who, no
doubt for special reasons to do with oral methods of composition,
repeat themselves or each other in ways which the brisker,
literate, fifth century would not countenance in the writers of its
own day).[34] Or take the recognition scene in Book iii:

The herald came to ask for the dead ... who had been killed in the
previous day's fighting ... When he saw the quantity of weapons
he showed surprise at it. Somebody asked why he was surprised,
and how many of them had been killed, supposing that this was
the herald from Idomene. He replied, 'About two hundred.' The
other replied, 'The arms you see here are of more than a
thousand.' The herald answered, 'Then they are not the arms of
those who fought on our side?' The other answered, 'Yes, they are,
if you fought at Idomene yesterday.' 'But we fought with no one
yesterday, but the day before yesterday.' 'Well, anyway, we
fought yesterday with those who came to reinforce you from

----

[33] Macleod, loc.cit.
[34] v 87ff. Note esp. 92ff: '*Melians*: And how could it be just as good for us to be
the slaves as for you to be the masters? *Athenians*: You, by giving in, would save
yourselves from disaster; we, by not destroying you, would be able to profit from
you. *Melians*: So you would not agree to our being neutral, friends instead of
enemies, but allies of neither side? *Athenians*: No, because it is not so much your
hostility that injures us; it is rather that, if we were on friendly terms with you,
our subjects would regard that as a sign of weakness in us, whereas your hatred is
proof [*paradeigma*, see above, p.106] of our power.' It is noticeable that 'verbal
contests in tragedy never solve anything, they merely intensify the conflict'
(Rutherford), and that is true of the Melian Dialogue also. Remarks of both
Rutherford and Hussey have helped me here. See now Hussey in P. Cartledge
(ed.) *CRUX, Studies in Greek History pres. de Ste Croix* (London, 1985), 126ff.

Ambracia.' When the herald heard this and realised that the reinforcement from the city had been destroyed, he groaned and was so stunned at the magnitude of the disaster that he went away without having done what he set out to do, and he stopped asking for the dead bodies back.[35]

This is very fast (the herald's confusion cleverly points up the confusion and sudden reversals of war), and like the Melian Dialogue it is closer to the drama of the fifth century than to epic. But a further dramatic feature is the way in which recognition (*anagnôrisis*) of the truth dawns.[36] Compare Euripides' *Bacchae*, where Agave slowly realises that what she holds in her hands is the head of her son Pentheus, a realisation achieved through cross-questioning.[37] There is a comparable, though cruder, recognition scene in Euripides' *Hercules Furens*, where Herakles is made to realise that he has killed his wife and children.[38] And in Sophocles' *Ajax* the hero comes to his wits before the end, and understands what he has done. Recognition scenes in Homer exist – Dionysius singles out Book xvi of the *Odyssey*, where Telemachus returns from the Peloponnese and meets his father Odysseus; and the most long-drawn out is certainly the recognition of Odysseus himself (Aristotle in the *Poetics* says that the *Odyssey* is 'one long recognition').[39] So perhaps the 'common source' is, again, ultimately epic. But recognition induced in a speaker by rapid question-and-answer technique is more in the style of Euripides than Homer.

Part of the explanation for the difference can be sought, not in a direct borrowing by Thucydides from tragedy, but more generally in the change in intellectual methods which took place in the fifth century. The Socratic method of question-and-answer is itself a product of the argumentative, verbally competitive style of discourse of the period after 462 – the age of the levelling Athenian reformer Ephialtes: dialectic is the enemy of political and intellectual authority, as Tacitus observes in the *Dialogus*, pointing out that free speech exists only in free states. Like a conflagration, it needs 'fuel and air, motion and excitement'. But

[35] iii 113.
[36] See H.-P. Stahl, *Thukydides*, 1966, 134f.
[37] Eur. *Ba.* 1269ff.
[38] 1113ff.
[39] Dion.Hal., *De comp.* 3 (Russell/Winterbottom, p.324) praising *Od*.xvi 1ff for its 'arrangement'. Ar. *Poetics* 1459b15.

'authority' had its limits even before 462 (above, p.74).[40]

We can offer a similar explanation for another ostensibly 'tragic' feature of Thucydides, the obsessive examination of single, often abstract, words and what they imply. The theme of justice, *to dikaion*, recurs again and again in the Corcyrean speech early in Book i, from the first word on.[41] There are plenty of other examples, like the remarks about *archê*, empire, in Alcibiades' speech at Athens in Book vi which includes the gnomic 'We cannot set limits in advance to our empire'.[42] Other words are turned over and over in shorter spaces (note *aischron*, disgraceful, or cognates of the word, in the Theban reply to the Plataeans in Book iii).[43] And the most celebrated analysis of words, and their re-evaluation under stress, occurs in the Corcyra *stasis* section (above, p.94 n.84). We might compare the exploration by Jocasta of the words *philotimia*, ambition, and (especially) *isotês*, equality, in Euripides' *Phoenissae*;[44] the whole relevant section[45] is in effect about *pleonexia*, greed, a thoroughly Thucydidean preoccupation: one sentence about the Corcyrean stasis specifically brackets *pleonexia* and *philotimia*.[46] (The latter incidentally is occasionally a derogatory word, although *philotimia* is normally something on which to plume oneself – an honourable sort of ambition.)[47] But here, again, it is safer to speak, not of Euripidean influence on Thucydides, but of a fondness, common to many of the greatest fifth-century intelligences, for the exhaustive analysis of words. The most systematic work was done here by the Platonic Socrates, but even on the most sceptical view of the 'Socratic problem' (the problem of the relation between the Socrates of real life and the Socrates of literature), the real Socrates surely dismantled and then reconstructed 'justice' and other abstract words in a way recognisably similar to the methods of the

[40] Tac. *Dial.* xxvi-xl; R. Syme, *Tacitus*, 1958, 106 paraphrasing xxxvi 1. See Lloyd, *Magic* and Goldhill, *passim*. For some qualifications, see above, pp.74f.

[41] i 32-6.

[42] vi 17-18; note esp. 18.3. Cf. ii 63.1 (obsessive on *archê*).

[43] iii 63.3-4.

[44] 532ff.; I am here specially indebted to Rutherford.

[45] 499ff.

[46] iii 82.8.

[47] Occasionally derogatory: cf. *Syll*[3] 543, Philip V's letter to Thessalian Larisa, line 34, *aphilotimôs*. Normal creditable sense: D. Whitehead, *The Demes of Attica*, Princeton 1986, 242ff. drawing on *Cl&Med.* 34, 1983, 55ff. See now R. Lane Fox, *Pagans and Christians*, 1986, 689 n.21.

Socrates in Plato's *Republic*. If we had to point to a single
'influence', it might be Prodikos of Keos, a contemporary of
Socrates, who was celebrated for the giving of precise definitions,
and for his attempts to distinguish between closely related
terms.[48] Thucydides' Pericles (see p.94) makes a very Prodikan
distinction-without-a-difference between *phronêma* and *kataphronêma*.[49] We shall return in Chapter Seven to Thucydides'
relation to Euripides, when we discuss Thucydides' judgment of
the demagogues and their methods.

It is logical to ask now what the relation was between
Thucydides and the philosophers, sophists and Socratics. We
noted above that Thucydides mentions virtually none of his
intellectual contemporaries, and those few whom he does
mention are not the expected ones. Thus Hellanicus is
mentioned – but not Herodotus, to whom his debt was
undoubtedly far greater. Of those who have any claim to be
called 'sophists', the only one whom Thucydides has ever been
thought to mention is Antiphon, in connexion with the events of
411.[50] But it is very doubtful whether this Antiphon is identical
with Antiphon the Sophist, the author of a surviving work 'On
Truth'.[51] We shall see in Chapter Six that Thucydides'
indifference towards the intellectual origins of the oligarchic
revolution has led him to neglect contemporary philosophy even
where it was directly relevant to his own, political, preoccupations: thus Prodikos' pupil Theramenes is treated as a
schemer not a thinker.[52] Gorgias' famous visit to Athens in 427 is
passed over,[53] despite its relevance to the Athenian involvement
in Sicily (Gorgias was acting as ambassador for his home town of
Leontini). Socrates never features in Thucydides' narrative as it
stands; perhaps he would have featured in a Thucydidean, as he
featured in the Xenophontic, account of the aftermath of the
sea-battle of Arginusai in 406. (The victorious Athenian generals
were put on trial after the battle for failing to pick up survivors.
Socrates, as president, by chance operation of the lot, of the
prutaneis or selection committee of the Council, for the one day

[48] DK 84 A17-20.
[49] ii 62.3; cf. J.H. Finley, *Three Essays*, 26.
[50] Hellanicus: i 97. Antiphon: viii 68.
[51] Andrewes ad loc.
[52] viii 89; below, p.141.
[53] Diod.xii 53.

of the trial of the generals, would not let them be tried *en masse*.)[54] But if Socrates' own pupil Xenophon was capable of referring to Socrates in a way ('Socrates son of Sophroniscus') which makes it impossible without other evidence to guess that this was the famous Socrates, Thucydides was certainly capable of it. (Indeed, we should allow for the possibility that in this early and deliberately Thucydidean section of the *Hellenica* Xenophon was showing an austerity which he assumed that Thucydides would have shown, had he got round to narrating these events.)

Thucydides' impatience with philosophical theory does not mean that he escaped its influence. But the extent, and the direction, of the influence, is disputed.[55] Plato's *Menexenus*, or Funeral Oration, certainly shows awareness of Pericles' Funeral Oration in Thucydides Book ii. And there are passages in the *Republic* which are strikingly close to Thucydides; the similarities are not just verbal[56] but conceptual. The account in *Republic* Book viii of the inversion of values which takes place within the soul of the democratic man (licence is re-evaluated as liberty, extravagance as generosity, shamelessness as courage, and so on) closely recalls the famous analysis of *stasis* at Corcyra in Thucydides Book iii.[57] Plato's age, the fourth century, was more prone to *stasis* than the fifth, when the superpowers Athens and Sparta guaranteed equilibrium of a sort, at least until 431. It is not surprising that *stasis* preoccupied Plato.[58] (But *stasis* was admittedly a condition which was bound to raise questions in all periods: the fifth-century dramatists make their choruses list it

[54] Xen.*Hell*.i 7.15.

[55] M. Pohlenz, *Aus Platos Werdezeit*, 1913, 247ff., thinks that Plato, especially in the *Menexenus*, followed Thucydides closely. Gomme, by contrast, minimised the extent of contact, *More Essays in Greek History and Literature*, 1962, 122ff. For a useful survey of parallel passages see O. Luschnat, *RE* supp.xii, 'Thukydides', cols. 1276ff. On Thucydides and the *Menexenus* see esp. Loraux ch. vi.

[56] For example *Rep.* 563 *eutrapelias te kai charientismou* ≈ Thuc.ii 41 *meta charitôn ... eutrapelôs*. Cf. too Macleod 151: Thucydides here echoes Solon's *eucharistôs* at Hdt.i 32.

[57] *Rep*.viii 650-1; Thuc.iii 82-3 with Chapter Four above, p.94 n.84.

[58] Dover, *Ancient Greek Literature*, 1981, 119 remarks that Plato's aim in the *Republic* was to create a society which would be immune from both internal *stasis* and external attack. For the fifth-century equilibrium see E. Ruschenbusch, *Untersuchungen zu Staat und Politik in Griechenland vom 7-4 Jh.v.Chr.*, Bamberg 1978. For Thucydides on *stasis*, Macleod ch.12 is now fundamental; see below, Chapter Seven.

among life's worst calamities – in the *Oedipus Coloneus* one of 'the worst things this life of pain can offer' – and the chorus in Aeschylus' *Eumenides* wishes Athens free from *stasis*.[59])

Stasis is negative and destructive, but there are similarities between the positive ideals of statesmanship held by Plato and Pericles in Thucydides. The prime Platonic text is the *Gorgias*, with its ideal of the good political *rhêtôr* or orator as one who 'works hard in saying what is best, whether it is pleasant or unpleasant to the audience', and who tries to educate rather than flatter his audience (compare the opening of Thucydides' Melian Dialogue for the distinction between educating *via* debate on the one hand, and, on the other, non-rational procedures such as preparing for war with closed minds).[60] But the *Phaedrus* also speaks of the ability of the *rhêtôr*,[61] actually Thrasymachus, to cool people down and warm them up according to need. All this is very like Thucydides' Pericles, who 'would reduce the Athenians to a state of terror when he saw them elated without cause, and when they were unreasonably depressed would restore their confidence'.[62] In a speech, Thucydides makes Pericles pride himself on his ability to 'know what policies were best and to expound them' (this echoes an authorial tribute to Themistocles in Book i).[63] An obvious difficulty is that Plato has, or is aware that one might have, reservations about Pericles' claim to be called a 'good politician':[64] he turned the Athenians into idlers and cowards by his introduction of political pay, and generally left them morally worse than when he found them (compare Aristophanes' *Wasps* on the effects of jury pay). Whether this is true or false – and it is arguable that Pericles was indeed not, or not always, concerned to educate the Athenians rather than to give them what they wanted[65] – it is a more cynical view than Thucydides', at least as

[59] Soph. *OC* 1234; Aesch. *Eum*. 977. Cf. also Hdt. viii 3.1.

[60] Plat. *Gorg*. 502-3; 514-19, esp. 503a; Thuc. v 86.

[61] 267cd. *Rhêtôr* as politician: see now P.J. Rhodes, *JHS* cvi, 1986, 140f.

[62] Thuc.ii 65.9; an example of this in action: ii 59.3.

[63] ii 60.5; i 138.3.

[64] *Gorg*. 515e; 516d.

[65] T. Irwin, *Gorgias*, 1979 (translated ed. with notes), remarks on 517c that 'Socrates is right on one point. Contrary to Thuc. 2.65 7-10 he insists that Pericles, like his successors, was guided by popular demands – he sought to give people what they wanted, in the long run, and took his aims and political values from their desires, not from a view of what would make them better and so benefit them.' Perhaps we should make a distinction between the young, more

expressed in the obituary in Book ii. The qualification is important: Edward Hussey has suggested that, despite that obituary, Thucydides implies criticism of Pericles elsewhere, by putting unattractive oratory into his mouth. Notable examples are in the Funeral Speech (which refers to 'unperceived death' as something desirable.[66] This is frigid, pompous and Gorgianic.) Or there is ii 62, which puts exaggerated and almost meaningless language into Pericles' mouth (see especially the last few sentences of the chapter). So perhaps Thucydides and Plato shared reservations about Pericles' rhetoric and its effects.

But there are other words given by Thucydides to Pericles whose meaning is plain enough, and which Plato can only have applauded. After all, Pericles' final speech comes very close to a Platonic view of the relation between the state and the individual, starkly expressed:

> 'When the whole state is on the right course it is a better thing for each separate individual than when private interests are satisfied but the whole state is going downhill. However well off a man may be in his private life, he will still be involved in the general ruin if his country is destroyed; whereas, so long as the state itself is secure, individuals have a much greater chance of recovering from their private misfortunes. Therefore, since a state can support individuals in their sufferings, but no one person by himself can bear the load that rests upon the state, is it not right for us all to rally to her defence? Is it not wrong to act as you are doing now? For you have been so dismayed by disaster in your homes that you are losing your grip on the common safety ...'

The same thought is voiced by a deplorable figure, Kreon, in Sophocles' *Antigone*:

> 'I would not count as my friend a man who was an enemy to my country; for I know that in our country is our salvation, and that unless the keel of *that* ship is even, we have no friends at all',

and by Erechtheus in a fragment of Euripides:

> 'No one man's house can be strong when the whole city falls'.

---

obviously demagogic, Pericles, and the mature statesman: see my *Greek World*, 122. For specific parallels between Plato, esp. in *Gorgias*, and Thucydides, see further Macleod 56f., 109 n.1, 138 n.33. Cf. Roberts, *City of Sokrates*, 1984, 61, 244.

[66] In *CRUX*, 125, citing ii 43.6.

LIBRARY ST. MARY'S COLLEGE

These parallels have been noted, one in a book called *Sophocles and Pericles*, the other in a study of Euripides and Thucydides. But there is a more menacing, because more notoriously totalitarian, parallel in the political thinking of Plato:

> The object of our legislation is not the good of any one class, but of the whole community ... Its purpose is to make each man a link in the unity of the whole.

These and other sentiments in the *Republic* and *Laws* drew from K. Popper the strong protest of *The Open Society and its Enemies*, a book which constantly contrasts the villain Plato with Pericles as Thucydides presents him. But I would suggest that a possible reply to Popper might be to start not from Plato but from Popper's own hero Pericles: the individualism of the society recommended by Thucydides' Pericles can be exaggerated. Both for Plato and for Thucydides' Pericles, the job of the statesman must be to calculate what will be best for the community, regardless of the unhappiness of individuals. That is why Pericles goes straight on to claim for himself superior insight and interpretative power, a claim which would otherwise be irrelevant straight after a disquisition on the relation of state and individual. There is, however, an important difference from Plato: Thucydides' statesman accepts that he is accountable to the critical, popular, assembly which he has convoked in order, as he says, to plead his own case. The Platonic philosopher-ruler, with direct access to the idea of the good in politics as in everything else, is not so humanly accountable.

But if it be accepted that there is common ground between Plato and the Pericles of the final speech, what follows? Is it conceivable that both Thucydides and Plato derived their notions from Socrates? The question is doubly difficult to answer: we do not know whether to speak of Socrates, or of Plato who may have traduced him; or whether to speak of Pericles, or of Thucydides who may have traduced *him*. Thucydides' own opinions, in so far as they are retrievable, may be left for another chapter. As to Socrates, it is fundamental to Popper's book that Plato was not Socrates' Boswell but his Judas: the 'real' Socrates was individualistic and egalitarian. There is a risk of circularity here, since the 'real' Socrates left nothing in writing. But on the reasonable assumption that the real Socrates was closer to the earlier dialogues of Plato, in which there is more question-and-answer exchange, than to the *Republic* and *Laws*, where there is so much system-building and monologue, we should look rather to works like the *Crito* – not forgetting the dialogues of Xenophon, who was surely no independent system-builder. In the *Crito*, which is agreed to be early (although there is no question-and-answer eristic), and which thus reflects Socrates' views rather than Plato's, we do in fact find the view, not accepted in the *Apology*, that the laws cannot be disobeyed: they are parents and masters. As a recent book on the *Crito* says, this model is 'disturbing' because it denies individual rights, and concedes to the state 'a metaphysical status which belongs to myth rather than to reason'.

Again, Xenophon's Socrates in the *Memorabilia* expresses something very like the view of Kreon and the Thucydidean Pericles which we have been considering.

The 'Socratic problem' is a treacherous topic, and enough has been said. I merely wish to raise the possibility that there is after all a line of descent from the paternalism of the historical Socrates to the exacting and even totalitarian view of the state which Plato and Thucydides put in the mouths of the literary Socrates, and of Pericles, respectively.

One obvious objection to what I have said above is that the psychology of the various remarks we have been considering – Kreon's, Pericles', Socrates' – is the product not of a single identifiable thinker, whether Socrates or some other, but of the conditions of fifth- and fourth-century Athenian life, or rather warfare. The *Crito* gives Socrates' answer to those of his friends who would have had him escape from prison; the *Apology* contains a more general defence of Socrates' adherence to his mission as he saw it. It is striking that both dialogues use a military metaphor for sticking to one's post, not giving ground but 'in war and lawcourts alike' doing whatever your country orders (as the *Crito* puts it). Greek infantrymen, or 'hoplites', were usually, and in Athens certainly, a citizen militia, not a paid professional army. Athenians doing their military service swore not to desert the ranks, as we know from inscriptions. This was not merely a pious inculcation of *esprit de corps* but a vital necessity: a hoplite depended, for the protection of his unshielded right arm, on the man next to him. Socrates, who fought at Delium and Potidaia, knew that.

All this is true and important, and is a further reminder that

Athens was a more corporatist and unforgiving place than Popper allowed. But it still makes sense to ask who intellectualised and generalised these military facts so as to produce what can, without absurdity, be called a theory of the state. Sophocles' Kreon is earliest in time (? 440s) but is meant to be repellent. Socrates means his arguments seriously. Thucydides' Pericles may indeed owe something to them.[67]

Just what Thucydides himself thought about Pericles and about the views he puts into his mouth (views which he may have reported without endorsing, or invented without endorsing) is a question to which we shall return when we examine Thucydides' opinions in Chapter Seven. But our conclusion must be that there are passages in Thucydides about rhetoric and political leadership which are similar enough in their presentation to passages in Plato to suggest a direct link. The link might be Thucydidean borrowing from Socrates, or Thucydidean desire to reply to Socrates, rather than Platonic echoing of Thucydides.

Rhetoric, as a technique of political control, is by its nature short-term in its effects (although Thucydides says that Pericles' position of ascendancy looked like being a fixture.[68] And the principle of debate is a long-standing Greek principle of stable government.) And *stasis* is by definition an aberration, a convulsion produced or aggravated by war. However, Thucydides was certainly capable of longer-term analysis of political change, of a kind which anticipates Plato (especially in *Laws* Book iii),[69] and especially Aristotle, and which goes well beyond anything in Herodotus. The best illustrations of this are in the *Archaeology*; the opening of i 13 is particularly impressive:

[67] Thuc.ii 60.2; Soph. *Ant.* 187ff., with V. Ehrenberg, *Sophocles and Pericles* 1954, 146 (see also M. Nussbaum, *Fragility of Goodness*, p. 59 and n. 28, and Simon Goldhill, *Reading Greek Tragedy*, 94) also Gomme on Thuc.loc.cit.; Eur. frag. 350, lines 20f. with J. Finley, *Three Essays*, 25; Plat. *Rep.* 519e; A.D. Woozley, *Law and Obedience: the Arguments of Plato's Crito*, London 1979, 73. (*Contra*, R. Kraut, *Socrates and the State*, 1984; but against his 'liberal' view of the *Crito* see C.C.W. Taylor, *CR* xxxv, 1985, 64. I am grateful to David Charles for telling me about Kraut.) Xen. *Mem.* iii 7.9, cited by Gomme, loc.cit. Military oaths: Tod 204 with P. Siewert, *JHS* xcvii, 1977, 102ff.; cf. Lyc. *Leoc.* 76, cf. 64. Note Goldhill 63, 145. Also Vidal-Naquet, *The Black Hunter*, 1986, 97.

[68] See p.70 n.97.

[69] Luschnat, op. cit. col. 1283 says that Plato became progressively more interested in history, and points to *Laws* iii in particular.

As Greece grew more powerful and the acquisition of wealth increased, tyrannies were set up in the cities, and revenues grew greater still. (Previously there had been hereditary kingships with stated privileges.) The Greeks now began to build navies and to take to the sea more boldly.[70]

We may compare a passage from Book iii of Aristotle's *Politics* on the kinds of kingship:

A fourth kind of kingly monarchy consists of those in heroic times which were both legal and traditional and by consent ... They controlled the command in war and such sacrifices as were not sacerdotal, and in addition they decided the lawsuits.[71]

With both these passages contrast Herodotus' treatment of tyranny. Much of our factual knowledge derives from him: for instance, the material about the Cypselids of Corinth in Books iii and v, about the Athenian Pisistratids in Book i, and about the Orthagorids of Sikyon in Book vi.[72] But Herodotus never once attempts a general explanation of tyranny, and offers no general comments, even in the Orthagorid section in Book vi, which describes the Homeric entertainment of the suitors for Kleisthenes' daughter Agariste. These chapters have drawn, from modern scholars,[73] generalisations about the tendency of the tyrannical dynasties to intermarry; but Herodotus leaves it all implicit.

Note also the concrete way in which Thucydides explains the rise of tyranny, in terms of *prosodoi*, revenues. And he brings out well the importance of colonising activity for the development of early Greece.[74]

Thucydides could surely have done a great deal more along these lines if he had wanted to, but his subject – a very short period of time, meticulously described – did not call for much of this kind of long-term analysis of political change.

If Herodotus was not the model, who (if anybody) was? Surely not local chroniclers like Antiochus of Syracuse. Perhaps the

---

[70] With Gomme ad loc.

[71] 1285b3, translated by Richard Robinson.

[72] See esp. v 92; i 65; vi 126ff.

[73] L. Gernet, 'Les mariages des tyrans' in *L'anthropologie dans la Grèce antique*, Paris 1968, 344ff.

[74] i 12. Revenues: cf. generally S.B. Smith, *HSCP* 51, 1940, 279.

influence was sophistic: Hippias of Elis may have addressed himself to problems of historical change, to judge from his interest in exact chronology; he compiled the first list of Olympic victors.[75] This shows an interest in periodisation and a new awareness of 'historical' as opposed to mythical time: with the first Olympic Games of 776 BC we are in from the dark. In the last years of the fifth century there are other manifestations of interest in the past: the purification of the island of Delos in 426, which revealed items of archaeological interest; the appearance of Hellanicus' *Attikê Sungraphê*, whose chronological incompetence earned Thucydides' censure; and the inscribing in the 420s of an archon-list in the Athenian agora. The list, which includes names of sixth-century archons, may itself be the product of the researches of Hippias.[76]

But Hippias forms a direct link with Socrates. Plato in the *Hippias Major* quotes Hippias' boast to Socrates that he knows by heart the genealogies of heroes and men and the history of the foundation of cities and antiquity (*archaeologia*) in general.[77] We must allow the possibility that Thucydides' interest in the periodisation of history owes something to the discussions which went on in the Socratic circle. But, as always, we must allow as much, or more, for the experience and acumen of Thucydides himself. As a general in the Archidamian War his access to the public records in the *Mêtrôon* would have been easier than that accorded to Hippias, who was not even an Athenian citizen, let alone an officer of the state.

The possibility that Thucydides drew directly on Socrates has arisen more than once, and we should ask whether there are contacts of a more purely philosophical kind between Thucydides, or his speakers, and contemporary speculation. In Chapter Four we saw that Thucydides' epistemology recalls that of Plato's Protagoras. And Thucydides' assumption that everyone always acts in his own interests is Socratic (above, p.77). Thucydides' Pericles 'Platonically' contrasts reason and sensation.

[75] *FGrHist* 6 F2.

[76] Thuc. iii 104 with p.2 above and p.184 below; i 97; ML 6. D. Bradeen, *Hesperia* xxxii, 1963, 205f., publishing new fragments of the archon-list, pointed out that even if Hellanicus' work did not appear until 407, as Jacoby thought, the earlier *Priestesses of Argos* would have called for general antiquarian knowledge: Hellanicus' Attic researches, as opposed to his finished *Atthis*, may date to the 420s.

[77] 285 = *FGrHist* 6 T3.

He also (we can add) puts forward an idea of courage like that in Plato's *Laches*.[78] But he does so in *speeches*; this shows merely that Thucydides was aware of, not that he agreed with, the ideas so ventilated.

But there are other identifiable philosophical influences: not just Prodicus, but perhaps Democritus. Hussey has argued for a connexion between Thucydides' political thinking and Democritus' optimistic ethics and psychology:[79] in particular (and this is the most important result of his paper) he shows that both men rejected the fashionable moral relativism of the sophists, which they would have regarded as diseased.[80] We can perhaps add that Thucydides' *Archaeology*, with its emphasis on human progress, is akin to other fifth-century writings, though it is not certain how much of it goes back to Democritus in particular. There is an imaginative reconstruction of the beginnings of the world and of animal and human life in Diodorus Book i, which is sometimes thought to derive from Democritus.[81] This kind of partly fantastic writing, perhaps the closest approach to science fiction known to the ancient world, is nevertheless comparable to the *Archaeology* of the realistic Thucydides, with his talk of revenues and fleets: the shared feature is a belief in progress and improvement. But the better view is that the origin of the Diodoran material is not so easily identified. Perhaps it was Anaxagoras at some remove, or just a Hellenistic manual in which rationalistic theories were pasted together.[82]

But even without the cosmology in Diodorus Book i, there is plenty of evidence that optimistic, evolutionist theories about

[78] Above, p.102 on ii 40.5. See now R. Sharples, *LCM* viii(9), 1983, 139f., and Plato, *Lach.* 194e (also *Protag.* 360d and *Rep.* 430b). On the Platonic aspect of ii 40.1-2 (Pericles on philosophy, wealth and politics) see most recently J.S. Rusten, *CQ* xxxv, 1985, 14ff.; L.B. Carter, *The Quiet Athenian*, 1986, chs.2 and 7 (on *apragmosunê*, quietism, etc., as ideas discussed by Thucydides' Pericles and by Plato. On *polupragmosunê* or meddlesomeness in Thucydides see J. Allison *AJAH* iv, 1979, 10ff.) Altogether ii 40 seems a very 'Platonic' chapter.

[79] E.L. Hussey, 'Thucydidean history and Democritean theory', *CRUX*, 118ff. (and note his p.119 n.2 on the ?Democritan treatise known as the Anonymus Iamblichi, with de Romilly, *Journal des savants*, 1980, 19f., there cited).

[80] Hussey, pp.133ff. See below, Chapter Seven p.173. Hussey at 129f. also argues that 'Diodotus [in the Mytilene Debate] seems Democritean', but I am anxious not to use speeches for the elucidation of Thucydides' own views.

[81] T. Cole, *Democritus and the Sources of Greek Anthropology*, 1967.

[82] E.R. Dodds, *The Ancient Concept of Progress*, 1973, 10f.; D. Furley, *JHS* xc, 1970, 240, reviewing Cole.

what we would call prehistory were in circulation in the fifth century. Another of Socrates' interlocutors, Protagoras, seems to have believed that the possession of *technai*, skills, leads man to the development of language and ultimately to the possession of the political virtues, justice and respect for others (*dikê* and *aidôs*).[83] This is an optimistic view,[84] comparable to Democritus' belief that human nature could be improved by education.[85] A more famous fifth-century expression of belief in progress is the chorus of Sophocles' *Antigone* – *polla ta deina* – which enumerates the achievements of human *technê*, or skill, including the conquest of the elements, the development of language, and *astunomous orgas*, city-dwelling instincts.[86] With this compare above all the growth of thalassocracy in Thucydides' *Archaeology*, the remarks about sea power and wealth in the Old Oligarch (420s), and Pericles' boasts in Thucydides Book ii that the Athenians have control over both land and sea.[87] If it is right to see foreboding, rather than straightforward Protagorean optimism, in the Sophocles chorus[88] (words like *deinon* and *orgê* are ambiguous: marvellous/terrible; instinct/anger), that might suggest a further similarity to Thucydides: we saw that Thucydides puts some vacuous rhetoric in Pericles' mouth, perhaps by way of criticism (see above). Sophocles' warning, if it is one, is directed against excessive ingenuity and confidence, but as always we should remember that it is the chorus not Sophocles himself who is speaking. (For the same reason we cannot make straightforward use of the Corinthian speaker in Thucydides who says that in politics as in every *technê* the latest inventions always have the advantage.)[89]

Thucydides, then, believed in technological progress. But control of the elements through technological progress leads to

---

[83] Plat. *Protag.* 322bc. Cf. J.H. Finley, *Three Essays*, 32, also citing Thuc. iii 45.3 (Diodotus on the development of law; but see above n.80).

[84] Hussey, unpublished paper, 'Protagoras and the importance of persuasion', delivered in 1985. See now R.A. McNeal, 'Protagoras the Historian', *History and Theory* xxv, 1986, 299ff.

[85] DK B33 with Dodds p.10.

[86] Lines 332-75.

[87] ii 62.2; cf.ii 39.3. See the important ch.ii of the Old Oligarch (ps. Xen., *Ath.Pol.*). On this work see below, p.161 n.29. Cf. Loraux 86ff.

[88] Dodds, ibid.; C. Segal, 'Sophocles' praise of man' in T. Woodard (ed.), *Sophocles*, 1966, 62f.

[89] i 71 with Dodds p.11. On use of choruses, see below, Chapter Seven p.170 and n.61.

the imperialism which the Hellenistic poet Lycophron was to call, in an emotive phrase, 'sceptre and monarchy over *land and sea*'.[90] Thucydides (below, p.173) was certainly critical of the greed, *pleonexia*, which was a concomitant of that imperialism: we should remember the often expressed ancient view that venturing on the sea was evidence of *hubris*. Like Sophocles' chorus, Thucydides was a believer in progress – but with qualms.

There are still other fifth-century texts which imply belief in progress. The medical writers expressed it without reservation.[91] *Ancient Medicine*, a Hippocratic treatise, claims:

> Many excellent medical discoveries have been made over a long time and still more remain to be made by some competent inquirer who knows about the discoveries which have already been made.

Again (*Art of Medicine*):

> To discover what was unknown before, when the discovery of it is better than a state of ignorance, is the ambition and the task of intelligence, and so also is the perfection of what is already half accomplished.

This is bold and optimistic, and provides a suitable cue for us to examine Thucydides' relation to medical thinking in general.

For Thucydides' Nikias, the job of the physician is 'to help or at least not to harm'.[92] This cautious and unassuming programme recalls the aims of the Hippocratic school of medicine, whose prescriptions were the opposite of violent.[93] How far does Thucydides' conception of his own task resemble that of a doctor, defined in this sense? And how far did he borrow from, and how far did he surpass, the intellectual

---

[90] *Alexandra* line 1229. For the history of the phrase 'land and sea', cf. A. Momigliano, 'Terra Marique', *Secondo Contributo alla storia degli studi classici*, 431ff. at 443 esp. n. 36 (=*JRS* xxxii, 1942, 53ff.); ibid., 57ff. 'Sea-power in Greek thought' (=*CR* lviii, 1944, 1ff.) at 57f.; C. Starr, *Mnemosyne* xxxi, 1978, 343ff; and see now P. Hardie, *Virgil's Aeneid: Cosmos and Imperium*, 1986, 302ff. and Loraux, loc. cit.

[91] Dodds, ibid.; R. Buxton, 'Blindness and limits: Sophokles and the logic of myth', *JHS* c, 1980, 22ff. at p.35.

[92] The Hippocratic passages are from the openings to the treatises; Nikias: Thuc. vi 14 (from a speech; but I am merely using it as a – presumably – uncontroversial contemporary definition of a doctor's role).

[93] See W.S. Jones's introduction to the Loeb *Prognostic* for the mildness of Hippocratic methods.

achievements of his medical contemporaries?

Wade-Gery, writing in the *Oxford Classical Dictionary*, compared Thucydides in certain respects to Shakespeare and Michelangelo; but immediately continued: 'Thucydides would no doubt prefer to substitute, for these great names, the practice of any honest doctor.' Wade-Gery had in mind the painstaking application of perfected *technê*.[94]

We saw in Chapter One, however, that the practice of 'honest doctors' in the fifth century BC was rather different from today. In particular, the frenzied self-advertisement and polemic, which we find in some Hippocratic treatises, show that doctors had to borrow oratorical skills in order to market their *technai*. The treatments dispensed by the Hippocratic doctors might be gentle, but their advertising technique was the 'hard sell'. Thucydides and (as we saw) Herodotus go in for abuse of predecessors, like Thucydides on Hellanicus, so that Wade-Gery's idea that Thucydides would prefer to be compared to honest doctors, rather than to great names of art and literature, should not be taken to imply that either Thucydides or the doctors were specially modest.[95]

It is true, though, that there are assumptions in common between Thucydides and the doctors about the purpose of their activities. The doctors did not merely gather together case-histories; they hoped that their collection of materials would be useful in identifying and treating disease, and that the *technê* would thus slowly advance. (See the opening of the *Prognostic*: the physician must practise *pronoia*, 'forecasting'; he 'will carry out the treatment best if he knows beforehand from the present symptoms what will take place later'.) All this resembles Thucydides' famous sentence about the plague:[96] 'I shall describe its character and shall provide information to enable anybody to recognise the symptoms beforehand if it should ever break out again.' Like the medical writers (*Regimen in Acute Diseases*),[97] Thucydides is aware that a phenomenon may vary in its character according as attendant circumstances change; he says[98] that the

[94] *OCD²*, 1970, 1069 col.2.

[95] Wade-Gery indeed goes on to say of Thucydides that he was 'not modest' (but he adds that he was 'singularly unaware of his unique equipment').

[96] ii 48.3.   [97] i ad fin.

[98] iii 82.2. Hussey in *CRUX*, 134, shows that Thucydides, like Democritus, regards *stasis* as a disease; but Thucydides gives only diagnosis, not cure. On iii 82.2 see also Vidal-Naquet, *The Black Hunter*, 1986, 46.

eidê (forms) of *stasis* vary with changes in the accompanying phenomena (Hussey compares this to 'boundary conditions' in modern physics).

But if the job of the doctor is to 'help or at least not to harm', as Nikias puts it, does Thucydides see it as his job to improve the reader? The answer must be an emphatic 'no'. There is no moralising tendency of this kind in Thucydides; and this sets him apart from most other historians of Greco-Roman antiquity. (In another sense Thucydides was a deeply moral writer. We shall return to this in Chapter Seven, where we shall also see that his view of morality was derived from an organic or medical view of the state.) Herodotus comes closest to Thucydides. He says that he wishes to keep great (rather than 'virtuous') deeds from oblivion; and although (ch.i) he believes that there is requital, *tisis*, for injustice, he does not labour the moral. In sharp contrast, Xenophon frequently makes his moral purpose explicit, and so do the Roman historians, especially Livy and Tacitus. Diodorus says frankly that he will regularly bestow praise and blame where appropriate.[99]

Thucydides' idea of 'usefulness' is by contrast *purely intellectual* (though medical *diagnôsis* is of course a largely intellectual business also). Statesmen need to be able to predict[100] and to interpret.[101] Thucydides' account of the Peloponnesian War will be useful for such men, and for anybody who wishes to be clear about the past; and about future events, because the constancy of the human condition means that patterns are likely to recur.[102] That is all. There is no programme of moral education here, no suggestion that Thucydides sees his job as the improvement of the soul or (to put it less grandly) the behaviour of human beings, in a way analogous to the improvement of the body at which the doctor aims. It is true, as we saw above, that Thucydides' political ideal implies that the

[99] On Xenophon see Grayson, *Stevens Studies*, 31ff.; Livy, *Preface;* Tac. *Ann*.iii 65; Diod.xi 46. Andrewes has suggested in a seminar that Diodorus preferred to follow Ephorus, rather than Thucydides direct, for the fifth century BC precisely because Ephorus' moralising was explicit.

[100] i 138.3: Themistocles.

[101] ii 60.5: Pericles.

[102] i 22.4. My view is close to that of A. Parry, *BICS* xvi, 1969, 106ff., who protests against the 'medical' Thucydides of Cochrane & co: Thucydides 'offers no hope at all of any cure'. But I do think that (see text) there are *indirect* ways in which, pace Parry, Thucydides offers help and hope.

true statesman will lead rather than be led, which resembles, but is less explicitly moral than, the political theory in Plato's *Gorgias*. But even so, the improvement is effected not by Thucydides directly, but by the politician himself; all that Thucydides aims to do by his writing is to *enable* the politican to predict and to interpret. In that sense his work has the permanent value which he claims for it:[103] provided that allowance is made for changes in attendant circumstances, Thucydides' subject-matter (human affairs) will never go out of date, and the material which he supplies and interprets will always stand as the basis for rational prediction.

This reservation – that Thucydides aims to inform, not to improve; at least not directly – is crucial, and means that Thucydides' conception of his task is different in an important way from that of contemporary doctors. What he does have in common with them is an articulate and polemical contempt for sloppy work, and a shared belief in the usefulness of detailed case-histories for the prediction of the future.

What though of Thucydides' borrowing from their intellectual achievements? In Chapter Four, I argued that Thucydides, even in an apparently 'technical' passage like the description of the plague, nevertheless distances himself by the phrase 'and other discharges of bile to which doctors have given names',[104] which implies that he himself is stopping short of uncompromising technicality. And although both Thucydides and the doctors practise empirical methods (autopsy and observation), in contrast to Plato,[105] nevertheless there are distinctions to be made between Thucydides and the medical writers. We noted at the beginning of this chapter a recent suggestion that he was aware, as they were not, of the concepts of contagion and acquired immunity.[106] The contagion point, however, may not prove quite as much as has been claimed: in the first place, what Thucydides actually says is that people were afraid to visit the sick because of the sight of people dying like cattle through having caught the disease as a result of nursing others. This

[103] Ibid. Jaeger, *Paideia* i, 390, rightly says that there is no *fabula docet* in Thucydides.

[104] ii 49.3, on which see above, p.97.

[105] The anti-empiricism of Plato is notorious. See esp. *Rep.* 530b, 'we shall neglect what is in the heavens' (said about the study of astronomy).

[106] See above, p.110, citing Holladay and Poole.

implies that observation of the effects of contagion was general.[107] But Thucydides should be given all credit for his *formulation* of the idea. In the second place, the 'silence' of the Hippocratics should not be over-interpreted: Hussey tells me that he is not convinced that the idea of contagion is *incompatible* with Hippocratic thinking, even if no precisely relevant passage can be cited from the extant writings. And it has been remarked that the Hippocratic writers were concerned for the most part with the pathology of isolated individuals rather than with epidemic illness.[108]

But the intellectual independence of Thucydides does seem to have been established, on these crucial issues, even if we choose not to damn the Hippocratics utterly for what they failed specifically to mention. Here as elsewhere in our examination of the intellectual affinities of Thucydides, we end by leaving a large place for his own originality: the methods, particularly the techniques of polemic and dialectic, which are such a feature of fifth-century poetry and prose have left their mark on him. But Thucydides – a lonely man, I think – ultimately went his own way.

---

[107] ii 51.5, with Jon Solomon, 'Thucydides and the recognition of contagion', *Maia* xxxvii, 1985, 121-3. I gather that Holladay will be replying in *Maia*.
[108] Solomon, ibid.

CHAPTER SIX

Development

Before examining Thucydides' opinions as a whole, we need to ask whether his views on any important issues changed or developed over time. This is bound up with the problem whether he wrote his account over a short or a long period. The first view is held by so-called 'unitarians', the second by 'analysts' – that is, by scholars who seek to break down or analyse Thucydides' thinking into the different stages of its assumed development.

We noted in the Introduction that Thucydides wrote only a single work. This means that our job is more difficult than that of the student, say, of Xenophon or Tacitus, each of whom wrote several works which can be ranged in some kind of order of composition. The problem is more like that faced by those Homeric scholars who see 'layers' of composition within a single large poem.

We may start with evidence external to Thucydides' own text – the solidest kind of evidence of all, if it could be shown to be independent of what Thucydides wrote and not fabricated to fit the text. Anecdotal material in the Hellenistic or later *Lives* of Thucydides, printed at the front of modern editions, cannot be trusted far, because it is not independent in this sense – though the story that the last surviving book, Book viii, was prepared for publication by Thucydides' *daughter* is so odd as to tempt one to believe it.[1] The biographies agree that Thucydides died shortly after 404 and the end of the Peloponnesian War. The assumption was challenged as recently as 1983 after the discovery of an inscription from the island of Thasos in the North Aegean which

---

[1] *Life of Thucydides* 43. The modern bibliography on the composition question is extremely large. Much relevant material is cited in J.H. Finley's 'The unity of Thucydides' history', *Three Essays*, ch.3. Add now the two appendixes, 'Indications of incompleteness' and 'Strata of composition', in the final (1981) volume of *HCT*. H. Konishi, *LCM* xii, 1987, 5ff. does not persuade me that Thucydides intended to take the narrative no further than 411.

seemed to prove that Thucydides was alive as late as 397. (It may show that a man, of whose death Thucydides certainly knew because there is an anticipatory mention of it in Book viii, was still alive in 397.) This inscription, and its possible implications for the composition of Thucydides' work, are discussed later in the present chapter, where I shall examine the possible implications for Thucydides' beliefs.

But most of the evidence we shall look at is internal; that is, it consists of statements by Thucydides himself. At the beginning of Book i he says that he began his work as soon as the war broke out, 'expecting that it would be a great war'. Then in Book ii, in the obituary notice of Pericles, he refers to the sending down of Cyrus by the Persian king in 407, and the final defeat of Athens. There is a further reference to the final defeat in Book v, the 'second preface', where he says that he has 'written down everything in the order that it happened, by summers and winters, until the Spartans and their allies put an end to the Athenian empire, pulled down the Long Walls, and took the Piraeus'. And a paragraph about Alcibiades early in Book vi also alludes to the final defeat.[2]

These few firmly autobiographical or authorial utterances tell us merely that Thucydides started to write when the war started in 431, and lived to record its end in 404. How did he spend his time in between these two dates? He was a soldier and a commander in the early years of the Peloponnesian War. He was exiled in 424 when he failed to relieve the northern city of Amphipolis, but it would not be safe to argue that he did not make serious progress with his book until exile gave him more leisure: after all, Julius Caesar found time to write copiously in a busy campaigning life.[3]

What of the work itself? Its unfinished state needs no proof: a book which several times mentions the end of the war in 404, but ends its continuous narrative in 411, is not in the final state which its author must at one time have intended. 'As soon as Tissaphernes arrived at Ephesus he sacrificed to Artemis' is no way to end an account of the greatest war known to experience or record. But how many other sentences were so provisional, either in their formulation or their placing? (We have seen that the

[2] ii 65.12; v 26; vi 15.
[3] Amphipolis: v 26.5. Julius Caesar: cf. for instance A.B. Bosworth, *A Historical Commentary on Arrian's History of Alexander* i, 1980, 23.

inclusion of inconsequential detail is not necessarily evidence of imperfect revision: above, Introduction p.10.)

We may begin by treating the two books which, taken as wholes, appear to be least finished. Book viii has features which no other book has, although Book v (on which see further below) comes closest.

Book viii has no speeches, though there are long sections of reported opinion, written in the dense and abstract style which characterises Thucydidean speeches. For instance, there is Alcibiades' advice to Tissaphernes, or the summary of Phrynichus' views,[4] both in indirect speech but both easily capable of being turned into speeches proper. This kind of thing is found elsewhere – for instance, the long account of Athenian war resources in Book ii is formally in indirect speech ('Pericles encouraged them, on the grounds that ...').[5] And indirect rather than direct speech cannot by itself be regarded as a *simpler* way for Thucydides to reproduce the opinions of Alcibiades or Tissaphernes; most people who have tried to write a Greek prose would say that the opposite was true. But indirect speech interrupts the narrative less, and is more suited to *summaries* of views, and so its presence may be proof that Book viii is less developed than, for instance, Book ii, which, despite the presence of a long section of indirect speech (see above), also contains a number of fully worked-up speeches.

Book v, also, has no speeches in monologue form, but it does contain the Melian Dialogue at the end, as polished a piece of prose as anything in Thucydides. But again we should recall that the book-divisions are arbitrary, and that the earlier part of what we call Book v is less polished than the later. For one thing it resembles Book viii in its inclusion of documents (texts of treaties, some in dialect). It cannot be shown that there was, at this time or ever in antiquity, any stylistic law banning such material from a finished product[6] (how could there be, at least in Thucydides' time, at so early a stage in the development of narrative prose?). But not all the treaties were of equal importance – some were provisional or abortive: in Book viii for instance there are three

---

[4] viii 46; 48.

[5] ii 13.3.

[6] Despite J.B. Bury, *The Ancient Greek Historians*, London 1909, 109, quoted by M.N. Tod, *Greek Historical Inscriptions* i, 178. Later examples would include Polyb. iii 22, text of a Roman-Carthaginian treaty.

successive attempts at treaties between Sparta and Persia, and one failed attempt between Athens and Persia. And not all the diplomacy in Book v and the end of Book iv was, we may think, worth recording in the precision of documentary detail which it gets from Thucydides. Certainly the documents are sometimes hard to square with the surrounding narrative.[7]

There is another reason for thinking Book v, at least, to have been unfinished and therefore presumably late in execution: Book v is, from the point of view of the modern historian, a very unsatisfactory book indeed because of what it puts in and what it leaves out. The diplomacy which we have mentioned above concerns Peloponnesian politics and was intricate and ultimately futile. It has been said recently that Thucydides gives such prominence to these minor negotiations 'because he wishes to focus attention upon the utter bankruptcy of Greek statesmanship at this time'.[8] This is a good, positive way of seeing the early parts of the book. But was it necessary to give Alcibiades' deception of the Spartan ambassadors so much space?[9] It all came to nothing very soon. We ought to be particularly grateful for *some* of the things which Thucydides uncharacteristically allowed himself to include: the squabble about the Olympic Games of 420, in which Lichas the Spartan entered in a Boiotian livery, is a reminder that it was not only in the archaic Greek world that athletic success conferred political prestige. Alcibiades' athletic boasts in Book vi, designed to get him the Sicilian command, are not a complete anachronism.[10] (The dispute which Thucydides relates also sounds very *modern*, in an age when South African athletes switch citizenship in order to compete in international competitions.) Perhaps Alcibiades' deception of the Spartans was included because it illustrated his slippery character; but its inclusion was dearly bought if the price was the material which he has omitted.

[7] For some problems arising from the Book v narrative see *HCT* v, 428-31.

[8] H.D. Westlake, 'Thucydides and the uneasy peace', *CQ* xxi, 1971, 315ff., at p. 323, a useful study. See also two other good treatments, R. Seager, 'After the Peace of Nicias: diplomacy and policy, 421-416 BC', *CQ* xxvi, 1976, 248ff. and J.B. Salmon, *Wealthy Corinth*, Oxford 1984, ch. xxiii. None of these accounts, however acute, seems to me to bring out the fundamental deficiency of Book v, viz. the *omissions*.

[9] v 43ff.

[10] v 49-50; vi 16. See above, p.62. Cf. iii 8 (with viii 35, 84): Dorieus; iv 121.1 (Brasidas).

What then are those omissions? Or rather perhaps, what were the developments whose importance Thucydides failed to see?

First, Persia. It was at some time in the Peace of Nikias period, 421-415, that Athens broke the Peace of Kallias by giving help – mercenaries and money – to the rebel Persian satrap Pissouthnes and then to his bastard son Amorges.[11] This was a radical and insane departure from the policy of détente pursued since 450 and reaffirmed as recently as 424.[12] In the end it lost Athens the war, because (as Thucydides says in the obituary of Pericles)[13] Cyrus' mission and internal dissensions, rather than the Sicilian disaster, were what caused Athens' fall, and Cyrus would never have been sent to help the Spartans if Athens had stayed on the right side of Persia. Since Thucydides saw the significance of this when he wrote the long chapter about Pericles in Book ii, which as we have seen is one of the few passages which we can be absolutely sure was written after 404, we may ask: should he not have traced the current phase of tension between Athens and Persia back to its beginnings in about 420? The explanation for his failure to do this seems[14] to be that Thucydides woke up too late to the importance of the Persian factor in the war (or was he still reacting against the Persian preoccupations of Herodotus?); and that the narrowly Peloponnesian focus of Book v is itself a sign that Thucydides' thinking was not at its final stage.

Second, Hyperbolus' ostracism and the reasons for it. This was an important event in Athenian domestic politics, and probably happened in 416 BC. Thucydides despised the demagogue Hyperbolus,[15] but he cannot be excused of negligence if Hyperbolus was indeed, as he seems to have been, behind an Argive alliance of 416 which envisaged the use of imperial tribute for operations in the Peloponnese.[16] If this serious policy issue was the real reason for Hyperbolus' ostracism, Thucydides' reportage, even of the Peloponnesian affairs which are his main concern in Book v, was culpably deficient.

Third and finally, central Greece. One of the major Spartan thrusts in the Archidamian War was towards the north – not just

[11] For the date see Andrewes, *Historia* x, 1961, 4f.
[12] ML 70 for the reaffirmation.
[13] ii 65.12.
[14] See the important article of Andrewes, 'Thucydides and the Persians', *Historia* x, 1961, 1ff.
[15] viii 73.
[16] Andrewes, *HCT* v, 261ff.

Brasidas' operations in Thrace, but the foundation of Heraclea Trachinia in 426. At the beginning of Book viii, Heraclea is in Spartan hands again after the Boiotian takeover of 420/19. But the Spartan reconquest is nowhere explicitly recorded: this is further evidence that the treatment of the Peace of Nikias period is incomplete.[17]

So in the east, the south and the north there were great events which deserved a place in a final version of Book v.

Book viii is so obviously a fragment that to accuse its author of incompetence, incoherence or omission may seem particularly silly. But we may single out two special features which suggest that what we have is a preliminary draft which was intended to be rethought and reworked.[18]

First, there is the failure, in the account of the oligarchic revolution of 411, to reconcile the essentially hostile picture of Theramenes and his motives (for instance, at one point the proposal to give power to 5000 voters is called a 'smokescreen') with the favourable judgment on the actual, later, constitution of the 5000 for which Theramenes is known from other sources to have been responsible.[19] The most recent commentator reasonably suggests that this was because Thucydides accepted an oral account from 'extremist refugees' (i.e. oligarchs), men who 'had every inclination to question the sincerity of Theramenes and his group'.[20] This inconsistency of judgment would have had to be resolved at some point, unless Thucydides seriously believed that a good constitution could be the work of bad and hypocritical men.

A second point is related to the first. We have an alternative account of the events at Athens in 411, in the *Athenian Constitution* (*Athenaion Politeia*) attributed to Aristotle. Since this work was discovered on papyrus a century ago scholars have generally opted for Thucydides' account in principle and in detail. But in one respect the *Ath.Pol.* has the advantage over Thucydides: Thucydides is not in the slightest interested in the attempts, which were certainly made at the time, to justify the new oligarchy intellectually. There is nothing in Thucydides about the so-called 'rider of Kleitophon'. This is an extremely

[17] iii 92; v 51-52; viii 3.
[18] Against J.H. Finley's view of viii, see below, p.149.
[19] viii 89; 97; Diod. xiii 38.2.
[20] Andrewes, *HCT* v, 253.

interesting amendment, recorded by the *Ath.Pol.*, to the original oligarchic manifesto, and runs as follows:

> Kleitophon moved that in other respects Pythodorus' proposal should be followed, but that the men elected should also search out the traditional laws which Kleisthenes had enacted when he set up the democracy, so that they might consider these too and deliberate for the best ...

The reference to Kleisthenes is constitutionalist in intention, and shows that there were moderates among the oligarchs. Again, there is nothing in Thucydides about the 'ancestral constitution' of which the theoreticians of the period, both right- and left-wing, claimed to be the champions.[21] There are no details, as in the *Ath.Pol.*, of the manifestos and protocols issued by the oligarchs. The atmosphere in Thucydides is pure terror, which may indeed be closer to the political reality, but probably does an injustice to those moderates (we should not shrink from the word) like Theramenes, who sought to make their actions philosophically defensible. This was after all the age of the sophists: the sophist Prodikos was the teacher of Theramenes.[22] Neither Prodikos nor any other sophist, philosopher or political theorist features as such in Book viii (see above, Chapter Five), although modern accounts rightly list intellectual disenchantment with democracy, alongside financial panic, as a major cause of the revolution.[23] But is this omission to be regarded as evidence of the incompleteness and unsatisfactoriness of Book viii, or just of Thucydides' realism and dislike of theory? Even if realism is the right explanation, Thucydides was surely wrong if he chose to deny, by implication, that people are prepared to kill, and be killed, in the name of ideas, and

[21] *Ath. Pol.* xxix.3. Ancestral constitution: see A. Fuks' book of that title, 1953. Aristophanes' version, if that is the word, of these events (on the relevant contemporary plays see *HCT* v, 184ff.) is as 'personal' as Thucydides', but so we should expect in a comic poet; see further below, p.167 n.52.

[22] DK 84 A6.

[23] For instance P.J. Rhodes, *Commentary on the Aristotelian Athenaion Politeia*, Oxford 1981, 372, after listing various other groups who wanted oligarchic change, says that 'some, pupils of the sophists, believed that democracy was a bad form of government' and mentions the Old Oligarch, a right-wing pamphlet preserved among the writings of Xenophon, in illustration.

that 'on recueille dans les rues les fruits qu'on a semés dans les livres'.[24]

So Books v and viii of Thucydides seem clearly to be unfinished, and this is probably evidence that these two books were written late.

Let us pass to the other books. Books i and ii contain passages which were certainly written 'early', for instance a passage in Book ii refers to the Oropians as subjects of Athens, which they had ceased to be by 411.[25] But these books also contain some undoubtedly 'late' passages[26] – not only the clear allusions to the end of the war in the Pericles obituary (above, p.137), but the possible references in Pericles' last speech.[27] In addition there is the material about King Archelaus of Macedon near the end of Book ii.[28] Here Archelaus is praised in general and retrospective terms for having done more for Macedon militarily than his eight predecessors put together. Now Archelaus died in 399 BC.[29] If Thucydides feels able to *sum up* the career of Archelaus, stopping only just short of the language of an obituary notice, Archelaus' life must surely have been either over or nearing its end. So this chapter was probably written about 400 BC. In any case, Archelaus' *accession* was in 413 BC, so that even if his military activity was crammed into the first years of his reign, Thucydides' remarks were written, or added, very much later than the events of 429 BC which are their immediate context.

But such tangible anachronisms are rare. And it is hard to point to many other passages which must have been written before or after some definite date during the war.[30] The last sentence of Book iii is reasonably secure: it speaks of the eruption

[24] This sentence is cited by Hugh Honour, *Romanticism*, Harmondsworth 1981, 237, from Ximénès Doudon, *Des révolutions du goût*, ed. H. Moncel, Paris 1924 (but the sentence was apparently written in 1832), p.xxviii.

[25] ii 23; viii 60. For the Pausanias-Themistocles excursuses see above, p.24 n.36.

[26] See Dover, *HCT* v, 405ff., 'Early and late passages'. Most of these passages, for example Oropus, have been much discussed – for instance by Finley, *Three Essays*, ch.3, and I omit references here, in the interests of brevity. For i 92-5 see my forthcoming commentary.

[27] Above, p.65, on ii 64 etc.

[28] ii 100.

[29] Diod. xiv 37.6, from the so-called 'chronographic' source.

[30] We saw (above, p.64), that the reference in Pericles' first war speech to *epiteichisis*, i 142.2, need not imply knowledge, on Thucydides' part, of the events of 425, the year which saw the most effective use in the whole war of the *epiteichisis* strategy – at Pylos.

of Mt Etna in a way which betrays no knowledge of an eruption in 396. Therefore, Thucydides was dead by 396.[31]

A more sophisticated technique is to try to distinguish between stages of Thucydides' thought, even where there is no certain pointer to show precisely when any of the thinking was done.

A good example of this method is the theory that Thucydides wrote Book i soon after the beginning of the Peloponnesian War, at a time when Corinthian ambitions and influence seemed to have been decisive in precipitating the war.[32] Later (it is argued) Thucydides saw that Corinth mattered much less than he had once thought, and substituted an explanation in terms of Athenian aggression and dynamism, the famous 'truest cause' of the war.[33] If this theory could be established it would be of prime importance for Thucydides' development. But the reasons offered are not compelling. First, the abrupt sentence about the 'truest cause' can, it is claimed, be easily detached from its context. This is so, but it may simply be a way of bringing the reader up short and of making the sentence sound as solemn and considered as possible – rather than evidence of hasty and subsequent insertion. Second, the 'truest cause' is not a mere afterthought expressed in a couple of authorial comments, but can also be found embedded deep in strata which the theory holds to be early. For instance, the Corcyreans say in the first speech in Book i that anybody can see that the Spartans are going to war through fear of the Athenians, which is exactly the thought contained in the 'truest cause'. Third, the theory rests in part on a complex analysis of the great tetralogy of speeches at Sparta. Only the Athenians and Sthenelaidas (it is held) address themselves to the 'truest cause' of Athenian expansion, so these two speeches were added later. But we have discussed this analysis of the tetralogy in an earlier chapter, and seen that the four speeches form an interwoven unit, and that the two pairs cannot so easily be separated.[34]

So we should reject the idea that Book i is seriously incoherent

[31] iii 116 with Gomme ad loc.
[32] Ed. Schwartz, *Geschichtswerk des Thukydides*[2] 1929; Andrewes, *CQ* ix, 1959, 223ff.
[33] i 23; cf. i 88.
[34] i 35 for the Corcyreans; i 68-86 for the tetralogy. See above, pp. 59f., and for the bearing on the composition problem, J.H. Finley, *Three Essays*, 119, drawing on Pohlenz; Dover *HCT* v, 415ff. (sceptical of the Schwartz/Andrewes view).

in its account of the causes of the war. On the contrary it seems to be remarkable for the degree of its finish.

I do however believe that we can see a change in Thucydides' deepest thinking, not on the causes of the war but on a very different topic: the role of individuals as opposed to collectives and impersonal forces. In *The Hedgehog and the Fox*, Isaiah Berlin discusses Tolstoy's view of history and his contempt for those historians who attributed causal importance to the cold in the head from which Napoleon suffered before the battle of Borodino. Tolstoy's view was that politicians and generals near the top of the pyramid delude themselves into thinking that they control events at the base. Tolstoy the 'hedgehog', the believer in simple, single determining forces and principles, is on Berlin's view at odds with Tolstoy the 'fox', who sees the casualness, complexity and detail of millions of unrelated human actions and emotions. At the beginning of his book, Berlin lists some great literary figures of the past and includes Herodotus among the foxes, those who have no over-arching, organising concept. It is tempting to play this game with other ancient historians. Polybius, for instance, is arguably like Tolstoy, a natural fox with a hankering to be a hedgehog: the 'cyclical' theories of his Book vi are mercifully without effect on the rest of the narrative. For Hieronymus of Cardia, the unity of Alexander's empire, or rather attempts by his Successors to recreate that unity, were a governing theme. But what of Thucydides (oddly not mentioned by Berlin)? In a way Thucydides is an obvious hedgehog, for whom *archê*, empire, was an obsessive preoccupation.[35] That is why it is 'the Athenians' (a collective: above, p.61) who are made to assert the legitimacy of the Athenian hegemony over Greece. But perhaps Thucydides' thinking developed in an unexpected direction, that is, towards a realisation of the power for good or damage of an effective or persuasive individual. This is the opposite development to that asserted by Beloch at the opening of his great eight-volume Greek History:[36]

Naive historiography sees only heroes; it is not troubled by the masses who stand behind them. So in Homer the Greeks are defeated because Achilles holds himself aloof from the battle;

[35] Isaiah Berlin, *The Hedgehog and the Fox: An Essay on Tolstoy's View of History*, London 1967; J. Hornblower, *Hieronymus of Cardia*, 1981, 170.
[36] K.J. Beloch, *Griechische Geschichte* i²i, Strasburg 1912, 1.

when he takes part again, he drives the Trojans before him like sheep.

But it does seem that Thucydides came round, or back, to the 'naive' view that individual human action can change the course of history.[37] In fact, he became less of a hedgehog and more of a fox. A similar idea, put in a more abstract way, is that, in Thucydides' judgment, chance, *tuchê*, took over from *gnômê*, intelligence, as the war went on; that is, Thucydides progressively abandoned a belief in confident human systems and structures.[38] Only Pericles enjoys, or thinks he enjoys, 'conscious mastery of men and events' – although Thucydides makes Pericles himself concede that events are 'unteachable.'[39]

What produced this shift in Thucydides? The answer is: Alcibiades. Alcibiades' charismatic leadership enabled him to achieve by his personality what Pericles had achieved by his policies, even if it be allowed that Periclean leadership was sustained by demagogic rhetoric to a greater extent than Thucydides chose to admit.[40] Thucydides can even say of Alcibiades that nobody else could have restrained the sailors of the fleet at Samos from sailing off to Athens.[41] In the fourth century, as we saw in the Introduction, histories were written round the personalities of individuals, and Alcibiades' career, his 'doings and sufferings', were singled out by Aristotle as the paradigmatic subject-matter of history. So Alcibiades' role in Thucydides looks forward to the individualistic fourth century. Incidentally the development here postulated is the exact opposite of that rejected above, according to which Thucydides replaced a 'personal' view of the war in terms of Corinthian pressure by one in terms of abstract expansion. (But I would not argue the other extreme, that i.23 is specially 'early'.)

It is possible to detect the point at which Thucydides' view of Alcibiades changed, and with it his view of the importance of human personality in history. The two books whose place in the economy of the whole work we have not so far examined are vi and vii, the books which narrate the Sicilian expedition. These

[37] This is the view of H.D. Westlake, *Individuals in Thucydides*, 1968.
[38] See above, p.69, on Lowell Edmunds' *Chance and Intelligence*.
[39] i 140.1. In *PBA* 1960, 56, Syme rightly stresses this passage; 'conscious mastery': R. Syme, *The Roman Revolution*, Oxford 1939, 53 (about Caesar).
[40] Above, p.122.
[41] viii 86.

books give the impression of having been written soon after the events which they describe, under the immediate impact of the disastrous end to the expedition. The counter-argument, that Thucydides could not have used the superlatives of the final chapter of Book vii ('the greatest work of the war ... most splendid ... most miserable ...') unless the war was already over, is too literal-minded, and mistakes the force of a Greek superlative, which is sometimes just a strengthening device. Even if 'of this war' governs *all* the superlatives used, Thucydides did not have to wait till 404 before calling the defeat the 'most miserable' of the war.[42] The idea that Sicily was written up in prompt passion may explain why Thucydides begins the narrative in such a pessimistic mood: most Athenians were ignorant of the size of the island, he says.[43]

This is an extraordinary statement: as early as 457 BC they had made an alliance with Segesta, a long way to the west in the interior of the island. The word which I have translated as 'size' is *megethos*; but it can also mean 'greatness' in a political and military sense, and it might seem tempting to think that Thucydides had in mind the power rather than the physical dimensions of Sicily. But this will not do, because he goes on to say that the journey round Sicily takes rather less than eight days sailing for a merchant ship. In other words, he *is* thinking of the island's physical dimensions. Another possible way out might be to take *apeiroi*, which I have translated above as 'ignorant', in its literal sense of 'personally inexperienced'. Thucydides would then be saying that most Athenians had not visited Sicily. But this would be a very obvious thing to say; and in any case the run of the rest of the sentence is against it.[44] So there is no escape: Thucydides means to say that most Athenians were ignorant of the most basic geographical facts about Sicily,

[42] J.H. Finley, *Three Essays*, 134, on vii 87.5.

[43] vi 1.1.

[44] *megethos*: LSJ[9] lists two distinct senses; Thuc.ii 38. 2 is perhaps an example of the second sense: the *greatness* of the city of Athens attracts imports from all over the world. 'Inexperienced': the whole sentence goes: 'Most of them were *apeiroi* of the greatness, *megethos*, of the island and of the mass of inhabitants, both Greeks and barbarians.' There are several genitives here: the genitive 'and of the mass' surely looks back to *apeiroi* rather than to *megethos*. That is to say, he is not talking about the *megethos* of the mass of inhabitants. They were *apeiroi* of the mass: 'inexperienced' would make no sense here.

and that this made the expedition an act of utter folly.[45]

That tone of gloom is kept up for most of the two books; they end with the solemn claim that Sicily was the greatest *ergon* of the war, and that the Athenian defeat was total: few out of many returned (a phrase we have discussed in an earlier chapter). Every conceivable tragic device is used to bring out the depth of suffering and the magnitude of the reversal.[46] In particular, the splendour and arrogance of Athenian resources and aims, at the beginning of Book vi, is brought out by vague superlatives rather than by the precise enumeration of detail which is Thucydides' more normal method.[47] This is the method of grand tragedy (Oedipus is 'the famous Oedipus', Agamemnon is 'king and conqueror'); the Athenian force in Sicily, like Oedipus and Agamemnon, will be brought down in the end, and the fall will be described in matching superlatives of suffering, in language which specifically suggests the destruction of Troy.[48] Thucydides draws on the full range of emotional devices, including pathetic or tragic *akribeia* (above, p.34), and a very Euripidean portrayal of the effects of the battle on spectators.[49] Aeschylus' *Persai* is verbally echoed at a couple of points.[50] I have suggested elsewhere that it is because Thucydides' whole approach to the Sicilian disaster is essentially literary and tragic that he has exaggerated its actual importance for effect.[51] I pointed to the awkward resumption of the narrative at the beginning of Book viii, which stresses the Athenian come-back, including some very energetic ship-building, in a way that reads uncomfortably after the finality of Book vii (I am not persuaded by those 'unitarians' who claim that the thought and texture of Book viii is essentially

[45] Plutarch, *Nicias* xii 1 describes how Athenians, young and old, drew maps of Sicily in the public places. Dover on vi 1 says this is not inconsistent with Thucydides, because veterans of the Sicily operations of 427-4 would have found willing audiences. True, but Plutarch speaks of *young* as well as old.

[46] Macleod, *Essays*, ch. ix.

[47] vi 31, passim, and note the desire for a 'never-ending source of revenue' at vi 24 (given as a popular motive for wanting to join the expedition). With this contrast the precision of ii 13 or vii 57.

[48] Soph. *OT* 8 with Macleod, p. 141; Aesch. *Ag.* 783; *panolethria*: Thuc. vii 87.6 with Hdt. ii 120 (Troy). Cf. Macleod, p. 142 for the reversal of fortune.

[49] Effects: cf. J.H. Finley, *Three Essays*, 47.

[50] Finley, ibid., compares *oimôgê*, groaning, at Thuc. vii 71.6 and *Persai* 426f.; add *nautikos stratos ... pezos*, 'land and sea army', at Thuc. ibid. and Aesch., *Persai* 727, which is still more clearly echoed at Hdt. viii 68.

[51] *Greek World 479-323 BC*, 1983, 141ff.

that of vi and vii.)[52] I pointed to the inconsistency between the catastrophic language with which Book vii closes and the casual remark late in Book viii, about the Euboian revolt, that it caused greater panic even than Sicily, great though that had *seemed* at the time. And finally I pointed to the concrete Athenian successes *after* Sicily, including a sea victory at Cyzicus as early as 410.[53] All this strengthens the suspicion that in Books vi and vii Thucydides was carried away by a desire to paint the Sicilian expedition in uncompromising black.

It is therefore a surprise to recall that in Book ii, in a passage written as we have seen after the end of the war, we had been told that the failure in Sicily was 'not so much an error of judgment' as of execution: the Athenians took decisions which were disadvantageous to those who *had* set out on the expedition (the past tense here implies that the mistakes were all subsequent to the initial decision to go). 'Disadvantageous decisions' is vague, but the phrase is normally and best taken to refer to the recall of Alcibiades; perhaps also to the failure to recall Nikias, and even to the support by Athens of Amorges, although this hardly 'blunted' the expedition. The king of Persia *may* have capitalised on the final Athenian failure in Sicily; hence the mission of Tissaphernes to stir up rebellion in the

---

[52] J.H. Finley, *Three Essays*, 136ff. lists 'ideas or turns of expression' common to viii and the two preceding books. Even if this be accepted (and some of Finley's instances are strange: for example viii 86.4 and vi 15 give as he himself acknowledges *contrasting* judgments on Alcibiades), it shows no more than that Thucydides' outlook on many points, and his style, remained more or less consistent. Finley's arguments on the central issue (p. 138) which is, as he puts it, that 'in emphasising the greatness of Athens' loss in Sicily, Thucydides failed to reckon with her partial later recovery' are not compelling. 'Partial' begs the question: the war, after all, went on for nearly another decade.

[53] H.D. Westlake, *JHS* cv, 1985, 213, objects to my use of the Spartan peace-offer after Cyzicus, arguing that the terms were disadvantageous to Athens. On the offer see also J.H. Finley, p. 139, who says that had Thucydides lived to describe Kleophon's refusal of peace 'he would doubtless have seen in it merely one more example of that extremism' which had underlain all Athens' reverses. Both Westlake's and Finley's points are equally true of Kleon's rejection of terms in 425 (iv 21). One could hardly argue from Spartan optimism and Kleon's extremism in 425 that Athens was weak *then*. Finley is concerned to show that Thucydides was constantly preoccupied with political disunity, i.e. that Book viii is of a piece with what had gone before. Perhaps; but it is too strong to say that Thucydides would have seen 'merely' this. Thucydides knew that for Sparta to sue for peace at all, on terms, was a surprise and a humiliation.

Athenian empire. But this did not damage those Athenians who were actually still at Syracuse.[54]

So in Book ii Thucydides reverses the entire implication of Books vi and vii: the Sicilian expedition could have succeeded after all, had Alcibiades been retained in his command. This is a change of mind not just about Sicily but about Alcibiades. The character-sketch early in Book vi, like the passage in Book ii, implies that the Athenians were wrong to recall him, and claims that his conduct of the war was excellent. This is surprising (nothing in Book v has prepared us for it) and hard to reconcile with the later statement, in Book viii, that Alcibiades' restraint of the fleet in 411, when the sailors wanted to sail to Athens, was the *first* time that he had done anything of real service to the city. That judgment implies that Alcibiades' behaviour hitherto, including his Sicilian strategy, was not worth much.[55]

The answer must be that the later successes of Alcibiades, in the period after Thucydides' narrative ended – that is, between the battles of Cyzicus in 410 and Notium in 407 – impressed Thucydides with Alcibiades' ability, and produced the favourable estimates in Books ii and in the digression early in Book vi.

This must mean that Thucydides wrote the bulk of Books vi and vii very soon after 413, the date of the final disaster, but before the Athenian revival in 411/10. There is a little internal evidence to support this, for instance the reference to Himera as a still-existing *polis*. (The point is that it was destroyed in 409.) On the other hand there are sections such as that in Book vii about the long-term effects of the Spartan occupation of Decelea in Attica, a reference which was surely added later. And so also, surely, was the Alcibiades digression in Book vi, for reasons which we have already discussed. More problematic is the reference, in the list of each side's forces before the final sea-battle, to the 'Aeginetans who then held Aegina'. This probably refers to the Athenian settlers who occupied Aegina

---

[54] ii 65.11. Mission of Tissaphernes and Sicily?: see D.M. Lewis, *Sparta and Persia*, Leiden 1977, 87 n.23 for the chronological problem. It seems that Darius cannot have heard of the final defeat when he sent down Tissaphernes (viii 5); but he may have been aware that Athens had, as Lewis puts it, 'over-extended herself by reinforcing the Sicilian expedition'.

[55] See Dover, *HCT* v, 423-7, 'Alcibiades and Sicily'; cf. id., 'Thucydides' historical judgment: Athens and Sicily', *Proc. Royal Irish Acad.* 81, C Number 8, Dublin 1981, 231ff., at p. 237.

between 431 and 404; in other words the passage was written after 404. The less likely alternative is that a contrast is intended with the period *up to* 431.[56]

So with the exception of a few passages, Books vi and vii were written soon after 413, the most important later strand being the revised estimate of Alcibiades.

Before we attempt to summarise the stages of the composition of the work, we should ask if there is any external evidence for the date at which Thucydides was working. The evidence is remarkably scant: like Shakespeare, Thucydides is a badly-documented genius in a well-documented period.

An exciting new possibility arose from the publication in 1983 of an inscription from the island of Thasos in the North Aegean.[57] It is a list of local magistrates, and includes under the year 397 the name of Lichas son of Arkesilas. Arkesilas is a royal name at Cyrene, the daughter city of Sparta's own daughter city Thera; and the combination of the two names invites at first sight an identification with the Lichas son of Arkesilas who appears in Thucydides Books v and viii. Now at one point in Book viii Thucydides, describing events at Miletus in 411, says that when Lichas 'subsequently' died of illness, the Milesians would not allow him to be buried where the Spartans wanted. If Lichas was still alive in 397, it would follow that Thucydides, who knew of Lichas' death, was himself still alive in 397. And this would mean that Thucydides survived the end of the Peloponnesian War by as much as seven years. (But no longer: the Etna passage (above, p.144) shows he was dead by 396). What are the other implications for the composition of his work? They are worth considering, though it must be stressed that, so far, few scholars identify Thucydides' Lichas with the Lichas of the inscription.[58] The doubters are probably right; but it is just

[56] Himera: vi 62.2; Decelea: vii 26-8 (vii 27.3 speaks of a *succession* of garrisons). Aegina: vii 57.2 with Dover ad loc.

[57] J. Pouilloux and F. Salviat, 'Lichas, Lacédémonien, archonte à Thasos et le livre viii de Thucydide', *CRAI* 1983, 376ff. The difficulties of the identification are discussed by P. Cartledge, *LCM* ix (7) 1984, 98ff. 'A new lease of life for Lichas son of Arkesilas?'. Lichas' death: Thuc. viii 84.2.

[58] In the *Bulletin Épigraphique*, which until Louis Robert's death in 1985 was the most authoritative annual discussion of Greek epigraphy in the light of new finds, Jeanne and Louis Robert pronounced firmly against the identification, on the grounds that the names in question were insufficiently rare for the argument to be convincing: *REG* 1984, 314. Westlake, *CQ* xxxv, 1985, 44 n.7 is also unconvinced, and so (as he kindly tells me) is David Lewis.

conceivable that more inscriptions from Thasos might prove them wrong. What follows is therefore tentative and provisional.

A number of passages actually make better sense on the new rather than the old assumption about the end of Thucydides' working life. First, the 'obituary' language about Archelaus of Macedon (above, p.143) is easily explained if Thucydides did indeed survive Archelaus, who as we saw died in 399. Second, there is the prophecy of Alcibiades in Book viii, that a Spartan victory in the Peloponnesian War would be very awkward for Persia because Sparta would start liberating Greek Asia Minor from Persia, just as she had liberated mainland Greece from Athens.[59] This prophecy was strikingly fulfilled after 400 BC when first Thibron (400), then Derkyllidas (399) and finally Agesilaus (396) invaded Asia Minor in response to appeals from the Greek cities there.[60] If Thucydides lived till 397 or later, the 'prophecy' was perhaps not a real prophecy at all, but manufactured *post eventum*, and we should speak not of Thucydidean acumen but of Thucydidean hindsight. Third, and perhaps most important of all, are the passages which imply knowledge of the end of the Athenian empire (above, p.65).

But here there is a difficulty. The years after 404 saw a remarkable resurgence of Athenian imperialism; in the mid-390s the Thebans said publicly at Athens that 'it is common knowledge that you Athenians want to recover your *archê*'.[61] If Thucydides lived to see any of this, it has left no *overt* trace in his work. The language of those passages which refer explicitly to the end of the war, and the pulling down of the Long Walls, is absolutely final.[62]

Is it reasonable to expect any trace of the 390s in a work which describes the events of 431-404? Much recent work on the historians of antiquity has sought to explain them by reference to their time of writing: 'all history is contemporary history'. In this way we are invited to see Hadrianic features in Tacitus' depiction of Tiberius, and anticipations of the 40s BC in Sallust's

---

[59] viii 46.

[60] Andrewes remarks ad loc. that 'Alkibiades' argument is by no means merely specious, as we can see from Sparta's performance in the 390s, when her quarrel with Artaxerxes was for the time beyond repair and it suited her to play the part of liberator'.

[61] Xen. *Hell.* iii 5.10; see generally, for the Athenian revival, my *Greek World*, 195ff.

[62] ii 65; v 26.

Conspiracy of Catiline. Livy's early books on Roman history of the fifth and fourth centuries are contaminated by the politics of the first century. In Greek history, Herodotus' account of the Persian War has become a warning message to the Athenians and Spartans of the time of the Peloponnesian War, and Xenophon's *Hellenica*, which covers events from 411 to 362, a sermon on panhellenism preached to the Athens of the 350s.[63]

With this in mind, let us return to Thucydides. It is surely fair to ask what, if any, traces of the imperialism of the 390s can be seen in Thucydides. We have admitted that there is no open mention. But if it is right to see Herodotus' work as a warning to the Greeks against fratricidal war, might there not be contemporary resonance in Thucydides' denunciations of *pleonexia*, imperialistic greed? Andokides in 392 was to chastise the Athenians for their desire to recover the perquisites of the old empire, the 'overseas possessions and the debts'.[64] Perhaps Thucydides felt the same way.

But this is pure speculation. The most that we can say is that the idea of a Thucydides alive in 397 would not clash with anything in the text, and could even explain some otherwise problematic details.

Is it possible to sketch any kind of conclusion, setting out the relative and absolute stages of Thucydides' thinking?[65]

The conclusions we have reached are as follows: Thucydides began work on the Archidamian War books before 411. That means that Book viii, which deals with events of 411, was written after i-iv. Book v, which resembles viii in its poor state of finish, was also written later than i-iv. Most of vi and vii were written soon after 413, but Thucydides' experience of the successes scored by Alcibiades led him to a different view about the viability of the Sicilian expedition. It also led him to a different view about the extent to which individuals can affect events. After the end of the whole Peloponnesian War, Thucydides

[63] R. Syme, *Tacitus*, 1958 and *Sallust*, 1964; R.M. Ogilvie, *Livy i-v Commentary*, 1965 (but note T. Cornell, *Past Perspectives*, edd. I. Moxon, J. Smart and A.J. Woodman, 1986, 67ff.); C.W. Fornara, *Herodotus, An Interpretative Essay*, 1971; Ed. Schwartz, *Gesammelte Schriften*, Berlin 1956, ii, 136ff.

[64] Thuc. iv 65 etc.; Andok. iii 12-15.

[65] The most recent attempt to discuss the problem, that of Dover in *HCT* v 1981 app.2, understandably declines to tabulate the results of his individual discussions.

added such passages as Pericles' obituary, which shows awareness of the final defeat, and perhaps other 'late' items like the notice about Archelaus at the end of Book ii. If he survived to the year 397, that would explain some ostensibly prophetic passages; and it might give extra point to his denunciations of imperial greed.

One important section I have left to the end, because it forms a natural transition to Thucydides' opinions: the Corcyra *stasis* material in Books iii and iv, which is of cardinal importance as giving the views of Thucydides himself. I agree with the recent commentary that the words with which, in Book iv, Thucydides 'signs off' this episode or episodes, were written 'well before' 410.[66] But I have a fundamental reason for seeing the main, analytical, discussion in Book iii as considerably earlier than e.g. the Pericles obituary, which represents the latest phase of the author's thought. Thucydides came to put more and more on to *identifiable* individuals (Kleon, Alcibiades, Hermokrates and – who knows? – the Spartan Lysander, whose prominence he did not live to describe). But the main Corcyra *stasis* section, though concerned with the behaviour of individuals more than with that of states,[67] names and is concerned with no identifiable individuals.[68] This seems to me to reflect an earlier outlook – Thucydides is not yet so concerned with outstanding *pleonectic* individuals but with *pleonexia* as a causal and abstract force. But this is to anticipate; we must return to *pleonexia* when we look at Thucydides' opinions in the next chapter.

---

[66] *HCT* iv, 411 on iv 48, a vexed passage. The main Corcyra *stasis* discussion is in iii 82ff.

[67] But see below, p.178: it is wrong to ignore the implications of the *stasis* chapters for state morality.

[68] At iii 70 there is personal material – about Peithias the *etheloproxenos* (above, p.99) and allegations about vine-props cut down on sacred land. I am thinking of Thucydides' more general analysis in the main chapters, 82ff. In the introduction to the Mytilene revolt. Thucydides passes over completely a story about heiresses, which we know from Aristotle (*Pol.*1304a) to have been relevant to the disturbances there. See *HCT* ii, 252f.

CHAPTER SEVEN

Opinions

Every sentence of Thucydides' narrative represents one of his opinions. But to an unusual degree this most magisterial of writers conveys the impression that all his pronouncements have the absolute authority of hard fact. Phrases like 'it seems to me' (*dokei*) or 'it is probably' (*hôs eikos*) are found more frequently in Book viii than in other books. This suggests (since Book viii contains more indications of incompleteness than any other book) that Thucydides aimed eventually to cut down the percentage of such tentative or diffident expressions – perhaps after further research, but perhaps merely after further *thought*. So Thucydides believed that the goal of both descriptive and analytic writing is *certainty*. This is more surprising than it may sound. Herodotus is far more generous with his acknowledgments of 'variants' in the source-tradition than is Thucydides. Thucydides very rarely admits to outright uncertainty, and very rarely offers alternative accounts without adjudication; in both these respects he differs not only from Herodotus but from many of the other comparable writers of antiquity. (In later times, Tacitus, Plutarch and Arrian, for instance, frequently indicate divergences in their sources without adjudication.) The few, exceptional expressions of serious doubt in Thucydides are soon listed: in Book vii he asks (a rare interrogative outburst), 'In such a night-battle [sc. as that at Epipolae], the only one which took place between large armies during the whole war, who could know anything for sure?' With this we might compare Herodotus' remark about the battle of Lade: 'It is not possible to say which of the Samians fought bravely and which did not, because they all accuse each other.' And there are a few explicit refusals in Thucydides to adjudicate between accounts: early in Book ii he says, 'That is what the Thebans say, and they claim they swore an oath. But the

155

Plataeans do not agree that they promised to return the prisoners immediately, but only if there was an agreement after discussion; and they deny that an oath was sworn.' Again, in the unfinished eighth book, Thucydides offers several views, including his own conjecture (but not what modern scholars think to be the correct reason) why the Persian ships in 411 got no further west than Aspendos.[1]

All this concerns the confidence, or diffidence, which Thucydides felt about factual questions to do with the war. Modern novelists – Stendhal in *The Charterhouse of Parma*, Tolstoy in *War and Peace*, Thackeray in *Vanity Fair* – equally recognise the confusion felt by people taking part in battles, and the difficulty of giving a narrative based on their accounts. Thucydides is on the whole remarkable for the confidence with which his factual opinions are expressed. But what of non-factual issues – that is, Thucydides' own political and moral opinions?

To begin, as we began this book, with war and politics: Thucydides' remark, that 'war is a violent teacher',[2] is so famous that it is easy to forget that it is an audacious and arresting personification. Theopompus in the next century was to personify war in a parable about War and *Hubris*, and Pericles said that he saw War approaching from the Peloponnese.[3] It seems that even for realists like Thucydides, Pericles and Theopompus, 'War' was an almost human agent, not an abstraction, long after most of the other unseen forces of human experience had lost their hold on the visual imagination. But the Thucydidean epigram is so powerful that it has elicited the comment, 'If Thucydides wanted his readers to draw any one moral from his work it was *biaios didaskalos ho polemos*', war is a teacher of violence.[4] Thucydides had in mind the distortion of morality and values for which war is responsible; he makes his comment in the course of his account of the Corcyrean *stasis*, and goes on to say that war 'removes people's ability to satisfy their daily needs and reduces their minds for the most part to the

---

[1] Expressions of opinion in book viii: *HCT* v, 399f. Thuc. vii 44; Hdt. vi 14; Thuc. ii 5.6; viii 87; D.M. Lewis, *Historia* vii, 1958, 393ff. 'The Phoenician fleet in 411'.

[2] iii 82.2.

[3] *FGrHist* 115 F 127; Plut. *Per.* viii 7. Cf. Macleod, p. 124 on i 122.1.

[4] Gomme, *HCT* i, 90.

level of their immediate desires'. In other words, brutality pays in wartime, and moral discernment is corrupted by the needs of the moment. There is implied condemnation here: Thucydides is distancing himself from the 'cynical doctrines of force' expressed by some of his speakers.[5] (We shall return to the problem of Thucydides and morality below.)

Yet Thucydides held military office himself; not as a 'professional soldier' in our sense but still as an elected *stratêgos* or commander – the only important Athenian office of state to which appointment was determined by election not the lot.[6] Among the historians of classical antiquity, military experience is surprisingly rare (unlike political or diplomatic experience): of writers whose works are extant, only Xenophon and Caesar commanded armies, and neither shows much compunction about war and its effects.[7] Xenophon was interested in practical and theoretical questions of military leadership, and was a man of sincere moral and religious conviction, but he never reflects on the moral issue, whether one should fight at all.[8] As for the far more intelligent Caesar, it has been said that 'the total of human suffering and misery occasioned by Caesar's Gallic campaigns is terrible to contemplate, and it is certain that much of it was unnecessary'.[9] Even before Thucydides, a speaker in Herodotus, namely Croesus, had observed that in peace sons bury their fathers, but in war it is the other way round: this expresses in simple, gnomic form Thucydides' point that war produces violent distortions. The thought is there in Homer: old Nestor in the *Odyssey* says that his dear son lies dead at Troy.[10] Homer's fighting, like Thucydides', is directly and personally described; we may also feel that Thucydides resembles some of the poets of the First World War: his condemnation issues from his own experience, which is the experience of a soldier. (But the individual disillusionment of a Graves or a Sassoon is absent.)

[5] Ibid. ii, 373.

[6] See above, p.125 for the conditions of fifth-century warfare. Note that *stratêgoi* were expected to command by land *and* sea. In what follows in my text, 'soldier' should be interpreted accordingly.

[7] I am not forgetting Arrian, but his extensive use of earlier writers (Ptolemy, Aristobulus, Hieronymus) makes his own views hard to get at.

[8] The remarks about war in Book ii of the *Memorabilia* are very general and theoretical.

[9] C. Hignett, *CAH* ix, 573.

[10] Hdt. i 87; Homer, *Odyssey* iii 111.

Only if we remember that he himself was a soldier can we understand how Thucydides, despite his reprobation of war for its morally levelling effects, can pass so many judgments about professional soldiering. In particular, he seems (rightly but still insufficiently) to have admired the generalship of Demosthenes,[11] the only man in Thucydides who learns from mistakes, his own (the Aitolian *pathos* or disaster), and those of others (in Book vii we are told that on taking up command in Sicily he wished to avoid the mistakes which Nikias had made).[12] Not all Thucydides' military judgments were sound: his praise of Phrynichus' *xunesis* or shrewdness in avoiding a confrontation with the enemy in 412 was misdirected if, as has recently been proved,[13] the Athenians had something like naval parity with the Peloponnesians at the time; they were certainly more experienced. This Jutland *could* have been a Trafalgar, had Phrynichus been less pessimistic.

It is the soldier in Thucydides who shows an interest in technical questions. For instance, he saw the potential of light-armed troops, which was to be fully realised in the warfare of the fourth century: it was because the Aitolians were light-armed that they were able to inflict so comprehensive a defeat on the Athenian forces in 426 BC. They pursued the Athenians into unknown forests and ravines: this was the calamity which Demosthenes is said to have wanted to avoid repeating.[14] Thucydides' own interest in light-armed operations is shown also in his account of the battle at Spartolus in the north of Greece, where the Chalcidian cavalry and light-armed troops defeat their Athenian opposite numbers, although the Athenian hoplites are victorious. This passage, it has been remarked,[15] is interesting for the military historian, because it is one of the first signs that the old hoplite tactics of Marathon and Plataea are outmoded. This is not quite right: the great battles of the fourth century – Leuctra, Mantinea, Chaeronea – were all fought with hoplites. It was the *combination* of heavy- and light-armed troops which was so effective;[16] so was the

[11] See V. Hunter, *Thucydides the Artful Reporter*, Toronto 1973.

[12] Aitolian pathos referred to: iv 30.1; errors of Nikias: vii 42.3.

[13] viii 27 with Andrewes, *HCT* ad loc. and excursus on ship numbers at pp. 27-32.

[14] iii 98.

[15] ii 79.3 with Beloch, *Griechische Geschichte* ii[2] 1, 310.

[16] See my *Greek World*, 1983, 132, 164.

combination of light-armed and mounted troops.[17] Thucydides also shows awareness of another phenomenon whose importance lay in the future: mercenary service.[18]

In naval warfare also, Thucydides enjoys analysing the detail of tactical innovation and professional expertise (see especially the paragraphs in Book ii on Phormio's operations).[19] His method is diagnostic. That is, he isolates the important features and writes them up, fully, just once. This is the treatment he accords to other phenomena that interest him. Thus the demagogue Kleon is examined fully, Hyperbolus hardly at all (above, p.41).

All this means that it is right to stress the interest that Thucydides takes 'in the tactics of battles: of normal battles, like Mantinea, and still more of unusual ones, as in Aitolia, on the beaches of Pylos, etc. He likes analysing the conditions, as well as narrating the details.'[20] (This interest makes it surprising that he was not more critical of Herodotus' wild figures for the Persian Wars: above, p.108.)

But even in a chapter like that describing the Aitolian disaster, Thucydides lets out a personal comment which shows how deeply he was moved by the deaths of the 120 Athenians, all in the flower of their youth, 'the finest men whom Athens lost in the whole war'.[21] (This can also be seen as at the same time a practical comment on the waste of excellent manpower. But Thucydides is generally very sparing in his comments on the waste of human life.)

The modern reader of Thucydides, even more than the ancient, must find himself wondering whether Thucydides thought that all the fighting which he records was worth it: did he believe that the political goals and gains justified those 120 deaths? We saw in the preceding chapter that Thucydides tends to neglect ideology as an ingredient in human motive – one of his most serious weaknesses. But this does not mean that he himself was without political opinions, or that he did not have a view about the Athenian empire for which the war was fought.[22]

[17] As at Thuc. ii 79; cf. above.
[18] vii 28; J. Roy, *Historia* xvi, 1967, 287ff. 'The mercenaries of Cyrus'.
[19] ii 83ff.
[20] Gomme *HCT* ii, 472.
[21] iii 98.
[22] i 23.6, for the cause of the war.

His most explicit political judgment is in Book viii.[23] It is about the so-called regime of the 5000, which was intermediate in time between the extreme oligarchy of the year 411 (the rule of the 400) and the full, restored, democracy. Of this regime Thucydides says that it was a moderate blending of the few and the many, and that under it the Athenians enjoyed, for the first time in his, Thucydides', lifetime, conspicuously good government. The whole paragraph is full of problems; I offer brief and dogmatic answers to them here. First, the expression 'blend of the few and the many' does, I think, imply that basic constitutional rights were denied to the *thêtes*, the bottom Athenian propertied class:[24] something more elitist than pure government by the many is envisaged; otherwise it would not make sense for Thucydides to claim that the political interests of the 'few' were represented under the 5000. Second, the two phrases which I have translated 'for the first time, in my lifetime' surely go closely together.[25] This is a material point: if the Greek means not 'during the first phase of this regime's existence' but 'for the first time', as it surely does, Thucydides' comment is far more sweeping, and implies censure even of Pericles' management of affairs. Third, the word for 'government', *politeusantes*, can mean both 'had a good form of government' and 'behaved well'. The former is surely the right meaning.[26] This makes the passage more interesting because it is very rare for Thucydides to use the language of political theory, rather than simply

---

[23] viii 97.

[24] See Andrewes' commentary (*HCT* v, 323ff.) against de Ste Croix, *Historia* v, 1956, 1ff.

[25] Here I disagree with Andrewes (cf. my review of *HCT* v in the *TLS* for 3 April 1981, p.388): *epi ge emou* surely qualifies *ton prôton chronon*. Andrewes' rendering of the latter expression as 'in the first phase' (sc. of this regime's existence) is said by him to 'leave *epi ge emou* out on a branch, not adding anything substantial to the sentence'; this is more than merely 'disquieting', as Andrewes puts it, but fatal. Andrewes' offered translation puts 'at least in my time' in a kind of parenthesis at the end of the sentence, but that distorts the Greek, in which the temporal indicator ('first') and the qualification ('in my time at any rate') are juxtaposed, at an early and emphatic point in the sentence. Andrewes could have cited, but does not cite, Xen. *Hell.* ii 3.15 in favour of his view, where *prôtos chronos* certainly means 'in the first phase', *vel sim.*, but in that passage the phrase is in the dative, which puts the meaning beyond doubt.

[26] Again, Andrewes seems to me wrong: the expression 'moderate blending' makes it clear that structure, not behaviour, is Thucydides' concern here. See also G. Donini, *La posizione di Tucidide verso il governo dei Cinquemili*, 1969, for lengthy discussion of viii 97 as a whole.

describing political or other kinds of behaviour.

The conclusion must be that Thucydides praises political arrangements which were not fully democratic. Syme said of him: 'Shall it then be supposed that Thucydides was an oligarch? If so, what kind of oligarch? Perhaps a lucid and non-practising oligarch.'[27] Certainly, to judge from the passage we have just discussed, not an extremist of the Kritias type. (When Kritias died, his friends put up a funeral monument on which was carved a picture of Oligarchy with a torch, setting fire to a personification of Democracy. The inscription announced: 'This is the monument of good men, who for a short while restrained the *hubris* of the accursed Athenian *demos*'.)[28] One would have ranged Thucydides with moderate oligarchs like Theramenes but for the sneer against this man a few chapters earlier, where he is accused of private ambition and of political insincerity. (We discussed this in Chapter 6, however, and accepted that Thucydides may here reflect merely the bias of his sources, who on this occasion were right-wingers with a grievance.) The *Old Oligarch*, a right-wing pamphlet, offers tempting parallels to Thucydides, but that document bristles with interpretative problems.[29]

Admiration for orderly oligarchic government is implied by other passages. He is critical of oligarchies *which take over from democracies*, because individuals pursue private advantage. But the words in italics are important: the whole passage is not, as it has been taken, a general comment on 'the characteristic weakness of oligarchy'.[30] Earlier in the same book (Book viii: note how much of our evidence so far has come from this least polished but most purely political of the eight) he says of the citizens of Chios that 'after the Spartans, they are the only people who to my knowledge have remained contented and

---

[27] *PBA* 1960. 51. L. Edmunds, *HSCP* lxxix, 1975 73ff. detects oligarchic sympathies in the Corcyra *stasis* section and elsewhere; but see n.32 below.

[28] DK 88 A13=Schol. Aeschin. i 39 p.261 Schultz. I confess that I do not quite understand 'good *men*' in the plural.

[29] On viii 89.3 see above, p.141. The *Old Oligarch* (Ps.-Xen. *Ath.Pol.*), a work probably of the 420s, says (i 9) that a respectable constitution would disfranchise 'mad' i.e. common people. On the *Old Oligarch* see Gomme, *More Essays*, 38ff.; Forrest, *Klio* lii, 1970, 107ff.; *YCS* xxiv, 1975, 37ff.; S. Cataldi, *La democrazia ateniese e gli alleati*, Padua 1984 (on i 14-18 but generally valuable). On the political viewpoint of Aristophanes, another tempting parallel, see below n.52.

[30] viii 89.3, further down the para. Characteristic weakness: Macleod, p. 129.

politically stable, increasing the security of their city in proportion to their prosperity'.[31] The word which I have translated as 'politically stable' is a cognate of *sôphrosunê*, which is an oligarchic code-word: it means generally prudence, temperance, sobriety, and came to have specifically conservative implications.[32] Thus Thucydides uses it of the wave of anti-democratic feeling in Athens after the failure of the Sicilian expedition.[33]

I suggest that what Thucydides admired about oligarchy of the 'long-term' Chiot sort (as opposed to upstart oligarchies, on which see the passage cited at the beginning of the preceding paragraph) was that it made *stasis* less likely. (The moral and material destructiveness of *stasis* itself is of course reserved for full treatment in Book iii, when events at Corcyra are put under the microscope; and Elizabeth Rawson is right in her book on the Spartan tradition in European thought to say that Spartan avoidance of *stasis* touches on Thucydides' basic preoccupations because stasis ruined other states involved in the war.)[34] This, rather than any doctrinaire conviction about the theoretically best form of government, lies behind his admiration for Chiot and Spartan arrangements. In the *Archaeology* he says specifically that Sparta had enjoyed orderly government (*eunomia*) and freedom from *stasis* and tyranny for a longer period than any other state known to him. The speeches are treacherous evidence on this as on all topics. There is lengthy praise of the Spartan way of life and education put into the mouth of King Archidamus in Book i, including a clear use of the word *sôphrosunê* in its semi-technical political sense.[35] Archidamus claims that Sparta was both free and glorious; but Pericles makes the same claims for Athens.[36] Which did Thucydides think was right? The speeches cannot tell us. But Thucydides' authorially expressed admiration for Spartan stability sounds genuine. If so, perhaps Socrates is the influence

---

[31] viii 24.

[32] See Helen North, *Sophrosyne*, Ithaca 1966, 111ff.; Andrewes, *HCT* v 159f. on viii 64 (Thasos: *sôphrosunê* ironic) is better than L. Edmunds, *HSCP* lxxix, 1975, 78, which Andrewes does not cite.

[33] viii 1.3.

[34] Oxford 1969, 21.

[35] i 18.1; 84.2 (Archidamus says Spartan *sôphrosunê* is sensible, *emphrôn*. On this passage see Andrewes, *HCT* v, 160).

[36] i 84.1; ii 37.2.

again. We looked at some aspects of the *Crito* in Chapter Five; in
that dialogue the personified 'Laws of Athens' are made to say to
Socrates: 'You chose neither Sparta nor Crete, which you assert
on every occasion to be states with good laws...'. This should be
given full weight: later, more Platonic and less Socratic,
dialogues also imply praise for Spcrta, but the *Crito* as we noted
is early, and more authentically Socratic.[37]

Naturally Thucydides was aware of Sparta's slowness and
proneness to suspect the motives of others. But it is a capital
error to mistake the abuse of Sparta, which Thucydides puts into
the mouths of certain of his speakers, for Thucydides' own views.
It is surprising to find, in a valuable and otherwise sophisticated
modern study of Euripides and Thucydides, that the Melian
Dialogue is quoted as showing that Thucydides thought of the
Spartans as 'in fact supremely guided by self-interest' or that a
passage from Pericles' Funeral Oration shows that 'the latter [sc.
Thucydides] feels that Athens at her best had a vigor and a
generosity' which contrasts markedly with Sparta.[38] It is fair
enough to cite,[39] in support of the claim that Sparta was in
Thucydides' view exclusively self-interested, her behaviour after
the 'trial' of the Plataeans, discussed above.[40] But against *that*
we must set his low view of Athens' leaders, to be considered
shortly (below, pp.166ff.). It cannot be emphasised enough that
the few authorial comments by Thucydides, and only such
comments, are the evidence from which we can hope to
reconstruct Thucydides' own opinions.[41] If we could safely

[37] *Crito* 42e with Woozley, op.cit. (1979) 154 n.1 and Rawson, op.cit. (1969),
p.28, rightly calling this passage the best evidence for Socrates' laconism. Popper
throws it out, but see Kraut (above, p.126 n.67) 216ff.

[38] On Spartan slowness, viii 96.5 (for instance) is authorial. The view criticised
in the text is that of J.H. Finley, *Three Essays*, ch.1, 'Euripides and Thucydides',
19f. On p.19 he says that on the subject of the Spartan character the 'thought of
the poet and of the historian is in close accord'. This is simply not a permissible
conclusion: Finley cites a large number of passages from Thucydides, drawn
indiscriminately from speeches and authorial remarks. I am less concerned (but
see below, p.169) to discuss Finley's treatment of Euripides, but it seems to me to
commit the same error, *mutatis mutandis*.

[39] Finley, p.19.

[40] On p.68. Strasburger, p.703, says that this and iv 80 (brutality to helots) are
the *only* blots on Spartan honour in Thucydides. I agree with Hussey (*CRUX*, 125
n.14) that this is too 'one-eyed' and we cannot say that Thucydides 'wholly
approved of Spartan institutions and foreign policy'.

[41] Colin Macleod, reviewing D. Proctor, *The Experience of Thucydides*, in the
London Review of Books for 21 Jan-3 Feb 1982, 26, was perhaps too pessimistic

ascribe to him every sentiment which he ascribes to his various speakers, the present chapter would be much longer – and much more self-contradictory. We have seen (Chapter Three) that speeches are by no means useless in arriving at what Thucydides thought: for instance, some speeches seem to be put in with a view to showing the futility, on a given occasion, of making speeches. That tells us something about Thucydides' view of the occasion in question, or the speaker on that occasion. And Thucydides' non-inclusion of speeches, when speeches were certainly made, implies warmly held opinions on his part.

Let us return to Thucydides' views on politics, resisting as far as possible the temptation to wish on him words of Archidamus or of Pericles, whether those words are the report, or the invention, of Thucydides (and for the present purpose it does not matter which answer we give to this, the problem of Chapter Three above).

The difficulty, to modern eyes, about Thucydides' equation of oligarchy with *stasis*-free stability, is this: the Athenian democracy was itself remarkably stable.[42] Thucydides himself comments, speaking of the oligarchic coup of 411, that it was not easy to deprive the Athenian *dêmos* of its liberty, a hundred years after the fall of the Pisistratid tyrants, especially when for more than half that period they had been an imperial people.[43] What strikes us is how little *stasis* there was at Athens from 510 to 403. The two right-wing movements of 411 and 404 were brief and happened for special reasons: the first because of an economic crisis and the temporary absence at Samos of the fleet, and the second because of Spartan interference. Thucydides does not try to explain Athens' freedom from class-conflict during the rest of the hundred-year period, in which the city saw the whole rainbow of political colours – tyranny, aristocracy, moderate Kleisthenic democracy, radical Ephialtic democracy, oligarchy

---

about the possibility of knowing what Thucydides himself believed (Thucydides, 'a man of whose life and opinions we know little'). But that is a better approach than the over-confidence and faulty method (below, n.105) of so much writing on this subject. I know of no really rigorous monograph or study of Thucydides' own opinions as a whole – rigorous in the sense of ruling the speeches out of account. Andrewes, *HCT* iv, 182-8 and v, 335-9 are exemplary on Thucydides' political views.

[42] On this see the 1986 Oxford D. Phil. thesis of my graduate pupil Carolyn Steppler, 'The nature of Athenian politics, 432/1-322 BC', final chapter.

[43] viii 68.

(briefly), radical democracy again. A proper explanation would have to mention the presence of metics (above, p.97), who provided cushioning against *stasis*: metics could not own land, which was a prerogative of citizens, so that the creation of new wealth by metics did not lead to social pressures for redistribution of land in their favour. Above all, the empire was managed in such a way that *all* classes benefited materially from it, not just the lower classes but the rich. It is a major defect of Thucydides' account and analysis of the empire – to anticipate a little – that he scarcely mentions the upper-class gains from the empire, our knowledge of which is partly derived from epigraphy.[44] The rich (as Phrynichus is made to hint briefly in Book viii) were for selfish reasons solid with the *dêmos* in desire to maintain the empire (the *Old Oligarch* has a hint to similar effect). Alcibiades might call democracy 'acknowledged folly', but Alcibiades' father Kleinias had been the proposer of a decree making tribute-collection more rigorous; outside the biassed pages of Thucydides, this kind of work was not left to democrats of the Kleon, Kleonymos or Hyperbolus type.[45] 'We are all democrats now', the Athenian aristocrats could have said, anticipating King George V. If the Athenian democracy was stable in the fifth century, that was largely because it was an imperial democracy. This does not quite explain why *fourth*-century Athens, after the loss of the empire, remained stable;[46] but this problem will seem less acute if we accept that fourth-century Athens was a less democratic place than the Athens of the fifth.[47]

There is none of this kind of analysis in Thucydides, though we saw in Chapter Five that he was alert, when discussing archaic tyranny, to the link between economic life and political change. Why the failure of understanding when he comes to his own day? I suggest that Thucydides was too close to his subject and too close to the prejudices of his own class. There is undoubted personal bias against men like Kleon (see further below), who were most vociferous and active in keeping imperial institutions

[44] In particular, the so-called Attic *stêlai*: see below, p.174 n.74.
[45] viii 48; vi 89; ML 46, 68, 69. *Old Oligarch* ii 20.
[46] See O. Murray, *TLS* for August 26, 1983 at p. 896, reviewing M.I. Finley, *Politics in the Ancient World*, Cambridge 1983.
[47] P.J. Rhodes, *Classical Journal* lxxiv, 1979-80, 305ff., 'Athenian democracy after 404 BC'.

going, and Thucydides failed to see that men of Kleinias' rich and aristocratic type (or like himself, with his mining concessions in Thrace, p.1 above) had a stake in the empire which meant that they had no interest in winding up the democracy – until Sicily and the events of 415-413 hurt them economically. There is a comparable problem about Aristophanes' view of the Athenian empire, as we were reminded recently.[48]

Bias against the volatility of the extreme Athenian democracy and its leaders takes the form of casual asides, of omissions, and of damaging attribution of motive – rather than sustained analysis of political and personal defects. Thucydides is fond of parenthetical remarks like 'as the people/crowd/mob is prone to do', usually said about something impulsive or silly.[49] Dislike of Kleon is shown by explicit rough handling in Book iii (where he is characterised as 'violent') and in Book iv, where his promises in the Assembly are 'mad' and there is a definite suggestion of cowardice about his avoidance of the Pylos command. (This is the prime instance of 'damaging attribution of motive': how did Thucydides know what Kleon knew?)[50] Thucydides' attitude to Kleon is, however, complex: he does not deny him some formidably effective oratory in the Mytilene debate, and this must be given its full weight, even if Kleon's knocks at his countrymen's passion for novelty and change do not straightforwardly reflect Thucydides' own views.[51] (This idea,

[48] W.G. Forrest, 'Aristophanes and the Athenian Empire', in *The Ancient Historian and his Materials*, 1975. I have discussed the implications of this article in the *Athenian Empire* LACTOR, p.21. See esp. Andrewes, *JHS* xcviii, 1978, 4.

[49] See, for example, ii 65.4 (about the reinstatement of Pericles); iv 28.3, where they egg Kleon on to take over the Pylos command from Nicias; viii 1 says contemptuously that 'they' (no subject is stated) blamed the orators, soothsayers etc. for getting them into the Sicilian commitment, 'as if they had not voted for it themselves'. Cf. *Old Oligarch* i 5 on the ignorance and indiscipline of the *dēmos*.

[50] iii 36.6; iv 39.3; iv 28. See above, p.78. Cf. p.140 n.15 on Hyperbolus.

[51] I say 'straightforwardly' because I agree, more or less, with Andrewes' guarded suggestions (*Phoenix* xvi, 1962, 75) on this point, best quoted rather than cited or summarised: '... Kleon's comment on Athenian delight in sophistry is prolonged well beyond its immediate tactical usefulness, and I cannot help suspecting that Thucydides through these speeches was trying to say something that he himself thought important about the assembly and its leaders. Not, presumably, that he endorses Kleon and his strictures: one would more readily believe that Diodotus was his mouthpiece ...' The word 'presumably' is strong; Kleon's complaint at the end of ch.38, that the assembly behaves like an audience at a sophistic performance, rather than like responsible parlia-

however attractive, must be rejected if we are rigorous in not using speeches to arrive at what Thucydides himself thought.) But as we saw in Chapter Three, there is 'bias by omission' against Kleon in Book iv: in the peace debate at Athens in 425 the unsuccessful Spartans are given a long speech but Kleon is allowed no speech in reply, although he prevailed on the Assembly to rebuff the Spartans. Again, we know from inscriptions that the level of the imperial tribute was dramatically raised in the same year, probably at Kleon's instance, and that heavy borrowing – a legacy of Periclean optimism – had made this measure necessary. But Kleon gets no credit for this from Thucydides, not because Thucydides was indifferent to the financial factor but – surely – because of purely personal distaste for the demagogues whom Plutarch, possibly drawing on the mid-fourth-century writer Theopompus, correctly associated with the tribute increase; so too did Aristophanes in the *Knights*, our other main literary source for the hostility which demagogues like Kleon could arouse.[52]

mentarians, is not unlike Thucydides' own comment at the beginning of Book viii, that it was illogical for the assembly to blame the orators, etc. (see above n.49) as if they had not voted for the Sicilian expedition themselves.; cf. *Old Oligarch* i 17 with Gomme, *More Essays*, 42. (Macleod observes, *Essays*, 92 n.17, that at i 22.4 Thucydides spurns rhetorical contests of the kind Kleon blames; here is a further 'endorsement' of Kleon). Consistent with his own view (Diodotus likelier to be the mouthpiece), Andrewes in his commentary on viii 1 (*HCT* v, 5) no less appositely cites *Diodotus* (iii 43.4-5) for the view that 'voters ought to be treated as equally responsible with their advisers'. Surely it is better to say that we cannot presume that Thucydides endorses *all* Kleon's strictures (any more than we can presume that he endorses all that Diodotus says). The fact, if it is a fact, that he endorses some of what Kleon says, and the fact that he explores the idea of assembly sophistry by giving telling sentiments to Kleon whom he disliked, imply some respect for the man, unless (as I do not believe) this section is a sustained exercise in irony.

[52] Tribute raised: ML 69, and commentary (I do not follow F. Bourriot, *Historia* xxxi, 1982, 404ff. who rejects one of the most important prosopographical arguments in Greek history, the identification of the Thoudippos who moves this decree as a son-in-law of Kleon, on the evidence of the 'Kleon son of Thoudippos' in Isaeus ix; this Kleon would be the grandson of the demagogue Kleon). Borrowing: ML 72 (temple accounts). Thucydides not indifferent to finance: above, p.33 n.81. Demagogues and tribute: Plutarch, *Aristides* xxiv, who however wrongly denied that the war made the increases necessary. From ML 72 we can confidently correct him. See further n.54 below. Aristophanes: *Knights* 313. Whether a clear and consistent political position can be ascribed to Aristophanes, and if so what it is, are much disputed questions; in my view the certainties are too few to justify trying here to compare his stance with Thucydides' (but see n.48 above); I hope to return to this topic.

Thucydides may have neglected the tribute increase for another reason too: if Kleon was right to raise the tribute, Pericles had been wrong to say that the war could be financed from existing resources.[53] In fact, he was responsible for failing to foresee the financial difficulties in which Athens was to find herself, and from which the demagogues extricated her; and to that extent Thucydides' praise of Pericles' *pronoia*, foresight, in the obituary notice in Book ii, was not justified,[54] nor was the disparaging contrast between Pericles' methods and those of his successors who 'did everything in the opposite way to Pericles'. We noted in Chapter Five that that obituary was too kind to Pericles in another respect also: it says that he was a genuine *leader* who did not indulge his supporters at all, but no politician, least of all an orator in the quicksilver Athenian assembly, could really get away with this sort of superior nonchalance.

These are serious distortions, and we must add that even on the most lenient view Thucydides changed the emphasis of his judgments on Alcibiades (Chapter Six above).

Can any generalisations be extracted from his preferences for people? He attributes virtue (*aretê*, see below) to Nikias, who he thought did not deserve his atrocious death; but that is essentially a private judgment, on Nikias as man and citizen, and not inconsistent with the judgment that Nikias' addiction to 'divination and that sort of thing' was excessive. The latter is surely a *military* judgment: superstitiousness in a civilian or a private soldier would not deserve comment, but since it led to indecisiveness it was a fatal flaw in a general.[55] Thucydides admired effective action (note *drastêrios*, used to sum up this quality in Book iv. That was said about Brasidas, who is also singled out for his oratory a few chapters later – 'not bad at speaking, for a Spartan'; a patronising remark. Wade-Gery commented of Thucydides that 'concentrations of energy were to

---

[53] ii 13.

[54] *pronoia*: ii 65.6, cf. para 5, *prognous tên dunamin*. See Andrewes, *Didaskalos* iv, 1972, 161: 'financial documents (notably Meiggs and Lewis no.72) conspicuously falsify Perikles' optimistic estimate of Athens' capacity to pay for the war, but that does not mean that Thucydides reported Perikles incorrectly, though he can be charged with failure to note the way things turned out in practice.' Leadership: above, p.122.

[55] vii 86.5; vii 50.

his taste', and instanced Athens and Alcibiades.)[56] But I doubt if
for instance Thucydides' praise for the *aretê* of Antiphon implies
admiration for more than this man's technical proficiency as a
speaker, and perhaps for the loyalty with which he would rally to
his friends when they were in trouble in the law-courts.[57] This is,
to invoke a modern distinction, 'competitive' rather than
'co-operative' *aretê*. Nikias and Antiphon are praised not for
their morals but for competitive, social, excellence.[58] As for
Alcibiades (to return to him), we have seen that Thucydides was
forced to modify his originally dismissive opinion, but even the
chapter giving the modified conclusion insists that Alcibiades'
behaviour, and resentment by others of that behaviour, was
disastrous for Athens. It might be better to say that Thucydides
was impressed by, rather than admired, the man. Andrewes
many years ago wrote severely that 'the trouble with Alcibiades
was that he wanted Pericles' position without undergoing
Pericles' apprenticeship or modifying the style of his personal
amusements'.[59] This perhaps approximated to Thucydides' own
view, except that he was not specially interested in Pericles'
apprenticeship, treating his ascendancy as a matter of charisma.
Other scholars have compared Thucydides' summing-up of
Alcibiades with 'the harsh portrait of the "young men" that
Theseus gives in rebuking Adrastus' (a reference to the *Supplices*
of Euripides).[60] This too is illuminating, provided we remember
that it is surely as true of Euripides as it is of Thucydides that his
own views are not necessarily identical with his speakers'; and
with Euripides the problem is worse because *all* 'his' views are
really those of his speakers: unfortunately he did not write
Prefaces like George Bernard Shaw and so we have no utterances
we can call authorial, in the way that some of Thucydides'
utterances are. (It seems agreed that tragic *choruses* cannot be
treated like Shavian Prefaces; and that 'it is wrong to treat
choral utterance as a direct indication of what the dramatist

---

[56] *Drastêrios*: iv 81; Brasidas' oratory: iv 84. Wade-Gery, *OCD²*, s.v.
Thucydides, 1069.

[57] viii 68.

[58] See A. Adkins, *Merit and Responsibility*, Oxford 1960; and on Nikias' *aretê*
specifically, *GRBS* xvi, 1975, 379ff.

[59] *JHS* lxxiii, 1953, 3 n.6.

[60] Macleod, *Essays*, 149; J.H. Finley, *Three Essays*, 23. (See Eur. *Suppl.* 232-7,
with Thuc. vi 15.)

wishes us to think about the enacted story'.)[61] Here is an
example of a very forced attempt to extract agreement between
Thucydides and Euripides, on a particular individual, from
insufficient evidence: Thucydides' remark about Nikias' *aretê*, it
is claimed, 'echoes what seems to have been the judgment of
Euripides, who at the end of the *Electra* (1351-2) sends the
Dioscuri off to Sicily to help the righteous' – and the Greek is
quoted, 'those who in their life love piety and justice'.[62] If this is a
Euripidean reference to Nikias, it is not in very good taste:
Euripides goes on to make the Dioscuri say they will *save* such
people from their troubles; Thucydides' comment was prompted
by Nikias' deplorable *end*. But the real objection must surely be
to the assumption, apparently based on nothing more than the
combination of the ideas of 'Sicily' and 'righteousness', that we
have here an authorial judgment by Euripides on Nikias.

We have not yet, however, exhausted Thucydides' praise for
individuals. Autocratic rulers like Archelaus of Macedon and
even the Pisistratids are commended with scarcely a qualification, though Syme observed of Archelaus: 'One of the

[61] K.J. Dover in Dover (ed.), *Ancient Greek Literature*, Oxford 1980, 60-5; the
quotation is from p.65. Note also Dodds, *The Ancient Concept of Progress*,
Oxford 1973, ch.v, 'Euripides the Irrationalist', at 80f. for a balanced view: 'There
are choruses in Euripides who affirm their belief in ... things which we have good
reason to think that Euripides did not believe in. On the other hand, there are
many places where Euripides does seem to speak through his Chorus, even at the
sacrifice of dramatic appropriateness, as when he makes the villagers of
prehistoric Pherae describe themselves as deeply read in poetry and philosophy
and convinced necessitarians'. On the other hand, some Sophoclean scholars
come close to identifying Sophocles with his choruses: Ehrenberg, *Sophocles and
Pericles*, 1954, 72, says: 'Not only the chorus is afraid of this; we can say that it is
the poet himself who expresses his highly emotional and pious beliefs ...' etc.;
and R.W.B. Burton, in the *Oedipus Coloneus* chapter of his *Chorus in Sophocles'
Tragedies*, 1980, seems to hanker after a similar view. But Dover's formulation is
hard to fault. Note that in another place Dover has excellent things to say about
the way Euripides 'uses fictitious characters as instruments for the development
of ideas which are interesting in their own right': see his 'The freedom of the
intellectual in Greek society', *Talanta* vii, 1976, 24ff., esp. 44. The best
conclusion is that neither characters nor choruses tell us where Euripides stood. I
reserve for this footnote a third possibility, that the *exodos* or final section of a
Euripidean tragedy is specially likely to allude to contemporary events (and so,
presumably, to betray authorial views). This idea was disposed of in some
withering pages by G. Zuntz, *The Political Plays of Euripides*, Manchester 1963,
64ff.

[62] By J.H. Finley, *Three Essays*, 46. Zuntz, op.cit. (1963) 66ff., discussing this
part of the *Electra*, does not specifically deal with the supposed reference to

interlocutors in the *Gorgias* of Plato (471b) comes out with a startling allegation: Archelaus pushed a boy prince down a well.'[63] As for the Pisistratids, they are credited with both *aretê* and *xunêsis*, intelligence; under them the city kept its laws – except that they ensured that one of their number should always hold high office. Like Cicero, for whom the Pisistratids stood for mild tyranny,[64] Thucydides could distinguish between such behaviour and that of monsters like Phalaris of Akragas, who roasted people alive in a brazen bull. But Thucydides certainly had no objection in principle to one-man rule. He admired success and had no time for the well-intentioned bungler. (George Cawkwell has remarked to me that Thucydides' judgments on people tend to be black and white; his characters never do the wrong thing for the right reason. This does not mean he is blind to the pathos of heroic failures like the Plataean resistance to Thebes in Books ii and iii.)

It is hard to say what our final judgment ought to be about the main preoccupation of the hedgehog Thucydides: the Athenian empire, the most strikingly successful phenomenon of the age, the eventual failure of which must have inflicted a trauma commensurate with that success. In the fourth century, Isokrates defends the empire by urging that Athens' fifth-century record had not been, on the whole, bad.[65] In the present day historians of left-wing leanings prefer to stress the way in which democratic Athens supported and exported democracy elsewhere; the tough imperialist measures attested by the inscriptions – tight grain controls at the Hellespont, and so forth – are then condoned by reference to the special needs of Athens as a state whose population was too large to be fed from her own resources.[66] Whatever one thinks of this (and the economic benefits enjoyed by individual Athenians went well beyond the satisfaction of hunger) these are not the terms in which Thucydides sought to explain or justify the empire. Notoriously, his speakers do not deny or palliate the harshness of Athenian

---

Nikias, but he hardly needs to since he shows that the phrase 'Sicilian sea' is quite vague, and rejects any association with the events of 415-413 at all.
  [63] *PBA* 1960, 51. See Thuc.ii 100 (Archelaus); vi 54 (Pisistratids).
  [64] *Ad Att.* viii 16.
  [65] Isoc. iv, *Panegyricus.*
  [66] G.E.M. de Ste Croix, 'The popularity of the Athenian empire', *Historia* iii, 1954/5, 1ff., and ch.v of *The Class Struggle in the Ancient Greek World*, 1981; above all his *Origins of the Peloponnesian War*, 45f.

methods, as Isokrates was to try to do; on the contrary, both
Pericles whom Thucydides liked and Kleon whom he disliked,
use the word tyranny about Athens (above, p.56). This takes us
no further towards Thucydides' own view. When Thucydides
describes the beginnings of the empire, he speaks only of revenge
against Persia, not of the economic necessities on which modern
commentators rightly insist.[67] Finally, although there is a
celebrated sentence in Thucydides, endorsed by the *Old
Oligarch*, which claims that democracies everywhere favoured
Athens, this sentence occurs not in an authorial passage but in a
speech (of Diodotus, in the Mytilene Debate), and can be
countered by Phrynichus' assertion that the allies would prefer
to be free of control by either Athens or Sparta.[68]

Certainty about Thucydides' own opinions is not to be so
easily won. The sentence, uttered about the Athenian Empire,
that 'everything that is born is destined to decay' is put into the
mouth of a speaker – Pericles towards the end of his life – who is
made to celebrate the Athenian empire in terms of power and
success, not of political or cultural benefits. The organic
metaphor is seriously meant, a point to which we shall return in
a moment, when we shall see that Thucydides himself conceived
the relation between state and individual in organic terms.
Applied to the empire, the organic view would imply that
Thucydides agreed with the views he attributes to Pericles: that
the end of the empire, which as a matter of fact he lived to see,
had been an inevitability from the start – a view of the rise and
fall of empires commonly held in antiquity.[69] The idea of organic
growth towards sea-power and imperialism is certainly present
(above, p.130) in the *Archaeology*, all of which represents
Thucydides' own words and thoughts: he speaks of the growth or
increase of navies, and lists the factors which inhibited that
growth; the word for increase is picked up at the beginning of the
Pentekontaetia, when he says: 'This is how the Athenians
reached the position where they "were increased" [i.e. grew
powerful].'[70] If things grow, they decay *naturally*, and

[67] i 96.1.
[68] iii 47.2; viii 48. *Old Oligarch* iii 10. The next para. of the *O.O.* however alludes
to occasional Athenian toleration of oligarchies; on this see my LACTOR
Athenian Empire 101ff.
[69] See J. de Romilly, *The Rise and Fall of States According to Greek Authors*,
Ann Arbor 1977. Pericles on the empire: ii 64.3.
[70] i 16; i 89.1.

Thucydides would not have needed to find a culprit. But in fact Thucydides also believed that the Athenian empire tended towards excess after success, and this was what undid it. This is shown by phrases in Book iv – they were greedy for more, they were puffed up by success at Pylos. As we have seen in Chapter Five, Edward Hussey has shown that both Democritus and Thucydides in his own person regarded stasis, and the corrupt theories of certain sophists, as a kind of disease afflicting a city. (At Corcyra, Thucydides explicitly says that the root cause is *pleonexia*). If Thucydides held that kind of organic view about the Athenian empire (which is simply another way of saying 'Athens, considered as an imperial city') we are entitled to ask what he thought were the causes of Athens' disease, given that decay is inevitable, disease not.[71]

And in fact Thucydides is specific about that: desire by politicians for private gain (he does not specify what kind of gain), and private quarrels between them, rather than particular disasters like Sicily, ruined Athens in the end. It is not strictly inconsistent with this that in Book vi he explains Athenian designs on Sicily as themselves due to a *popular* desire for a never-ending source of pay or revenue.[72] But the main objection to Thucydides' view is that it puts too much on to that one particular generation of which Thucydides had personal experience. Moses Finley has objected to what we might call the 'harshness-of-Kleon error',[73] the view that the really aggressive features of the empire were all the work of Kleon and his generation. His objection was based partly on the correct grounds that the activities of Kleon, fully reported by Thucydides and ridiculed by Aristophanes, are merely better-documented than, but not really different from, the behaviour of

[71] iv 21.2; 65. Hussey: above, p.129 n.79. *Pleonexia* the root cause at Corcyra: iii 82.8 ad init., where the word is coupled with *philotimia* on which see above, p.119 n.47. Gomme renders: 'The cause of it all was power pursued for the sake of greed and personal ambition', and says rightly that not all *archê* (power), obviously, brings such bad results, only that pursued, etc. In other words greed and ambition are the root causes, and *archê* is only superficially the 'cause'.

[72] ii 65.7 and 12. Motive for Sicily: vi 24. Thucydides gets full credit from M.I. Finley (*Ancient History: Evidence and Models*, London, 1985, 77) for thus stressing the 'profit-motive', which Finley says modern historians too often do not.

[73] M.I. Finley, 'The fifth-century Athenian empire: a balance-sheet', in *Imperialism in the Ancient World*, Cambridge (1978) edd. P. Garnsey and C. Whittaker, 103ff.

Kimon, and Kleinias, earlier in the century. We can add that it is clear, from inscriptions rather than from Thucydides, that the Athenian upper class owned land in the territory of allied states;[74] we do not know when this abuse started, but we have no right to think it was an innovation of the Peloponnesian War period. It was strongly resented, as we see from the clause in the charter document of the Second Athenian Confederacy (377 BC) which explicitly forbids individual Athenians to acquire land in allied territory.[75] What of Pericles himself? There was blood on his hands after the suppression of the revolt of Samos in 440/39, when he had the Samian trierarchs brutally killed, an item reported by Plutarch not Thucydides.[76] As Andrewes said when discussing the Melian Dialogue,[77] 'the concrete implications' of Pericles' advice to *keep the allies in hand*[78] are 'not reassuring'.

We must conclude that in Thucydides' view the responsibility for the failure of the Athenian Empire lay with the generation in whose time the failure happened, even if we should prefer to trace the policies of that generation back to Pericles and earlier. The better view is surely that Athens' mistake was in allowing the war to happen at all, by provoking Corinth in various ways – by the pressure put on Megara and Corcyra; also on Potidaea, not only by raising the tribute of this Corinthian dependency but by the founding of a large-scale Athenian colony at nearby Amphipolis in 437. All this happened in the 430s. This, rather than the events of 425 and Pylos, was the 'culpable' greed or *pleonexia*; the inverted commas are there because the criterion of culpability is simply success or failure: Thucydides makes no facile connexion between immorality and failure. If the above argument is right, the real mistakes were after all mistakes of the 430s and earlier. That means that they were Periclean mistakes. Personal prejudice – the spell of Pericles and the nostalgia for

[74] *Hesperia* xxii, 1953, 225ff.; xxv, 1956, 178ff. These are the so-called 'Attic *stēlai*' recording the sale of property of rich men convicted after the profanation of the Mysteries and the mutilation of the herms, two major scandals of the year 415 BC. Cf. M.I. Finley, 'The fifth-century Athenian empire' 116; J.K. Davies, *Wealth and the Power of Wealth in Classical Athens*, 1981, 55ff. I have discussed the implications of this for our view of the empire in LACTOR *Athenian Empire*, 146ff., 'The Athenian upper class and the empire'. *Old Oligarch* i 19 may refer to such properties. Cf. generally Andrewes, *JHS* xcviii, 1978, 4f.

[75] Tod 123, lines 135ff.

[76] Plut., *Per*.xxviii 2-3 with R. Meiggs, *The Athenian Empire*, 1972, 191f.

[77] *HCT* iv, 185; Gomme, *More Essays*, 104.

[78] ii 13.2.

Pericles induced by experience of his less stylish successors –
stood between Thucydides and a correct assessment of the
moment at which *pleonexia*, which had been there from the
Periclean period, and indeed from 479 and the beginning of the
empire, began to have effects which would be fatal.

What are the implications of this for Thucydides' own view of
human action and suffering? In Chapter Five we saw that
Thucydides makes use of epic and tragic techniques (we declined
to follow the sceptics all the way in their denial that Thucydides
was influenced by tragedy). But Thucydides' judgment on the
reasons for Athens' defeat in the war, and the loss of her empire,
carries very different implications from much contemporary
tragedy. Thucydides absolutely declines to conclude that 'the
doer shall suffer', *drasanti pathein* in the phrase of Aeschylus; in
this he is unlike Xenophon, an explicit moralist (above, p.133),
who said that the Spartan defeat at Leuctra was a punishment
for their impiety on an earlier occasion, or Aeschylus'
Agamemnon, who suffered for killing Iphigeneia. Nor is there
any idea that one generation pays for the mistakes of a previous
generation, as Croesus in Herodotus pays for those of his
predecessors in the Mermnad dynasty: imperial Athens was not
the house of Atreus. Avoidable mistakes, Thucydides implies,
were made *during the war itself*; that is the only possible
conclusion from Pericles' obituary.[79] It happens to be a wrong
conclusion, if the arguments above are correct. But in any case
Thucydides goes less far than even the most unpoetical modern
scholars would wish to do, in his refusal to trace the end of the
empire back to its beginning, or to mistakes made *en route*.[80]

In these respects Thucydides the general has got the better of
Thucydides the poet; were it not for the crucial passage in Book i
where the fact of the Athenian empire is said to be the 'truest
cause' of the war, we might want to say that the journalist in

---

[79] ii 65. For the events of the 430s (Potidaea, etc.) see my *Greek World* ch. 8.
Amphipolis: Thuc. iv 102.

[80] The *Pentekontaetia* in Book i is not adequate, being too baldly factual (and
jumping right over the crucial years 439-434). The statement that Themistocles'
wall-building in the 490s 'laid the foundations of the empire' (i 93.4) is a piece of
rare percipience. It was the continuation of this wall-building after the Persian
Wars which began the Atheno-Spartan tensions: i 92. Unfortunately, though,
this line of explanation is not consistently followed through, because i 95 implies
ready Spartan acquiescence in Athenian leadership in the early 470s. See my
Greek World, ch.2.

Thucydides has made the usual journalistic error of sacrificing the long view to the vivid, snap judgment ('the greed of the demagogues ruined Athens') which makes for better copy. What he failed to see was that the 'truest cause' of the war, which he correctly diagnosed, and the 'truest cause' of the Athenian defeat, which he incorrectly saw as the greed of a particular generation of Athenians and politicians, were identical: the empire was built on greed. The 'truest cause' of the war could have done double duty as the 'truest cause' of the Athenian defeat.

It is time to come back briefly to Thucydides' view of the empire itself. We have desperately little to go on, once we have ruled out statements in speeches and have accepted that there is no firm authorial pronouncement. But we can now argue backwards from Thucydides' impatience with the generation which (he thought) ruined the empire;[81] from the way he is impressed by effective and successful individuals; and from his tendency to assimilate the conditions of states and of individuals. In this sense he was impressed by Athens (it is better to avoid the word admiration, with its moral implications)[82] and by her splendour and success; but he was unable, for personal reasons, to identify the early date

[81] ii 65. Andrewes, in what must now rank as the basic discussion of Thucydides' view of the empire (*HCT* iv, 182ff., prompted by the Melian Dialogue), writes at p. 186 that Thucydides' 'feeling that the power of Athens was somehow admirable seems to me beyond question'. In support of this he cross-refers to his p. 184, where two points are made: first, it is said, 'the rhetoric of (for example) ii 64.3 is too warm'. This point must however be discarded: ii 64.3 is a speech of Pericles, and 'endorsing Pericles' at ii 65 does not involve Thucydides in endorsing all that Pericles says in ii 64 (contra Andrewes, *PCPhS* 1960, 6). We are left with Andrewes' second point: Thucydides' 'regret (even exasperation) at Athens' eventual defeat [is] too evident at ii 65'. This is indeed, I believe, *all* we are left with if we place the speeches to one side, as even the famous study of this topic by Strasburger (678ff.) fails to do. The same is true of D. Grene, *Man in his Pride: A Study in the Political Philosophy of Thucydides and Plato*, Chicago 1950 – a remarkable book nevertheless. (It was later re-issued with the dull title *Greek Political Theory*). On Loraux, *Invention of Athens*, 1986, see above, p.62 n.66. Note also E. Lévy, *Athènes devant la défaite de 404*, 1976, 62ff.

[82] Andrewes in *PCPhS* 186, 1960, 6, an earlier study of the dialogue, says that Thucydides admired the empire *and* thought it immoral, by the standards of private justice (on Andrewes' 'for empire itself there can be neither praise or blame' see below). Wade-Gery's phrase about 'what was to [Thucydides'] taste' is better (see above, p.168). The word 'impressed' may seem pathetically weak, but we are trying to deal in certainties. Grene, op.cit., p.54, concludes too much from 'the absence of any moral censure of the empire' comparable to that visited on the democracy.

or phase at which excess, greed, or *pleonexia* began to operate. It should be immediately added that Thucydides was impressed by Spartan success also, as authorial comments show; but since he did not see Sparta defeated he did not need to ask 'when did it all go wrong?' (Xenophon, in the period of whose writing life it all *did* start to go wrong for Sparta, did not have the mental equipment to ask, let alone answer, that question in sophisticated terms.) From what has been said earlier in this chapter I do not think that Thucydides' attitude to the Athenian empire has much to do with the fact that it was a democracy. We are left with small certainty: Thucydides is interested in and impressed by effective action and stable arrangements: the more effective and the more stable, the more deeply he is impressed. Disorders in the physical constitution of individuals suggested to him, as to others of his contemporaries, an analogy for the way in which states break down and fail. Athens broke down; Sparta did not. Impatient with that failure, Thucydides permitted himself to blame the culprits. But he got the wrong culprits. This reprobation is partly moral reprobation. Of course: we shall see that he is perfectly capable of making clear moral judgments in his own person; and Kleon and the demagogues, in their way, are (in his one-sided view) a disorder like the moral rottenness which he reprobates when discussing the Corcyrean *stasis*: see below. (These are 'moral' views; but there is another sense of 'moralist', already discussed, in which Thucydides is not a moralist – he does not seek straightforwardly to improve his readers.) However, reprobation of the greed, which in his view destroyed the empire, does not imply either moral approval or moral disapproval of the empire as an institution: wicked men might be the undoing of either a generally virtuous or a generally vicious system, just as a particular disease might attack and destroy either a body which was in other respects healthy or one which was in other respects unhealthy. To the extent that Thucydides (wrongly) regarded demagogic Athens as a declension in all respects from Periclean Athens, he must have approved of Periclean Athens *more*. (But note the reservations about even Periclean Athens implied by the praise of the 5000: above, p.160.) Similarly, if he (wrongly) thought that the word *pleonexia*, greed, was appropriate to the empire in Kleon's day but not earlier, he approved of earlier arrangements *more*. But it was faint Thucydidean praise of the empire before Kleon if the most we can say is: he (wrongly) thought that things became much worse in the 420s than they had been at unspecified earlier dates. And that really is the only judgment that can safely be extracted from his authorial remarks.

Before we leave Thucydides' purely political views, we ought to return to a question left suspended in Chapter Five: did Thucydides share the 'totalitarian' view of the state which he puts into Pericles' mouth? There is nothing explicit. We have noted more than once that Thucydides had an organic view of the state, and it is time to give the evidence. The most striking expressions of the view are in the mouths of his speakers: Pericles' parenthetical remark that imperial Athens will perish in the end like everything else; or Alcibiades' view that if a *polis* remains at rest it will wear itself out (he goes on to use the metaphors of old age and decay);[83] or Nikias' words, quoted in Chapter Five, about the duty of those who hold political office to imitate doctors and help or at least not harm the city. But if Pericles, in an earlier speech, makes a generalisation in the form 'whether a state or an individual', so too does Thucydides in his own person, in one sentence of the Corcyrean *stasis* section where he speaks of *states and individuals* having a particular moral outlook.[84] I wish strongly to emphasise the importance of this short phrase, undramatic compared to what Alcibiades is made to say, but authorial and thus usable in the present chapter in a way that a speech by Alcibiades is not. Such a view is surely also implied by the medical approach towards the Corcyrean *stasis*; by the collective seizure which attacked Athens at the time of the Sicilian expedition (the Greek is certainly metaphorical, and the metaphor is that of individual pathology);[85] and we can add that Hussey's work on Democritus and Thucydides (above) implies that both men held the 'organic' view of the state in general.

But can a 'Periclean' imperative, about the need for individual

[83] ii 64.3; vi 18.6.
[84] vi 14; i 144.3. The authorial passage is iii 82.2. (Note also ii 8.4. – again authorial – 'cities and individuals eagerly supported each side'.)
[85] vi 24.3; on *erôs enepese* here, see Hussey, *CRUX*, 132 and n.28. On the Corcyra *stasis* as disease, Hussey, p.134; cf. Cochrane, op.cit. (1929), 133f.: 'This analysis, which begins with a *katastasis*, and then proceeds to a description of symptoms, curiously resembles that of the plague at Athens ...' Hussey reminds me that the very first words (*ômê ... prouchôrêse*) are medical. So is *pasa idea katestê*, iii 81.5, cf. ii 51.1. See also Adam Parry, *YCS* 1972, 47ff. 'Thucydides' historical perspective', at p. 56.

interests to be subordinated to those of the state, be derived from this organic view? Surely not. On an organic view, the health of the whole organism depends on the health of its parts. It would be odd to say 'the failure of part of an organism is *better* than the failure of the whole', because the failure of each carries with it the failure of the other. The point is important: Thucydides does not in his own person make any such austere claims as he puts into Pericles' mouth; nor can we derive any such claim from statements which Thucydides *does* make in his own person. If this is right, it follows inexorably that Thucydides has fathered two distinct views on Pericles: the organic view and the totalitarian view.[86] I cannot explain this except by supposing that the isolated passage in the final speech, which as we saw in Chapter Five resembles things said by Sophocles' Kreon, Euripides' Erechtheus, and Plato's Socrates, is no more than an expression of a fashionable view, one which Thucydides himself did not cherish and so did not trouble to bring into line with things which he himself believed and which he elsewhere attributes to the same speaker and to others.

The arguments above make me reluctant to admit that Thucydides made any 'Hobbesian' distinction between the morality which prevails between individuals and the 'war of all against all' which prevails between states.[87]

[86] The 'totalitarian' view: ii 60.2; cf. above, p.125. By 'two distinct views' I do not mean 'two necessarily inconsistent views'. The 'totalitarian' Plato certainly held organic views: justice in the soul is discovered by examining the justice in the state (but the latter is defined very idiosyncratically). What I mean is that the organic and the totalitarian approaches represent two different ways of looking at the relation between state and individual: the former stresses the interdependence of, and the similarities between, state and individual; the latter stresses the subordination of individual to state. ii 60.2 is easily the most extreme statement in Thucydides of the second of these views. It is perhaps relevant that such very chill comfort is administered to *individual* grief in the Funeral Oration; but that hardly amounts to evidence for a 'totalitarian' outlook on the part of the Pericles whom Thucydides reported or created here.

[87] This view is held by de Ste Croix, *OPW*, 25ff. Hussey seems to endorse it as far as Thucydides goes, in his *CRUX* article. As for Democritus, Hussey says we have 'no indications' whether Democritus believed in 'moral interdependence' between states, but he goes on (p.122) to suggest how Democritus might in fact have seen states as having 'a legitimate moral interest' in maintaining peace, etc., in inter-state relations. He concludes, however, that there might still be 'no real basis for a notion of "justice" in international affairs'. I conclude that on this issue any attempt to illuminate what Thucydides thought by appeal to Democritus would be to seek to explain *obscurum per obscurius*. I have quoted Hussey at length because I do not wish to seem to invoke him for more than (a)

It may be objected to the above that Thucydides may indeed generalise psychologically about states, but his concern in what follows the passage about 'moral outlooks' is not the behaviour of states towards each other; it is an interior phenomenon which concerns him. This is true (but see below on the Athenian aspect at Corcyra). This does not settle the question, however: if Thucydides had given us anywhere a disquisition on inter-state morality (or lack of it) and behaviour, there would be no problem at all about discovering his views. My point is that there is nothing in his writings to suggest that he saw states as a moral category apart, in some metaphysical mysterious and frankly modern way. (There was of course a set of purely inter-state codes and practices about, for example, burial of the dead, Olympic truces, proxeny arrangements and so on.) It is a banal but relevant truth that ancient 'states' were tiny, in area and population, compared to the states with which Hobbes was familiar, let alone the twentieth century. (So my own talk of the 'super-powers' is anachronistic.) The slowness of Sparta – that is to say, her handful of decision-makers – is a psychological characteristic; but it affected foreign policy. Surely the same is true of moral outlooks. At the outset of the work Thucydides speaks of the whole war as a convulsion or disturbance affecting both the principal states at the acme, a biological word, of their power. This is inter-state talk, if you like. And he says specifically that the 'convulsion' at Corcyra later gripped the whole Greek world.

But perhaps (a problem to which we shall return) he thought states *do* always operate on an amoral level. Sparta (Chapter Three) discounts her allies' speeches with their talk of justice, and goes to war for practical reasons, and 'punishes' the Plataeans for motives of policy. Yes; but it is not only states who are said to disregard speeches and their appeals (see above, p.68 on Alcibiades and the impulse to dissolve democracy). It is certainly not true that the *profession* of moral motives is denied to

---

the view that both Thucydides and Democritus had a medical or organic approach to politics, and (b) the view that neither man was a sophistical relativist. Hussey tells me that he does not see DK 68 B267 (*phusei to archein oikeion to kressoni*, cf. S. Cagnazzi, *La spedizione ateniese contro Melo*, Bari 1983, 30 n.4; Gomme, *HCT* on i 76; J.H. Finley, *Three Essays*, 13) as evidence that Democritus had 'Thrasymachan' views. The fragment if genuine does not tell us what Democritus thought was *right*.

states. Discounting actual speeches (because I want an example
of something we *know* was actually said) I would stress the
passage early in Book ii where Sparta is said to have the goodwill
of 'Greece' (the biggest such generalisation in all Thucydides)
because she *poses* as liberator (above, p.5). Liberation implies
servitude or tyranny, which are moral notions; whatever one
thinks, and Thucydides thought, of Sparta's actual subsequent
record (and Plataea and her early behaviour in Ionia soon
aroused misgivings), the *notion* was surely of Spartan
manufacture; though it developed from a historical fact
mentioned in the *Archaeology*, namely Sparta's deposition of
archaic tyrants in the neutral descriptive sense of 'tyrant'. Here
(in Book ii) Thucydides says authorially that the Spartans had a
moral programme: *proeipein* (announce) is the verb. We cannot
moreover say 'but Thucydides (unlike most of Greece) must have
thought they were not sincere' without a circular appeal to his
supposed view that states never act without moral motives. (And
should 'were not' read 'were not all'?)

Another obvious objection to my view is that I have taken too
literally what for Thucydides was just a medical *façon de parler*:
he did not literally believe in a 'body politic' which had arms you
could amputate and a gall-bladder you could remove and which
suffered from nervous breakdowns. But if it is a figure of speech
for Thucydides himself, it is not a mere and explicit simile, as in
the speech he gives to Nikias, which speaks of the politician as
like a doctor. For Thucydides it is a whole-hearted and pervasive
metaphor (much more so than, say, the analogies between men,
on the one hand, and cities or Earth, on the other, in Sophocles'
Oedipus Coloneus). What is it to say that Thucydides saw the
world in a certain metaphorical way? One reply would be to say
that a great deal of what passes even now for scientific writing is
phrased in metaphor: 'that was a way of putting it', in T.S.
Eliot's words. The organic view was indeed, perhaps, 'not very
satisfactory'. But it does not follow, from our agreement that the
organic view was a metaphor, that it is unusable for the purpose
of finding what he thought about the morality of states. If we
recall what was said above about the small size of
decision-making groups, and the undoubted linguistic fact that
in political contexts the Greek for Athens is, as everyone who
learns to write a Greek prose is taught, not *Athênai* but *hoi
Athênaioi*, 'the Athenians', we shall find it easier to understand

how Thucydides made the slide (slide, not jump) to generalising psychologically, and I suggest morally, about states.

Thucydides' morality is however a topic to which I shall return soon; first I wish to examine briefly his attitude to religion. We have looked at his use of oracles. A passage about the evacuation of the Pelargikon at Athens is the closest he gets to scepticism. It does not make sense to ask if he 'approved' of oracles. It does make sense to ask that about religion. But even his few value-judgments here tell us nothing new. He approved of the Pisistratids for maintaining, he deplored the plague for undermining, conventional religious observance. That is, he liked order and stability and disliked the opposites. This we knew already (above, p.177).

After this it may seem superfluous to examine Thucydides' religious 'views'; it follows from what has been said already that Thucydides did not think that the interference of the gods is a force in human affairs. In this he is unlike his predecessor Herodotus and his successor Xenophon, but resembles the author of the Hippocratic treatise *On the Sacred Disease*, who said that epilepsy was no more 'sacred' than any other. It is not possible to say confidently that Thucydides had no personal religion; he may simply have believed, like the Prophet in Plato's Myth of Er, that 'the blame is that of the chooser; the god is blameless'.[88]

It has however been claimed that Thucydides did after all believe in religion in a stronger sense than this; certainly he allows for 'the unexpected' as a factor in human affairs, and he realises (for instance) that the superstitiousness of Nikias, and of the Spartans, were relevant to the historical situation.[89] But not only does he himself not claim, he does not allow any of his apologists for the Athenian empire to claim, that Athenian rule was divinely sanctioned; the most that any speech claims is divine complicity. 'We know it to be true of men, and we infer it

[88] Sacred Disease i; Plato, *Rep.* 617e.
[89] The approach of N. Marinatos, *Thucydides and Religion*, 1981 (cf. *JHS* 1981, 138) is not followed here. Note H. Meuss, *Neue Jahrb*, 1892, 225ff.; C. Powell, *Historia* xxviii, 1979, 15ff.; J. Mikalson, *Sterling Dow Studies*, 1982, 217ff. Pelargikon: ii 17. Pisistratids and plague: vi 54.5; ii 52. Nikias, Spartans: vii 50; 18; add i 118 with p.82 above, and see A.J. Holladay and M. Goodman, *CQ* xxxvi, 1986, 152ff. 'Unexpected', 'chance', etc.: see the very useful collection of references in de Ste Croix, *OPW*, 25 n.52, 31 n.57; but he fails to distinguish speeches from authorial matter.

to be true of the gods, that they rule where they can': that is the Athenians in the Melian Dialogue.[90] Perhaps Thucydides went too far here: were all Athenians so sceptical and cynical? Brunt, discussing the differences between Athenian and Roman imperialism, shrewdly said of the Athenians that 'it seems very doubtful if many of them acknowledged publicly or in their own hearts that their empire was a tyranny and unjustly acquired' – but he goes on to say that Roman belief that their rule was divinely sanctioned was new. Is that true? That is, can we point to any evidence that Athenian rule was thought to be so sanctioned? The oracle at Delphi, about the middle of the fifth century, hailed Athens as 'an eagle in the clouds for all time'. And much use was made of religious themes in the imperial architecture of the Acropolis – an assertion of Athenian empire which Thucydides notoriously neglects. One of the few relevant items is the long chapter of Book iii which describes the purification of the island of Delos in 426, which was perhaps part of a bid for the political prestige conferred by control of the religious festivities of the old Ionian League.[91] Religious propaganda is not the same thing as religious belief; but it presupposes such belief on the part of those at whom it is aimed. If Thucydides deliberately suppressed any evidence suggesting that the empire had a religious justification, that implies an opinion of his own, namely that such considerations were irrelevant. What was his motive? Perhaps not *just* 'anti-clericalism', a word which Dodds once used to describe Euripides.[92] Part of the explanation may be that, as we saw in Chapter Four, he was blinkered in his use of archaeological evidence (I mean that expression in the sense of 'material remains'): he very rarely uses it except to make a point about the distant past. *Contemporary* buildings such as the Parthenon and the temple of Athena Nike, which arguably commemorated the battle of Marathon and the Peace of Kallias respectively,[93] were a category of evidence which he rejected in favour of *erga*,

[90] v 105.

[91] Brunt, *Imperialism*, 162. Delphi: Parke/Wormell, *The Delphic Oracle*. ii: *The Oracular Responses*, no.121. Delos: iii 104, a passage I have discussed in *Historia* xxxi, 1982, 241ff. The religious propaganda of the empire is well discussed in J. Barron, *JHS* ciii, 1983, 1ff., 'The fifth-century *horoi* of Aigina'.

[92] Dodds, *The Ancient Concept of Progress*, 78.

[93] Parthenon: J. Boardman in *Festschrift for F. Brommer*, 1977; Athena Nike: ML 44 and commentary.

political and military acts. If we ask, why the long chapter in Book iii, the answer may be personal: I have sometimes wondered if the 'purification' of Delos was entrusted to Thucydides himself, with his known interest in ancient history. There were sound propagandist and other considerations as well, but perhaps there was an antiquarian aspect to the project: we have seen (p.128) that the 420s were a decade of intense interest in the past. In the *Archaeology*, Thucydides draws on the 'purification' for an archaeological fact about the distant past (above, pp.93, 105). At least, Thucydides was in a good position in 426 to have a look at the Delos excavations for himself: the mid 420s are the years when we know he was prominent in public life. Just the man to be called in when the 'rescue dig' found some interesting old bones and armour. But this is the merest conjecture.

We must conclude that if Thucydides had religious beliefs they have not affected his historical judgment. Nor can we argue from them about his moral beliefs – the last topic we must look at.

Thucydides is often held to be some kind of 'amoral' thinker, at least in his attitude to relations between states.[94] Certainly the Melian Dialogue beautifully exemplifies a remark of one Kleochares of Chalkis, quoted by the fourth-century orator Aischines, which sums up much of Greek history: 'The small states fear the secret diplomacy of the great.'[95] But what did Thucydides himself think of this? It does not seem to me to be right to distinguish sharply between Thucydides' conception of public and private morality, between inter-personal and inter-state justice (see above). The difficulty with this distinction is well illustrated by the Corcyra *stasis* chapters in Book iii; is this 'public' or 'private' behaviour? Thucydides

[94] De Ste Croix, *OPW*, 18f. Contrast Andrewes, *PCPhS* 186, 1960, 6: 'Thucydides is not an amoral author', and his remark, quoted above, n.82, that Thucydides regarded the empire as immoral by the standards of private justice. De Ste Croix, *OPW*, 15 cites approvingly Andrewes' words on the same page, 'for empire there can, morally speaking, be neither praise nor blame', and writes that Andrewes gives this as 'Thucydides' assertion'. No; Andrewes is much more cautious: he is talking about a 'doctrine' expressed in the speeches, and says that for Thucydides the exclusion (in those speeches) of moral considerations constitutes a problem; that the 'empire-is-a-fact-of-nature' assertion ('this assertion', not 'Thucydides' assertion') was a rather imperfect resolution of the problem; and that even the austere Thucydides may not have felt at ease with this 'automatic' view of imperialism. This is wobbly support for de Ste Croix.

[95] Aischin. ii 120.

appears to be speaking of the way in which individuals treat individuals, but he also makes it clear that the *stasis* was worsened, perhaps even produced, by the presence, in the neighbourhood of Corcyra, of representatives of the super-powers Athens and Sparta. It has been rightly noted that Eurymedon, the Athenian general, could have intervened to stop the terror but stood aside; also, that Thucydides does not explicitly condemn Eurymedon for this.[96] Certainly, at the beginning of his whole analysis, Thucydides explicitly runs together public and private values, in a passage we have already stressed: what he says is that in peace and prosperity *both cities and individuals* have a morally better outlook.[97]

The Corcyrean *stasis* section is crucial for us because here for once we have sustained political and moral comment by Thucydides in his own person: nothing can be straightforwardly extracted from the Melian Dialogue, or the Camarina debate, about Thucydides' own position. But every sentence of the Corcyra section, difficult (and sometimes impossible) though the Greek is, represents pure Thucydides. In chapters 82-83, it has been well said, 'Thucydides makes it clear where he stood'; it is not with the sophists 'who denied the validity of any principle of morality but a short-sighted self-interest'.[98] This is the fundamental respect in which, for all his speakers' affinities with speakers in Plato's *Gorgias* and the first book of the *Republic*, with their identification of might and right, the essentially conservative Thucydides stands apart. (We cannot assume that the Aristophanes of the *Clouds*, who ridicules the sophists and their methods, felt strong *personal* disapproval: *mutatis mutandis*, I believe he should be treated as warily as we treat Euripides.) Even the Athenians in the Melian Dialogue do not unambiguously identify might and right, like Plato's Kallikles or Thrasymachus; rather they appeal to the truths of history and politics to argue that might excludes right, as a matter of fact: 'If Kallikles or Thrasymachus had argued thus, Socrates could have refuted them only by appeal to historic facts and not by the tricks of dialectic.' So Brunt, putting it very strongly indeed. Hussey by contrast says of the Athenians in the same passage that they go 'almost as far as "might is right" ' when they assert a Thrasymachan-sounding *nomos* or law of nature that one rules

[96] Gomme, *HCT* ii, 369, 385.
[97] iii 82.2.
[98] Gomme, *HCT* ii, 386.

whatever one can get control of: not a law *we* laid down, the Athenians say. I suggest that part of the trouble here is that the word *nomos*, 'law', a much discussed notion at this time, is being used in two ways: it is established *practice* to do as we are doing; but we did not lay down this *law*.[99] No other passage comes even this close to 'might *is* right'.

Perhaps Thucydides himself held the factual beliefs which he attributes to his Athenian speakers. We cannot say. What matters is that Kallikles or Thrasymachus could not have deplored, as Thucydides does, the disappearance in civil war of that 'simplicity, *euêthes*, which is the largest part of noble character'.[100] It is right to say that Thucydides in the 'faction'

---

[99] On the *Clouds*, I appeal again to Dover: see the cautious pp. lvi f. of his 1968 Oxford commentary.

The Brunt quotation (which concerns, specifically, v 105) is from *CR* xix, 1969, 200, a review of von Fritz, *Die griechische Geschichtsschreibung* i, 1967. Andrewes also carefully distinguishes the 'might-is-right' view from the 'empire-is-a-fact-of-nature' assertion, *PCPhS* 1960, 6.

Hussey on the Melian Dialogue: *CRUX*, 126. He distinguishes an initial Athenian position from a later and more extreme one. The first he thinks is at v 89: justice in international relations is just an unenforceable fair name. But Thucydides is not making the Athenians into 'Hobbesians' as this paraphrase implies; better to take the passage with Andrewes, *HCT*, 164: the Athenians allow that justice between cities is a usable concept if they are on the same level of power, but Athens is disproportionately stronger than Melos. Both Hussey and Andrewes think the Athenians are well short of a Kallikles or Thrasymachus position here. Grene, *Man in his Pride*, 62f. on force as 'the new natural justice' in Thrasymachus and the Melian Dialogue refers I think to my second passage.

The second passage is the one mentioned in my text. Andrewes, *HCT* iv ad loc. (pp. 174-5), comments: 'for the "law" of the stronger see the similar expression of it in i 76 by the Athenian delegates at Sparta'. But the Greek there is *kathestôtos*, which means 'established practice' in a much more unambiguous way than *nomos* at v 105, which thus seems to me to be uniquely difficult and close to a truly sophistic assertion (though Brunt is right that the appeal is essentially to the supposed *facts* that men and gods rule where they can, the fact in the case of the latter being a matter of inference). For *nomos* here see now Goldhill, *Reading Greek Tragedy* pp. 239 ff.

In any case none of this tells us what Thucydides believed. He says in his own person that the enslavement of Naxos by Athens was *para to kathestêkos* (i 98.4), which Gomme takes to mean 'against accepted Greek usage'; cf. above on *kathestôtos*. But the thought is odd anyway: how do you enslave somebody *according to kathestêkos*? In any case we cannot argue back from i 98 to a non-factual meaning for i 76.

When in Chapter Six I argued that Thucydides gives insufficient space to political theory I was not overlooking his coverage of crude doctrines of the i 76 or v 89 and 105 type. On all this, Jaeger, *Paideia* i, 391, 402 seems to me misguided.

[100] *To euêthes*: iii 83.1. The translation of this vital sentence is disputed. It is odd that so many of Thucydides' most important authorial comments should be

chapter is describing the *evils* of sophistic instruction.[101] To
return to a problem which has exercised us on other issues: how
far did Euripides share Thucydides' view? A famous passage in
the *Supplices* denounces the politician who makes wrong use of
his skill in speaking and puts private gain first.[102] The passage is
'anti-intellectual' in a way that corresponds to the anti-sophistic
mood of Thucydides' Corcyra chapters; and Euripides'
characterisation of such politicians as a kind of 'illness' is
specially interesting if we are right that this was Thucydides'
opinion also (p.173). But the passage is a *speech*, by an Argive

---

hard to translate: see p.160 for viii 97. and note that vii 86.5 on Nikias' *aretê* is
formally ambiguous (see *HCT* ad loc. for *nenomismenê*, and on the whole
judgment Adkins, art.cit. (1975)). Did Thucydides find these personal judgments
particularly awkward or embarrassing to formulate? Or is it just that we
scrutinise these interesting texts too closely? At iii 83.1 the problem is to know
whether nobility is the ingredient of simplicity or the other way round. Gomme
ad loc. and Adcock, *Thucydides and his History*, Cambridge 1963, 73 take *to
gennaion* to be the ingredient of *to euêthes*. But most translators (Hobbes,
Jowett, Warner in the Penguin, also Shorey, *TAPA* xxiv, 1893, 75) make
simplicity the ingredient: 'simplicity, which is so large an element in a noble
nature' (Jowett). This certainly makes an easier sentence in English. (Gomme's
'simplicity, in which a sense of honour has so large a part' is just about
intelligible, but at the cost of a rather free rendering of *gennaion*. Adcock's
'simple-mindedness, of which nobleness is a large ingredient' does not seem to me
to mean very much). The question has now been re-opened by Martha
Nussbaum, *The Fragility of Goodness*, Cambridge 1986, 507f. n.24, who has
convinced me that Gomme was wrong, and that *euêthes* is the ingredient. She
appeals to Plato, *Symp.* 211a (but Plato's usage may not be conclusive for a point
of Thucydidean exegesis) and Thuc. i 84.3, which is exactly comparable to iii
83.1. (*Aidôs sophrosunês pleiston metechei* ought in the context to mean that
moderation is a large element in shame.) Nussbaum does not cite Classen-Steup,
who adduce i 84 but nevertheless translate: ' "an welchem ein edler Sinn den
grössten Antheil hat" d.h.mit welchem er innig verwandt ist, vgl. i 84.3.' Only
thus, i.e. by taking *metechei* to refer vaguely to the 'intimate relationship' of
euêthes and *gennaion*, can i 84 be adduced as support for their view of iii 83.
Perhaps there is something in this and Thucydides meant to do no more than
express such a relationship, i.e. we should not read him too closely (it is
unnerving that instinct leads different scholars to opposite conclusions without
discussing other possibilities). But anyone who wishes to overturn Nussbaum's
view will have to deal with her argument about i 84, unless the passage is vaguer
than she and most commentators have assumed. *Thucydides' own factual
beliefs*: Andrewes, again admirably cautious, says (*PCPhS*, 1960, 6) that it is
'likely enough' that Thucydides subscribed to the view that the domination of the
stronger is one of the 'less attractive constants' of human nature. But it must be
insisted that no authorial statement can be produced to prove this, and
Andrewes' 'likely enough' is a recognition of that absence.

[101] Macleod, *Essays*, 128, in his paper on the Corcyra *stasis* chapters.
[102] Eur. *Suppl.* 412ff.; J.H. Finley, *Three Essays*, 22f.

herald: does it tell us anything at all about Euripides' own views? One feature of the speech has been noted: 'The herald scores a shrewd hit against democracy, which Theseus does not even try to answer ...'[103] That is, it is significant that Euripides leaves the herald's points unanswered, just as it is significant that Thucydides does not allow Kleon a speech in answer to the Spartan envoys in Book iv. But Theseus is not denied a speech; he merely prefers to defend democracy positively not negatively. Euripides' own views remain an enigma.

With the Corcyra chapters we are back where we started, with Thucydides' belief in the morally corrosive effect of war, the 'violent teacher'. We can now qualify that: the *pleonexia* which caused the *stasis* should not have been treated so sweepingly as a purely war-time phenomenon. Why did he do this? For the answer, we may perhaps return to the main result of the preceding chapter. We saw there that Thucydides came more and more to recognise that he had underestimated the importance of individuals. Now the most sustained discussion in Thucydides of the linked ideas of *pleonexia* and the end of the empire is in the obituary of Pericles in Book ii. This was certainly written late, at a time when the impact of men like Kleon, and above all of Alcibiades, had convinced him that the blame for Athens' downfall could be laid at the door of individuals, specifically, the individuals who came to prominence after Pericles' death. But, logically, Thucydides ought to have been led by this realisation to overhaul his account of earlier periods, and of earlier but equally dynamic individuals and the effects *they* had on the course of events, and to see that in Book iii he had made too tight, too exclusive and too abstract a connexion between war-time conditions and *pleonexia* in general (for this, and for the date of the Corcyra section, see also Chapter Six, p.154).

None of this invalidates Thucydides' view that war *aggravates* the effects of *pleonexia*. Belief in progress, as we saw in Chapter Five, is implied by the *Archaeology*. Macleod sees in the Corcyra chapters a more pessimistic belief that war undoes progress, or rather induces a specially twisted sort of progress: 'By learning from their predecessors men thought up new arts of aggression

[103] Macleod, p.148. Zuntz, op.cit. (1963), 21 says that according to Theseus' reply, democracy is the natural and ideal form of common existence. It is the freedom of all under the norm of equality; on this basis the tyrant's herald is conveniently refuted. 'Conveniently' is a recognition of Macleod's point that the herald is not really answered at all.

and revenge.'[104] In Chapter Five we compared the qualms voiced by a chorus in Sophocles' *Antigone*, about human *deinotês*, the Greek word for cleverness which also has implications of the terrible. We have seen that Thucydides is not a moralist, in the sense that he does not try to improve the reader directly, or distribute praise or censure on every page. But the Corcyra sections are the closest Thucydides gets to moral condemnation of that behaviour, and those actions, by states and individuals, which his eight books describe in, for the most part, such neutral language. It is astonishing, though, that his own position could ever have been mistaken, by any reader of the *euêthes* passage quoted above, for that of the fashionable immoralists of his generation;[105] or even that he could ever have been thought of as

---

[104] Macleod, pp. 125ff.

[105] I am not here arguing against a view which nobody holds. On the contrary see Oswyn Murray's chapter on the Greek historians, in the 1986 *Oxford History of the Classical World*. This chapter has brilliant things to say throughout, and has excellent and stimulating thoughts on Thucydides in particular. Nevertheless the two pages (195f.) on Thucydides' 'theory of politics' seem to me to suffer from the two main confusions which I have been discussing. Murray starts: 'Thucydides seems to accept as a general fact about human society that "might is right" – societies are in fact organised in terms of self-interest ...'. This confuses 'might-is-right' doctrines with 'might-excludes-right' factual beliefs; cf. n.99 above. Which is Murray talking about? The second, to judge by 'are in fact organised'. But we cannot just substitute 'might excludes right' because he goes on to say that Plato's Thrasymachus gives the clearest philosophical expression of 'such views'. However, Thucydides' speakers (see text for *nomos* at v 105) are not attempting, like Thrasymachus, to redefine justice, *to dikaion*.

The other confusion, one against which much of this book has been directed, is between Thucydides' views and those of his speakers. Murray speaks of Thucydides' 'acceptance of this type of social theory', but the only evidence offered is a speech of Pericles, the famous statement that Athens holds her empire as a tyranny, 'which it may have been wrong to acquire, but is dangerous to surrender' (ii 63.2). The two main authorial discussions in Thucydides. the Pericles obituary and the Corcyra *stasis*, are dismissed as occasions when Thucydidean analysis is 'less successful' than the speeches which 'serve more as a vehicle for exploring the consequences of the *Thucydidean view of politics*' (my italics).

On both points, the equation of Thucydides' position with the immoralists of his day, and the equation of Thucydides' view with his speakers', I believe Murray's account to be unacceptable. What he goes on to say about Sicily as tragic pride and calamity, after the tyrannical arrogance of the Melian Dialogue in 416, is a much better approach – we have seen that the *placing* of a speech at a given point in the narrative may be informative about the opinions of Thucydides – but does not save what has gone before. The idea that the juxtaposition of Melos and Sicily gives a clue to Thucydides' own view – Cornford; Zimmern, *Greek Commonwealth*[5], 443 – is not new. It is true that Thucydides was

morally, as opposed to linguistically, neutral ('amoral') in view of the devastating power of those admittedly rare passages where in both language and thought he drops all pretence of neutrality.

responsible for the *emphasis* he gives to the two events; but he did not invent the fact that the year 416 preceded the year 415 (or that the plague followed Pericles' Funeral Speech): cf. Dover, quoted above, p.111 n.5, for the banal but basic differences between 'Creon' and 'Cleon'. More important, though, Thucydides is – see text above – no facile Xenophontic *drasanti pathein* moralist: we cannot arrive at Thucydides' judgment on the imperialists of Melos by exclaiming, 'Look what happened to Athens next.'. His opinion may indeed have been that pride often leads to a fall, as Colin Macleod says, p.157. But perhaps we can apply to Thucydides something said about Herodotus: 'The mighty did fall – this was a fact of life, not the subject for a sermon (in any case proselytising was not an early Greek vice)': Forrest, p.xxxii of his introduction to Herodotus in Trevor-Roper's Great Historians. It was indeed no more than a 'fact of life' for Thucydides that the might of Athens would come to grief, if we are right that Thucydides saw such things 'organically'.

Conclusion
Thucydides' Virtues Illustrated

In the Introduction I said that Thucydides' influence was in one important respect malign: he narrowed the focus of *historia*, inquiry, so that matters other than war and politics were henceforth treated as secondary. Later (Chapter Six) I argued that Thucydides' vision was defective in another respect also: he allowed too little influence to theoretical ideas (such as sincerely held political beliefs) in his accounts of human action.

These are serious defects, and if I am right, why do I nevertheless regard him as a very great writer? One answer might be that it was precisely the seriousness and intensity of Thucydides' gaze which disqualified him from taking pleasure in the human landscape as a whole, so that ethnography, political theory, trivial Herodotean motivation in terms of the pursuit of women, and so on – even humour – got left out;[1] but he was thereby enabled to develop, for the first time in European thought, a conscious, secular theory of causation in terms of deep and superficial political causes (Chapter One, p.30). But in this final chapter I wish to take four passages, two famous two less so, and use them to illustrate Thucydides' strengths in detail.

---

[1] Serious defects: I pass over for the present purpose possible mistakes in judgment, such as his praise of Pericles' foresight or Phrynichus' military *xunesis* (ch. vii); or his neglect of the all-important Persian factor in the war (ch. vi). Such errors, if errors they are, *might* have been put right had he gone on working (though Oswyn Murray, *Oxford History of the Classical World*, 195 pertinently asks whether Thucydides would 'ever have faced the fact that ultimately it was Persian gold which defeated the Athenians?', despite ii 65. Conversely, the culpable lack of space given to theory in Book viii, at least, *may* be due to imperfect revision, p.142, rather than to a congenital or progressive tendency to see things in terms of personalities). *Humourlessness*: deliberate, cf. i 22.4 and (on puns) above p.94 n.88. There is only iv 40 (the spindle story: very grim) and vi 2.1 (Cyclops). Lateiner, *TAPA* cvii (1977) 175 n.6 notes that there are three mentions of laughter in Thucydides, and that each time the laughter is unpleasant (iv 28.5; vi 35; iii 83.1).

In Book iii Thucydides describes the implementation of the Athenian decision to reprieve the Mytileneans: they sent a second vessel out at high speed to overtake the first,

> since they feared that, unless it overtook the first trireme, they would find on their arrival that the city had been destroyed. The first trireme had a start of about twenty-four hours. The ambassadors from Mytilene provided wine and barley for the crew and promised great rewards if they arrived in time, and so the men made such speed on the voyage that they kept on rowing while they took their food (which was barley mixed with oil and wine) and rowed continually, taking it in turn to sleep. Luckily they had no wind against them, and as the first ship was not hurrying on its horrible mission, while they themselves were pressing on with such speed, what happened was that the first ship arrived so little ahead of them that Paches had just had time to read the decree and to prepare to put it into force, when the second ship put in to the harbour and prevented the massacre. So narrow had been the escape of Mytilene.

This is graphic and exciting; like much else in Thucydides it would make an excellent piece of cinema. (The detail about the food stays in the memory.) The point about the first ship not hurrying on its horrible mission has psychological insight, but the way Thucydides makes the point is unpretentious and even casual. As usual we are left guessing. Is the (implied) attribution of motive here the result of inquiry or inference or – more likely – a bit of both? Note also the prosaic and realistic addition about contrary winds, which could still have undone the Mytileneans even after the softening of hearts at Athens. Would Thucydides in that event have given us a Mytilene Debate at all? He knows that the wind on that occasion was not a divinely sent wind like that which delayed the fleet of Agamemnon. The final phrase 'so narrow ...' will be picked up at the beginning of Book vii when the arrival of Gylippus enables the Syracusans to scrape clear of danger.[2] With the next chapter, which I have not given, Thucydides changes gear after braking with this phrase about the narrow escape. What follows is a severe piece of prose with the administrative and financial detail of the settlement imposed (the land divided into 3000 holdings, rent of two minae

---

[2] iii 49; vii 2.4. The parallel is not noted in *HCT*, commenting on either passage. Robert Parker observes to me that the Athenians had 'moral luck' over the wind. For the notion see M. Nussbaum, *Fragility*.

for each holding, etc.). This is not, I think, 'tragic *akribeia*' as I have called it; this is the *epibda*, the 'day after' (but the untranslatable Greek word has connotations of 'hangover'): after the emotional turmoil and exhaustion of the chapter I have quoted, there was sober and not specially generous sorting out to do. The balance between the dramatic and the dreary could not have been held with a surer hand than in these two chapters of Thucydides.

In the chapter towards the end of Book vii where Nikias makes his final address to the Athenians before the disastrous sea-battle in Syracuse harbour, Thucydides reports his desperate efforts in indirect speech. Nikias felt, Thucydides says,[3] as men tend to do in a great struggle, that he had not said or done nearly enough, so he addressed the trierarchs individually by name, patronymic and tribe, invoking their own or their ancestors' reputations, their wives, children and family gods, and generally behaving as men do in such a situation, when they are no longer careful to avoid old-fashioned appeals. (The word for the last idea is *archaiologein*.) Since Nikias was to die shortly after this moment, these two paragraphs cannot be based on any report by Nikias of his own state of mind. What Thucydides gives is inference about a man staring disaster in the face. The two phrases which refer to wider human experience – that is, to the desire in a crisis to leave nothing undone, and the tendency to forget fastidiousness about sounding traditional – are in fact concealed autobiographical statements: Thucydides had commanded men in battle himself. This chapter reminds us that behind the subtleties of so many of Thucydides' speeches lies an awareness that intellectual fashions and movements like the sophists might come and go but family and honour are timeless in their ability to move the deepest emotions. It ought also to warn us not to think of Thucydides as too inscrutable and impersonal: he has here told us something about himself as well as about Nikias. It is not so easy to say of this passage, as of the Mytilene passage, why it is admirable; it sounds wholly sincere and convincing, but that is a subjective impression. It is an example of *to euêthes* – see previous chapter – in action, and if we sympathise with Thucydides' rejection of sophistic values we

---

[3] vii 69. The idea that Thucydides here 'faults' Nikias (D. Lateiner, *CP* lxxx, 1985, 203) seems to me extraordinary.

will sympathise with his attitude to this occasion too.

I should like finally to take two less celebrated passages of Thucydidean narrative, one long one short, which seem to me to illustrate him at his best. The first is from Book ii and describes a Peloponnesian attack on Akarnania in 429 BC:[4]

> The same summer, not long after this, the Ambraciots and Chaonians persuaded the Spartans to equip a fleet from allied resources and to send an army of 1,000 hoplites to Akarnania. Their object was to conquer the whole of the country and to detach it from the Athenian alliance, and they said that if the Spartans joined them in simultaneous operations by land and sea, the Akarnanians on the coast would be unable to combine for defence, that after gaining possession of Akarnania they could easily subdue Zakynthos and Kephallenia, and that this would make it more difficult for the Athenians to send their fleets round the Peloponnese; besides this there was a possibility of capturing Naupaktos.
>
> The Spartans were won over by these arguments and immediately sent out the hoplites on a few ships under the command of Knemos, who was still admiral. They gave orders for the fleet to get ready as soon as possible and to sail to Leukas. In all this the Corinthians were particularly energetic in supporting the Ambraciots, who were colonists of theirs. So the ships from Corinth and Sikyon and the other towns in that area made ready for the voyage, and the ships from Leukas, Anaktorion, and Ambracia, which arrived there first, waited for the others at Leukas. Meanwhile Knemos with his 1,000 hoplites crossed over from the Peloponnese without being observed by Phormio, who was in command of the twenty Athenian ships on guard off Naupaktos. They then immediately prepared for their march overland. The Hellenic troops with Knemos consisted of Ambraciots, Leukadians, and Anaktorians, in addition to the 1,000 Peloponnesians with whom he arrived. He had also contingents of native troops: there were 1,000 Chaonians, a tribe that is not governed by a king. This force was led by Photius and Nikanor, members of the ruling family who were in office for that year. With the Chaonians there were also some Thesprotians, another tribe that is not ruled by a king. The Molossians and Atintanians were led by Sabylinthos, the guardian of King Tharyps, who was still a minor. The Parauaeans were led by their King Oroidos and with them marched 1,000 Orestians who were subjects of King Antiochos and had been put by him under the command of Oroidos. Perdikkas also, without revealing his

---

[4] ii 80ff.

intentions to the Athenians, sent 1,000 Macedonians, who arrived too late to take part in the expedition. With this force Knemos set out on his march, without waiting for the fleet from Corinth. Going through the territory of Amphilochian Argos, they sacked the unfortified village of Limnaia, and arrived in front of Stratos, the biggest town in Akarnania, thinking that, if they captured this place first, the rest of the country would easily fall into their hands.

When the Akarnanians saw that they were being invaded by a large army by land and that also they would soon be confronted by an enemy fleet on the sea, they took no combined measures for defence, but stayed where they were to protect their own particular areas. They sent an appeal for help to Phormio, but he replied that he could not leave Naupaktos undefended at the moment when a fleet was just about to sail from Corinth. Meanwhile the Peloponnesians and their allies in three divisions were advancing on Stratos. Their intention was to camp near the city, and if they failed to win it over by negotiation, to make an attack on its fortifications. In their advance the Chaonians and other native troops were in the centre; on their right were the Leukadians and Anaktorians and those with them; and on the left was Knemos with the Peloponnesians and Ambraciots. There were large gaps between the divisions, which would sometimes be out of sight of each other. The Hellenes advanced in good order, keeping a proper look-out, until they pitched camp in a good position. But the Chaonians, who had the greatest reputation for their warlike qualities among the tribes in these parts of the country, felt so sure of themselves that, without waiting to occupy the ground for their camp, they rushed forward with the other native forces, thinking that they would capture the town at one blow and so win the credit for the whole action.

When the Stratians realised that they were still advancing they came to the conclusion that, if they could defeat this isolated division of the army, the Hellenic part of the force would be much less likely to attack them later. They therefore placed parties of men in ambush all round the city, and when the Chaonians drew nearer, they made a concerted attack on them both from the city itself and from the ambushes. This caused a panic among the Chaonians; great numbers of them were killed, and when the other natives saw them giving way, they also broke and fled. Meanwhile neither of the two Hellenic divisions knew that the battle was taking place, because the Chaonians were far in front of them, and it was assumed that they were hurrying on to find a position for a camp. But when the native army came rushing back on them in flight, they took them in behind their lines, brought their two divisions together into one force and stayed where they were for the day. The Stratians did not come to close quarters with them, since their reinforcements from the rest of Akarnania had not yet arrived; but they harassed them from a distance with their slingers and caused them much trouble in this way, since it was impossible to move except under arms. Indeed, it seems that in this form of warfare the Akarnanians are remarkably effective.

As soon as it was night, Knemos hurriedly retreated with his army to the river Anapus, which is about nine miles away from Stratos. Next day he recovered the bodies of the dead under an armistice. The friendly tribe of the Oiniadai were with him, and he retreated through their country before the Akarnanian reinforcements arrived. From there the contingents of his army dispersed to their various homes, and the people of Stratos put up a trophy for their victory over the Chaonians.

This passage is a straightforward piece of writing, and that is one of the reasons why I have chosen it: in this book I have emphasised, perhaps to excess, the assault which Thucydides' prose can sometimes make on the emotions. But he is able to startle us precisely because the mask slips so rarely. That is, the reaction against a 'positivist' view of Thucydides has been too extreme.[5] Here we have a solid slab of clear and unaffected writing, to remind us that Thucydides' emotions are not always engaged very intensely.

That does not mean that the factual material has been inartistically arranged. There is a gentle descent from the very general to the very particular. First, we are given the explanation, in terms of grand strategy, for the Ambraciot approach to Sparta: a suggestion that the ultimate prize of a successful invasion of Akarnania would be control of the Ionian islands Zakynthos and Kephallenia and thus of the sea-lanes which made it possible for the Athenian fleet to circumnavigate the Peloponnese. 'They might even hope to take Naupaktos'. The importance of Naupaktos, which dominated the narrows at the west end of the Corinthian gulf, is not insisted on; but we know from the inscription on a statue dedicated at Olympia, the famous and very beautiful *Niké* or Victory sculpted by Paionios, that Naupaktos played an active part in the Archidamian War on the Athenian side.[6] The occupants of the site at this time were former Spartan helots from Messenia, settled there by Athens after the great helot revolt in the middle of the fifth century. One

[5] See Connor, 'A Post-modernist Thucydides?'.
[6] ML 74.

of the advantages for Athens of the Thirty Years Peace, which ended the First Peloponnesian War in 446, was that it left these Messenians in possession of Naupaktos. They were not Athenians themselves and so could not be dislodged diplomatically in 446, however total an evacuation of other such distant bases was imposed on Athens. On the other hand, the sympathies of the Naupaktan Messenians were all with Athens and against Sparta – and against Corinth (a few words later, Thucydides reveals that the Corinthians were specially keen on the whole plan and egged Sparta on). All this gave the Messenians at Naupaktos great nuisance value in the 420s.

Herodotus might have handled this rather differently. Instead of the six-word sentence about Naupaktos which Thucydides gives us, we might have had a retrospective digression recording the original capture of the place by Athens in the 460s (an event obscure to us); something about the helot revolt; a mention of the dedication of the statue of Nike with perhaps an anecdote attached; an apologetic formula announcing the end of the digression; a short speech by somebody stressing the attractions, and exaggerating the size, of Zakynthos, Kephallenia and Naupaktos; and finally some resumptive words about the Peloponnesian plan against Akarnania in 429 BC, this time with a note saying, 'But events were to show that the Akarnanians were not destined to come to grief as a result of this expedition'. (Compare Herodotus on the Persian designs against Naxos in 500 BC. Aristagoras tells the Persian satrap Artaphernes that the conquest of Naxos may bring with it the conquest of the Cyclades and of Euboia, a fertile place the size of Cyprus (!) and easy to take; but Herodotus comments that 'events were to show that the Naxians were not destined to come to grief as a result of this expedition'.)[7]

Thucydides has been criticised[8] for neglecting the middle ranges between the methods of tragedy and of the laboratory note-book; in particular, for providing no intelligible account of strategy. That is certainly not true of the motive given for the founding of the Spartan colony at Heraclea in Trachis in Book iii, which is explained clearly in terms of a dual desire to coerce Euboia (where Athens kept food supplies) and to control the

[7] Hdt.v 31.3; 33.2.

[8] By Wade-Gery in *OCD²*, 1068 – said about the Archidamian war only; but my counter-instances are from that war too.

LIBRARY ST. MARY'S COLLEGE

passage to Thrace and the north generally.[9] Nor is it true of the present passage: the strategy here set out may have been wrong; or Thucydides may have misunderstood it; but there is no question that this is 'strategic' writing. It has been said recently:[10] 'We cannot judge whether Thucydides had access to good information about the arguments used by the Ambraciots, Corinthians and Chaonians, or about the Spartan motives for agreeing to the proposals; but the plan seems most unreal.'

The point here made about access to good information is sound (is this Thucydidean reportage or Thucydidean inference? What comes after 'they said' is in effect a tiny speech, and as we saw in Chapter Three we always have to ask, 'Is this *ta deonta* or *alêthôs lechthenta*?'). Typically (Chapter Seven, p.155), Thucydides does not disclose his source. Incidentally, knowledge of the eventual failure of the whole enterprise would not have committed him to the view that it was impracticable *ab initio*: the great Sicilian expedition failed, but Thucydides came to think that it could have succeeded if differently managed. Given what we have seen (p.68) about Thucydides' ironic use of speeches, we might want to say that the tiny speech here was so ludicrously belied by the outcome that a judgment is after all implied. If so it is *kept* implicit. On the Akarnanian plan itself, however, the author of the sentence I have just quoted very honestly cites another modern view in a footnote: 'the appeal was persuasive, and the prospects seemed good.'[11] So there is no scholarly consensus on the soundness of the plan. What of Thucydides' manner of giving it, dry and, if censorious, only implicitly so? I would re-emphasise here a point made in Chapter Two: the one influence on Thucydides which is absolutely certain, since we know that he was a soldier and *know* very little else about his life, is the influence of his own military career. (It was perhaps unkind towards the military profession to make that point there, rather than in the chapter on *intellectual* affinities). The way Thucydides offers or reports the more distant objectives, without Herodotean exaggeration, owes something to the spareness of the military appraisal. This was a major legacy to later historiography.

There is, however, one point on which Thucydides seems

<hr/>

[9] iii 92.
[10] J.B. Salmon, *Wealthy Corinth*, 309.
[11] Kagan, *Archidamian War*, 107.

clearly open to criticism. The Spartan readiness to dispatch Knemos and 1,000 hoplites is one of those items which, like the founding of Heraclea in Trachis in 426 (see above), prove that there was adventurous military thinking at Sparta even before the advent to prominence of the unusually energetic Brasidas; and that Sparta was being forced to recognise the importance of the naval factor although sea-fighting was not her *forte*. As Gomme remarked of a comparable Spartan embroilment in 426, 'Sparta is not accused of rashness';[12] that is, Thucydides unfairly saves for Athens the strictures and credit appropriate to such ambitions and opportunism. (See above, p.177: what would he have said, had he covered the 'Xenophontic' period, about the occupation of the Cadmea? Not that 'this was to incur divine displeasure shortly', but that 'this was sheer *pleonexia*'.) True, Thucydides does make clear, as we noted above, that Sparta was in the present instance under pressure from Corinth, the mother-city of Ambracia (note the stress, as often in Thucydides, on the colonial factor, in the words 'who were colonists of theirs'. One of his best insights was to see the way the war cut across such traditional ties, a point I have made elsewhere.)[13] But if we say 'Sparta wanted to do a good turn to Corinth', we must also say 'and Corinth wanted to do a good turn to Ambracia'. That is, the original idea was neither Spartan *nor* Corinthian, but Ambraciot. (Ephorus, in Diodorus' bald summary,[14] omits the Corinthian aspect entirely.) What matters is that Sparta, for whatever reason, committed a large force to a plan which was bold if not downright speculative, so that this incident tells against (for instance) Thucydides' own comment, near the end of this whole work, that the Spartans were generally slow and timid, the Athenians generally quick and audacious (above, p.163).[15] We can fairly complain that Thucydides here reports a ready Spartan response, which comes close to being a Spartan initiative, without commenting on its political implications, and its implications for the Spartan national character.

From the account of the object of the expedition, Thucydides moves on to describe the barbarian contingents in Knemos'

---

[12] *HCT* ii, 413.
[13] LACTOR *Athenian Empire*, 90f. discussing the curious erasures in ML 89. See also above, Chapter Four, n.96.
[14] xii 47.4.
[15] viii 96.

army. Of this the standard commentary remarks: 'a characteristic multitude of names and other details, obviously from
notes made at the time.' I should like to protest at this if the
suggestion is that what we have here is a jumble which would
have looked very different in a final draft (Introduction, p.10, cf.
p.138). As for 'characteristic', the information about forces is
indeed not untypical – so we need not feel that we have chosen
too exceptional a passage for the illustration of Thucydides'
virtues. Nevertheless I wish (see above on Thucydides' lack of
ethnographic material for its own sake) that there were more not
less in Thucydides of this kind of thing,[16] so culturally and
socially, as well as politically, informative about the parts of the
Greek world (in the geographical sense of that term) which were
normally beyond the horizons of our literary sources.

The information about the Epirot and Upper Macedonian
tribes is precious and has been duly exploited.[17] The Chaonian
system of command – two members of the royal house holding
office for a year – has been compared to the Roman system of
consular *imperium*. Chaonian primacy among the Epirotes is
obvious from this chapter, and from their role in the subsequent
action. Tharyps, mentioned by Thucydides as the under-age
king of the Molossians, here makes his first appearance in
history; from Thucydides' careful description of the tribal
alignments it can be inferred that Atintania was dependent on
the Molossians; but that the Parauaeans (i.e., simply, the people
along the river Aous) and the Orestae were equals. Furthermore
it is clear that Orestis, on the upper section of the great gorge of
the Haliakmon river, is not yet, as in Philip and Alexander's
time, part of Macedonia. Then comes Perdikkas of Macedon,
treacherously providing troops for Sparta, despite his supposed
commitment at this time to Athens. Note in all this what
Thucydides does *not* tell us: the information about Tharyps and
Molossia is purely political. We have to go to the opening part of
Plutarch's *Life of Pyrrhus*, and to Justin, for an account of
Tharyps' later hellenising activities, and the fact that the boy
was educated at Athens. Justin expresses Tharyps' achievement
as the provision of 'laws, senate and magistrates' – a regular
Latin formula for *Romanisation* (Corbulo imposed these three

---

[16] On the Odrysians of ii 97 and the allegedly raw meat-eating Aitolians of iii 94
see J. Hornblower, *Hieronymus* 151f.
[17] Above all by Hammond in *Epirus*, 1967; cf. *History of Macedonia* i, 1972.

institutions on the Frisii) or for constitutional government (Velleius makes Augustus restore authority to the *law*, dignity to the *senate*, and power to the *magistrates*).[18] Thucydides was perfectly capable of discussing achievements of this sort in appropriate terms; witness his account of the reign of Archelaus at the end of Book ii, or his reference to the hellenisation (cultural, not just linguistic) of the Amphilochian Argives, earlier in the same book. Nor (we may suppose) would Thucydides have had much time for the attempts to exploit mythology in support of Athenian designs in Epirus, which scholars detect in the *Andromache* of Euripides (cf. above, p.83, on Thucydides and Hellanicus and p.183 on religious propaganda). Finally, Thucydides mentions Stratos, of which he says merely that it is the 'greatest polis of Akarnania'. This is true, but very sparingly put; we might compare his very jejune information about the resources of Sicily (above, p.32). Stratos is indeed the key to Akarnania, with two strong lines of fortifications running along its ridges and a commanding situation.[19]

With the next chapter we pass to the narrative of the attempt on Stratos and Akarnania as a whole. This is an excellent, clear and intelligible piece of narrative. That is eminently worth saying, because so little ancient military writing is any use at all (witness the trouble which scholars have had making sense of Herodotus on Marathon or Arrian on Gaugamela, not to mention the Roman historians, who are surprisingly poor at this kind of thing despite their more militarily oriented culture). Near the end of the previous chapter we had been told that Knemos did not wait for ships from Corinth; Thucydides reserves treatment of their fate until a section which comes outside the chapters I have quoted. Knemos' failure to wait for them is clearly half the reason, though Thucydides does not say so explicitly, why the whole operation was unsuccessful. The other half is the impetuous behaviour of the Chaonians who went ahead of the rest of the force. They were ambushed by the Stratians who (Thucydides says: inference or information?) thought that a

---

[18] Justin xvii 3; Tac. *Ann.* xi 19; Vell. Pat. ii 89.

[19] ii 100; ii 68, cf. above, p.95 n.91, for *hellenizō* here. For the Molossian aspect to the *Andromache*, see R.L. Beaumont, *JHS* lxxii, 1952, p. 65 and references. This article also exploits Thuc.ii 80 extensively. R. Hoffmann, *GRBS* xvi, 1975, 374, by contrast, doubts Perdikkas' involvement at ii 80, thus rejecting Thucydides in favour of his own conjectures about 429 BC.

Chaonian defeat would lower the morale of Knemos' Greek troops, whose own defeat is then recorded (with a comment on Akarnanian sling-power. This I *would* call characteristically Thucydidean; cf. Chapter Seven above, p.158). The narrative ends in simple fashion, with Knemos' retreat to Oiniadai and the erection of a trophy by the Stratians. The descent to the particular is thus completed and Thucydides passes to naval operations in the next chapter, not bothering to sum up (contrast the Mytilene passage, and Herodotus' sentence about what was 'destined' to happen). He hardly needed to sum up (contrast the most recent modern account of the episode, 'The plans failed in every respect').

Before leaving the passage I would like to comment on a feature of Thucydides which is surely one of his very greatest virtues, and is illustrated by this passage. We have seen that he failed to make a very telling point against Herodotus which he could have made: David Lewis has complained, with much justice, of the innumeracy of Thucydides for not taking issue with, for instance, Herodotus' Persian army of 5,283,320, preferring instead to disparage the Persian Wars by reference to the fact that they were settled in four battles only.[20] We also noticed that such figures as the 20,000+ slaves who deserted after the Spartan occupation of Decelea are hardly likely to be the result of statistical research by Thucydides (above, p.36). And it takes some desperate argumentation to save some of Thucydides' financial material about the tribute; what impresses us favourably here is the assured *tone* of his statement that, for instance, the Athenians hoped that a 5 per cent maritime tax would bring in more than the tribute had done.[21] But that is by no means the whole story. Quite apart from the occasional 'pathetic' use of *small* numbers (cf. above, p.34), Thucydides deserves much credit for the believably small scale of the forces he gives. The most sustained section on population figures is in the long chapter on Athenian human and financial resources in Book ii. There is fierce argument about the population of classical Athens among scholars; but we *can* say

[20] See above, p.108. See also C. Reid Rubincam, art. cit. (1979) on hyperbolical 'qualification' of numerals.

[21] vii 28.4. for the 5 per cent tax, cf. above, p.33 n.81. The 460 talents of i 96, and the tribute totals of ii 13.3 have provoked much argument; this is not the place to give bibliography. 600 talents at ii 13 is credible.

that on no plausible view can Thucydides be said to have got things widely and discreditably wrong, especially if we accept that there was no central hoplite register as was once believed.[22] One set of figures, his numbers for the Spartan turn-out at Mantinea, has, it is true, been recently impugned on the serious grounds that Thucydides missed out a whole stage in the calculation so that his figures should be doubled; but more recently still an equally careful study has returned to the view that Thucydides was right.[23] This is not the place to attempt to adjudicate on this point; what is important is that the orders of magnitude in Thucydides' accounts have not been definitely shown to be ridiculous. To return to the present passage. Like countless other routine slices of narrative, this contains totals which we can believe in. A thousand hoplites here, a thousand there – round or paper totals perhaps, but small. It was a force of a mere 120 which prompted the lament we discussed in Chapter Seven (p.159). Even the great set-piece encounter of Mantinea was a matter of a few thousands, casualties being numbered in hundreds (Argives, Orneans and Cleoneans 700, Mantineans 200, Athenians and Aiginetans 200; on the other side Spartiate losses of 300, with very little allied loss. But 300 is not negligible given Spartiate numbers; that is to say, there has been no attempt to make out that the victors came off unscathed – a fault of many ancient battle accounts). Fleets are similarly described. The Athenians with a kernel of 44 ships beat a Samian fleet of 70 towards the end of Thucydides' *Pentekontaetia*. At Syracuse the *combined* total of the two sides was less than 200.[24] Thucydides' sobriety in giving troop and fleet totals does not establish his accuracy. But he must be given his rightful place at the head of an honourable tradition which avoided inflated figures. Another writer in this tradition is the Hellenistic historian Hieronymus of Cardia; the books (xviii-xx) of Diodorus which draw on him are noticeably more careful and plausible in this respect than the 'Ephoran' and 'Kleitarchan' books which have gone before.[25]

[22] M.H. Hansen, *Demography and Democracy*, 1985, for full discussion and literature. No hoplite *katalogos*: Hansen, *Symbolae Osloenses* lvi, 1981, 19ff.

[23] Impugned: Andrewes, *HCT* ad loc. Defended: Cawkwell, *CQ* xxxiii, 1983, 385ff., 'The decline of Sparta'.

[24] v 74; i 116; vii 70. On the supposedly impossible 500 ships of ii 7 see *HCT* v, 10. On cost of a siege, ii 70 is plausible, cf. ML 55.

[25] J. Hornblower, *Hieronymus of Cardia*, 1981, 108f.: the reliability of his military narrative compared to Thucydides.

There is a rhetoric of numbers as of words, and though Thucydides may use pathetically small numbers for, in effect, rhetorical purposes and sometimes 'qualifies numerals hyperbolically', he was (Chapter Two) too much of a soldier to exaggerate in this way in his routine narrative.

I turn now to the final passage I have chosen, which is short.[26] It covers events of 413 BC: the final phase of the Athenian attack by night on the strong Syracusan position at Epipolae. In itself the chapter contains little of historical importance: it rates a mere six lines in the standard commentary, four concerned with a possible gloss which has crept into the text, the other two with the (for once) more specific numbers of casualties given in Plutarch and Diodorus (2000; 2500).

> Next day the Syracusans put up two trophies, one at the approach to Epipolae and one at the place where the Boeotians had first made their stand. The Athenians took back their dead under an armistice. Many had been killed, both Athenians and allies, though the quantity of arms captured was out of proportion to the numbers of the dead, since those who had been forced to jump down from the cliffs had abandoned their shields, and, while some were killed, others of them escaped.

The chapter deserves a word or two more than it has hitherto received; the style of narration is as brisk as the Book ii section which we have just considered. But there is a difference. The statement, that those who had been forced to jump from the heights had thrown away their shields, refers to a sentence in the preceding chapter of Thucydides:

> The way down from Epipolae was only a narrow one, and in the pursuit many men lost their lives by throwing themselves down from the cliffs.

The discrepancy noted by Thucydides, between the numbers of the dead bodies and the total of weapons found after the battle,

---

In this chapter I have decided, after thought, not to discuss Thucydides' basic *topographic* reliability, in which I believe, against his many critics. The individual issues are too boring and technical to be discussed here. Only the most methodologically important, e.g. Pylos 425 BC (cf. Cawkwell, *CR* 1981, 132 on J.B. Wilson's book of that title) will be treated (briefly) in the two-volume commentary which I have undertaken for Oxford University Press.

[26] vii 45.

is factual enough. But here, I suggest, we *do* have an instance of what I have called tragic *akribeia*. The fact to be explained is a purely arithmetical oddity; the explanation, however, is the ghastly end of a large number of human beings. Thucydides does not rub the point in but it is there. If the passage helps us to understand the Peloponnesian, or any other, war, it is hardly through its factual content (who cares how much armour was found?) but because of its implications for people's lives and the way they can end. Note the conscientious addition, in the second passage (the first quoted) to the effect that some also escaped though we have just been told that many were killed.

These two passages contain much that is admirable. The first is clearly and artistically constructed, and politically and militarily informative; but emotionally neutral. This is the Thucydides with whom the 'positivist' modern historian feels most at home. The second has little factual value (it would be a very full modern history indeed which picked up the point about discrepancy in numbers of suits of armour) but is powerful: it seems at first reading to be as emotionally neutral as the other (contrast the Mytilene passage, where we hold our breath); but this time the neutrality is deceptive. Its implications are not comfortable. Taken with the two other passages we looked at near the beginning of this chapter – the feelings, about their horrible mission, of the first contingent of Athenian sailors sent to Mytilene; and the old-fashioned harangue of Nikias – they illustrate the range of Thucydides' handling, and the strengths which make him a great writer.

In his preface, Thucydides expresses contempt for those who do not take trouble in the search for truth.[27] From the context, he clearly has factual accuracy in mind, since he has just corrected a string of factual errors. It is to his own diligent factual inquiries that we owe the material, discussed above, about the tribal structure of Epirus. Other kinds of truth, like the knowledge of the kind of occasion when men resort to appeals which would normally sound absurdly old-fashioned, were less easily come by through 'taking trouble', and Thucydides' grasp of this kind of truth is as mysterious as that of any artist gifted with psychological understanding. No account of Thucydides will be complete which neglects his grasp of either sort of truth.

[27] i 20.3.

Bibliography

Adcock, F., *Thucydides and his History* (Cambridge 1963).
Adkins, A., *Merit and Responsibility* (Oxford 1960).
'The *arete* of Nicias: Thucydides 7.86', *GRBS* xvi (1975) 379ff.
Allison, J., 'Thucydides and *polypragmosyne*', *AJAH* iv (1979) 10ff.
Aly, W., *Volksmärchen, Sage und Novelle bei Herodot und seine Zeitgenossen* (Göttingen 1921).
Amit, A., *Athens and the Sea* (Brussels 1965).
Andrewes, A., 'Thucydides and the causes of the war', *CQ* ix (1959) 223ff.
    'The Melian Dialogue and Pericles' last speech', *PCPhS* 186 (1960) 1ff.
    'Thucydides and the Persians', *Historia* x (1961) 1ff.
    'The Mytilene Debate', *Phoenix* xvi (1962) 64ff.
    'Modern work on the history of Athens', *Didaskalos* iv (1972) 155ff.
    'The Opposition to Pericles', *JHS* xcviii, 1978, 1ff.
    see also under Gomme, Andrewes & Dover.
Armayor, O.K., 'Did Herodotus ever go to the Black Sea?', *HSCP* lxxxii (1978) 45ff.
Astin, A., *Scipio Aemilianus* (Oxford 1967).
Badian, E., 'Archons and strategoi', *Antichthon* v (1971) 1ff.
Barron, J.P., 'The sixth-century tyranny at Samos', *CQ* xiv (1964) 210ff.
    'The fifth-century *horoi* of Aigina', *JHS* ciii (1983) 1ff.
Beaumont, R.L., 'Corinth, Ambracia, Apollonia', *JHS* lxxii (1952) 62ff.
Beloch, K.J., *Griechische Geschichte²*, 4 vols (Strasburg, Leipzig, Berlin 1912-1927).
Bender, G.F., *Der Begriff des Staatsmannes bei Thukydides* (Würzburg 1938).
Berlin, I., *The Hedgehog and the Fox: an essay on Tolstoy's view of history* (London 1967).
Berwick, K., 'Die "Rhetorik ad Alexandrum" und Anaximenes, Alkidamas, Isokrates, Aristoteles und die Theodekteia', *Philologus* cx (1966) 212ff. and cxi (1967) 47ff.
Bétant, E.-A., *Lexicon Thucydideum*, 2 vols (Genf 1843, reprinted Darmstadt 1969).
Birley, A., *Marcus Aurelius* (London 1966).
Boardman, J., 'The Parthenon frieze: another view', *Festschrift für Frank Brommer* (Mainz 1977), 39ff.
Bosworth, A.B., *A Historical Commentary on Arrian's History of Alexander*, vol. i (Oxford 1980).

Bourriot, F., 'La famille et le milieu social de Cléon', *Historia* xxxi (1982) 404ff.

Bowra, C.M., *The Creative Experiment* (London 1948).

'Euripides' epinician for Alcibiades', *Historia* ix (1960) 68ff., reprinted in *On Greek Margins* (Oxford 1970) ch. xii.

Bruns, I., *Das literarische Porträt der Griechen* (Berlin 1896).

Brunt, P.A., Review of von Fritz, *Die griechische Geschichtsschreibung*, *CR* xix (1969), 198ff.

Italian Manpower (Oxford 1971).

(ed.), Loeb Arrian, 2 vols (London 1976, 1983).

'Laus imperii' in *Imperialism in the Ancient World*, ed. P. Garnsey and C. Whittaker (Cambridge 1978) 159ff.

Burton, R.W.B., *The Chorus in Sophocles' Tragedies* (Oxford 1980).

Bury, J.B., *The Ancient Greek Historians* (London 1909).

Busolt, G., *Griechische Geschichte*, 3 vols[1-2] (Gotha 1893-1904).

Buxton, R.G.A., 'Blindness and limits: Sophokles and the logic of myth', *JHS* c (1980) 22ff.

Cagnazzi, S., *La spedizione ateniese contro Melo* (Bari 1983).

Cairns, F., 'Cleon and Pericles: a suggestion', *JHS* cii (1982) 203f.

Canfora, L., *Totalità e selezione nella storiografia antica* (Bari 1972).

Carter, L.B., *The Quiet Athenian* (Oxford 1986).

Cartledge, P., 'A new lease of life for Lichas son of Arkesilas?', *LCM* ix, (1984) 98ff.

Cataldi, S., *La democrazia ateniese e gli alleati (Ps.-Senofonte, Athenaion Politeia, 1, 14-18)* (Padua 1984).

Cawkwell, G.L., 'The crowning of Demosthenes', *CQ* xix (1969) 163ff.

'The fall of Themistocles', *Auckland Classical Studies presented to E.M. Blaiklock* (London 1971) 39ff.

'Thucydides' judgment of Periclean strategy', *YCS* xxiv (1975) 53ff.

Review of J. Wilson, *Pylos 425 B.C.*, *CR* xxxi (1981) 132.

'The decline of Sparta', *CQ* xxxiii (1983) 385ff.

Classen, J. & Steup, J. (eds), *Thukydides*[3-5] (Berlin 1892-1922).

Clark, S.R.L., *Aristotle's Man: Speculations upon Aristotelian Anthropology* (Oxford 1975).

Cochrane, C., *Thucydides and the Science of History* (Oxford 1929).

Cogan, M., *The Human Thing: the speeches and principles of Thucydides' history* (Chicago 1981).

Cole, T., *Democritus and the Sources of Greek Anthropology* (Western Reserve 1967).

Connolly, C., *Enemies of Promise* (Harmondsworth 1961).

Connor, W.R., *The New Politicians of Fifth-Century Athens* (Princeton 1971).

'A post-modernist Thucydides?', *Classical Journal* lxxii (1977) 289ff.

'Thucydides' in *Ancient Writers* ed. T. Luce, 2 vols (N.Y. 1982) vol.i, 267ff.

Thucydides (Princeton 1984).

Cook, R.M., 'Thucydides as archaeologist', *BSA* 50, (1955) 266ff.

208 *Thucydides*

Cope, E.M., *An Introduction to Aristotle's Rhetoric* (London 1867).

Cornell, T.J., 'The formation of the historical tradition of early Rome' in *Past Perspectives* ed. I.S. Moxon, J.D. Smart, A.J. Woodman (Cambridge 1986) 67ff.

Cornford, F.M., *Thucydides Mythistoricus* (London 1907).

Davies, J.K., *Athenian Propertied Families* (Oxford 1971).

Wealth and the Power of Wealth in Classical Athens (N.Y. 1981).

Deffner, A., *Die Rede bei Herodot und ihre Weiterbildung bei Thukydides* (Diss. Munich 1933).

Detienne, M., *Les maîtres de vérité dans la grèce archaique* (Paris 1973).

Diels, H. & Kranz, W. (eds), *Die Fragmente der Vorsokratiker*[6], 3 vols (Berlin 1952).

Dittenberger, W., *Orientis graeci inscriptiones selectae*, 2 vols (Leipzig 1903-1905).

Sylloge inscriptionum graecarum[3], 4 vols (Leipzig 1915-1924).

Dodds, E.R., *The Ancient Concept of Progress* (Oxford 1973).

Donini, G., *La posizione di Tucidide verso il governo dei Cinquemili* (Turin 1969).

Doudon, X., *Des révolutions du goût* (Paris 1924).

Dover, K.J. (ed.), Aristophanes, *Clouds* (Oxford 1968).

Thucydides; Greece and Rome New Survey in the Classics No. 7 (Oxford 1973).

'The freedom of the intellectual in Greek society', *Talanta* vii (1976) 24ff.

Chapters 4 ('Tragedy') and 7 ('Classical science and Philosophy') in K.J. Dover (ed.) *Ancient Greek Literature* (Oxford 1980) 50ff., 105ff.

'Thucydides' historical judgment: Athens and Sicily', *Proc.Royal Irish Acad.* 81, C, no.8 (1981) 231ff.

'Thucydides "as history" and "as literature" ', *History and Theory* xxii, 1983, 54ff.

See also under Gomme, Andrewes & Dover.

Drews, R., *The Greek Accounts of Eastern History* (Harvard 1973).

Edmunds, L., 'Thucydides' ethics as reflected in the description of stasis (3.82-83)', *HSCP* lxxix (1975) 73ff.

Chance and Intelligence in Thucydides (Harvard 1975).

Egermann, F., 'Zum historiographischen Ziel des Thukydides', *Historia* x (1961) 435ff.

Ehrenberg, V., *Sophocles and Pericles* (Oxford 1954).

Fehling, D., *Die Quellenangaben bei Herodot* (Berlin 1971).

Finley, J.H., *Thucydides* (Oxford 1942).

Three Essays on Thucydides (Cambridge, Mass. 1967).

Finley, M.I., (ed.) *The Portable Greek Historians* (Harmondsworth 1977).

'Myth, memory and history', *History and Theory* iv (1965) 281ff., reprinted in *The Use and Abuse of History*[2] (London 1986) 11ff.

'The fifth-century Athenian empire: a balance-sheet', in *Imperialism in the Ancient World* ed. P. Garnsey and C. Whittaker (Cambridge 1978) 103ff., reprinted in *Economy and Society in Ancient Greece* ed. B. Shaw and R. Saller (London 1981) 41ff.

Politics in the Ancient World (Cambridge 1983).

'The ancient historian and his sources', *Tria corda* (Studies in honour of A. Momigliano) ed. E. Gabba (Como 1983) 201ff.

Ancient History: evidence and models (London 1985).

Fornara, C.W., *Herodotus: an interpretative essay* (Oxford 1971).

'Evidence for the date of Herodotus' publication', *JHS* xci (1971) 25ff.

'Andokides and Thucydides' in *Panhellenica (T.S. Brown Studies)*, (Lawrence, Kansas 1980) 43ff.

Forrest, W.G., Introduction to *Herodotus* in *The great historians* series, general ed. H.R. Trevor-Roper (N.Y. 1963).

'Two chronographic notes, I: the tenth thalassocracy in Eusebius', *CQ* xix (1969) 95ff.

'The date of the pseudo-Xenophontic Athenaion Politeia', *Klio* lii (1970) 107ff.

'An Athenian generation gap', *YCS* xxiv (1975) 37ff.

'Aristophanes and the Athenian empire', in *The Ancient Historian and his Materials: essays in honour of C.E. Stevens*, ed. B. Levick (Farnborough 1975), 17ff.

*A History of Sparta*² (London 1980).

'A lost Peisistratid name', *JHS* ci (1981) 134.

Fraser, P.M. & Rönne, T., *Boiotian and West Greek Tombstones* (Lund 1957).

Some More Boiotian and West Greek Tombstones (Stockholm 1971).

von Fritz, K., *Die griechische Geschichtsschreibung*, 2 vols (Berlin 1957).

Gernet, L., 'Les mariages des tyrans', in *L'anthropologie dans la grèce antique* (Paris 1968) 344ff.

Gill, C., 'The question of character-development: Plutarch and Tacitus', *CQ* xxxiii (1983) 469ff.

Goldhill, S., *Reading Greek Tragedy* (Cambridge 1986).

Gomme, A.W., *Essays in Greek History and Literature* (Oxford 1937).

The Greek Attitude to Poetry and History (California 1954).

More Essays in Greek History and Literature (Oxford 1962).

'Thucydides' in *Encyclopaedia Britannica* (1963 ed.).

Gomme, A.W., Andrewes, A. & Dover, K.J., *A Historical Commentary on Thucydides*, 5 vols (Oxford 1945-1981).

Grayson, C., 'Did Xenophon intend to write history?' in *The Ancient Historian and his Materials: essays in honour of C.E. Stevens*, ed. B. Levick (Farnborough 1975) 31ff.

Grene, D., *Man in his Pride: a study of the political philosophy of Thucydides and Plato* (Chicago 1950), re-issued as *Greek Political Theory: the image of man in Thucydides and Plato*.

Griffin. J., *Homer on Life and Death* (Oxford 1980).

Review of Veyne, *Les grecs ont-ils cru ...*, in *TLS*, 22 April 1983.

Latin Poets and Roman Life (London 1985).

'Words and Speakers in Homer', *JHS* cvi (1986), 36ff.

Griffith, G.T., 'Some habits of Thucydides when introducing persons', *PCPhS* 187 (1961) 21ff.

Griffith, J.G., 'A note on the first *eisphora* at Athens', *AJAH* ii (1977) 3ff.

Halliwell, S., *Aristotle's Poetics* (London 1986).

Hammond, N.G.L., *Epirus* (Oxford 1967).

History of Macedonia vol.i (Oxford 1972).

'The particular and the universal in the speeches of Thucydides, with special reference to that of Hermokrates at Gela', in P. Stadter (ed.) *The Speeches in Thucydides* (N. Carolina 1973) 49ff.

Hammond, N.G.L. and Griffith, G.T., *History of Macedonia* vol. ii (Oxford 1979).

Hands, A.R., 'Postremo suo tantum ingenio utebatur', *CQ* xxiv (1974) 312ff.

Hansen, M.H., 'The number of Athenian hoplites in 431 BC', *Symbolae Osloenses* lvi (1981) 19ff.

Demography and Democracy: the number of Athenian citizens in the fourth century BC (Herning 1985).

Hardie, P., *Virgil's Aeneid: cosmos and imperium* (Oxford 1986).

Hart, J., *Herodotus and Greek History* (London 1982).

Havelock, E.A., *Preface to Plato* (Oxford 1966).

Herter, H. (ed.), *Thukydides*, Wege der Forschung Bd. xcviii (Darmstadt 1968).

Hill, G.F., *Sources for Greek History between the Persian and the Peloponnesian Wars*, revised by R. Meiggs and A. Andrewes (Oxford 1951).

Hinrichs, F.T., 'Hermokrates bei Thukydides', *Hermes* cix (1981) 46ff.

Hoffmann, R., 'Perdikkas and the outbreak of the Peloponnesian war', *GRBS* xvi (1975) 359ff.

Holladay, A.J. & Poole, J.C.F., 'Thucydides and the plague of Athens', *CQ* xxix (1979) 282ff.

'Thucydides and the plague: a footnote', *CQ* xxxii (1982) 235f.

'Thucydides and the plague: a further footnote', *CQ* xxxiv (1984) 483ff.

Holladay, A.J. & Goodman, M., 'Religious scruples in ancient warfare', *CQ* xxxvi (1986) 152ff.

Honour, H., *Romanticism* (Harmondsworth 1981).

Hope, C., *Titian* (London 1980).

Hopkins, K., 'Rules of evidence', review discussion of Millar, *Emperor JRS* lxviii (1978) 178ff.

Hornblower, J., *Hieronymus of Cardia* (Oxford 1981).

Hornblower, S., 'Thucydides, the Panionian festival, and the Ephesia (III 104)', *Historia* xxxi (1982) 241ff.

The Greek World 479-323 BC (London 1983, revised 1985).

Review of R. Bichler, *Hellenismus, CR* xxxiv (1984) 246.

Hornblower, S. & Greenstock, M. (eds), *The Athenian Empire*, LACTOR sourcebook³ (London 1984).

How, W.W. & Wells, J., *A Commentary on Herodotus*, 2 vols (Oxford 1912).

Humphreys, S.C., 'Family tombs and tomb cult in ancient Athens: tradition or traditionalism?', *JHS* c (1980) 96ff., reprinted in *The Family, Women and Death* (London 1983) 79ff.

Hunter, V., *Thucydides the Artful Reporter* (Toronto 1973).

Past and Process in Herodotus and Thucydides (Princeton 1982).

Hussey, E., *The Presocratics* (London 1972).

'Thucydidean history and Democritean theory' in *CRUX: Essays in Greek history presented to G.E.M. de Ste Croix on his 75th birthday*, ed. P. Cartledge and F.D. Harvey (London 1985) 118ff.

Immerwahr, H., 'History as monument in Herodotus and Thucydides', *AJP* lxxxi (1960) 261ff.

Irwin, T. (ed.), *Plato, Gorgias* (Oxford 1979).

Jacoby, F., 'Herodotus' in *RE* supp.vol. ii (1913), reprinted in *Griechische Historiker* (Stuttgart 1956) 7ff.

Die Fragmente der griechischen Historiker, 15 vols (Leiden 1924-1958).

'*Patrios nomos*: state burial in Athens and the public cemetery in the Kerameikos', *JHS* lxiv (1944) 37ff., reprinted in *Abhandlungen* (see below) 260ff.

Atthis (Oxford 1949).

Abhandlungen zur griechische Geschichtsschreibung, ed. H. Bloch (Leiden 1956).

see also under Zahn.

Jaeger, W., *Paideia*, tr. G. Highet, 3 vols (Oxford 1945).

Jebb, R.C., 'The speeches in Thucydides' in *Hellenica*, ed. E. Abbott (London 1898) 244ff.

Jones, J.W., *Law and Legal Theory of the Greeks* (Oxford 1956).

Jowett, B. (tr.), *Thucydides*, rev. by W. Forbes and E. Abbott (Oxford 1900).

Kagan, D., *The Archidamian War* (Cornell 1974).

Kelly, D.H., 'The Athenian archonship 508/7-487/6', *Antichthon* xii (1978) 1ff.

Kirchhoff, A., *Thukydides und seine Urkundenmaterial* (Berlin 1895).

Kitto, H.D.F., *Poiesis* (California 1966).

Knox, B., *Oedipus at Thebes* (Oxford 1957).

Kraut, R., *Socrates and the State* (Princeton 1984).

Kurz, D., '*Akribeia*', *Göppingen Akad. Beiträge* 8 (1970).

Kyle, D.G., *Athletics in Ancient Athens* (Leiden 1987)

Landmann, G.F., *Interpretation einer Rede des Thukydides: die Friedensmahnung des Hermokrates* (Diss. Basel 1932).

Lane Fox, R., *Pagans and Christians* (London 1986).

Lateiner, D., 'The speech of Teutiaplus (Thuc. 3.30)', *GRBS* xvi (1975) 175ff.

'No laughing matter: a literary tactic in Herodotus', *TAPA* cvii (1977) 173ff.

'Nicias' inadequate encouragement (Thucydides 7.69.2)', *CP* lxxx (1985) 201ff.

Lévy, E., *Athènes devant la défaite de 404: histoire d'une crise idéologique* (Paris 1976)

Lewis, D.M., 'The Phoenician fleet in 411', *Historia* vii (1958) 393ff.

Sparta and Persia (Leiden 1977).

Limentani, I. Calabi (ed.), *Plutarchi vita Aristidis* (Florence 1964).

Lloyd, G.E.R., *Polarity and Analogy: two types of argumentation in early Greek thought* (Cambridge 1966).

Magic Reason and Experience (Cambridge 1978).

Lloyd, M., 'Croesus' priority: Herodotus 1.5.3', *LCM* ix (1984) 11.

Lloyd-Jones, H., *The Justice of Zeus*[2] (California 1983).

Long, C.R., 'Greeks, Carians and the purification of Delos', *AJA* lxii (1958) 279ff.

Loraux, N., *The Invention of Athens: the Funeral Oration in the Classical City* (translated by A. Sheridan, Harvard 1986).

Luschnat, O., 'Thukydides', *RE* supp. xii (1970) cols 1147ff.

Macdowell, D. (ed.), Andokides *On the Mysteries* (Oxford 1962).

Macleod, C. (ed.), Homer, *Iliad xxiv* (Cambridge 1982).

Review of D. Proctor, *The Experience of Thucydides*, London Review of Books (21 Jan.-3 Feb. 1982) 26.

Collected Essays (Oxford 1983).

McNeal, R.A., 'Protagoras the Historian', *History and Theory* xxv (1986) 299ff.

Marinatos, N., *Thucydides and Religion* (Königstein 1981).

'Thucydides and oracles', *JHS* ci (1981) 138ff.

Marshall, M.H., 'Urban settlement in the second chapter of Thucydides', *CQ* xxv (1975) 26ff.

Martin, R., *Tacitus* (London 1981).

Martin, T.R., *Sovereignty and Coinage in Classical Greece* (Princeton 1985).

Meiggs, R., 'Herodotus', *History Today* (November 1957) 729ff.

The Athenian Empire (Oxford 1972).

Meiggs, R. & Lewis, D., *A Selection of Greek Historical Inscriptions to the end of the Fifth Century BC* (Oxford 1969).

Meuss, H., 'Thukydides und die religiöse Aufklärung', *Neue Jahrb.f.kl.Philol.* 146 (1892) 225ff.

Meyer, C., *Die Urkunden im Geschichtswerk des Thukydides*[2] (Munich 1970).

Meyer, Ed., *Forschungen zur alten Geschichte*, 2 vols (Halle 1892, 1899).

Geschichte des Altertums vol.i[2] 1 (Stuttgart 1907).

Mikalson, J., 'Religion and the plague in Athens 431-427 BC', *GRBS* monograph x (1982) (*Studies presented to Sterling Dow on his 80th birthday*), 217ff.

Millar, F., *The Emperor in the Roman World* (London 1977).
'Epigraphy' in M. Crawford (ed.) *Sources for Ancient History* (Cambridge 1983) 80ff.
Momigliano, A., 'Terra marique', *JRS* xxxii (1942) 53ff., reprinted in *Secondo contributo alla storia degli studi classici* (Rome 1960) 431ff.
'Sea-power in Greek thought', *CR* lviii (1944) 1ff. reprinted in *Secondo contributo* (see above) 57ff.
Studies in Historiography (London 1966).
Alien Wisdom (Cambridge 1975).
'Persian empire and Greek freedom' in *The Idea of Freedom, Essays in Honour of Sir Isaiah Berlin* (Oxford 1979) 139ff.
Moraux, P., 'Thucydide et la rhétorique', *Les études classiques* xxii (1954) 3ff.
Murray, O., 'Herodotus and hellenistic culture', *CQ* xxii (1972) 200ff.
Early Greece (London 1980).
Review of M.I. Finley, *Politics in the Ancient World*, *TLS* (26 Aug. 1983) 895ff.
'Greek historians' in Boardman, J., Griffin, J., & Murray, O. (eds) *The Oxford History of the Classical World* (Oxford 1986) 186ff.
'The Ionian revolt' in *Cambridge Ancient History*[2] vol. iv (Cambridge 1987).
Myres, J.L., 'On the "list of thalassocracies" in Eusebius', *JHS* xxvi (1906) 84ff.
Nestle, W., 'Thukydides und die Sophistik', *Neue Jahrb. f.kl. Alt.u.Päd.*, xxiii, Jg.17 (1914) 649ff., reprinted in *Griechische Studien* (Stuttgart 1948).
Nilsson, M., *Geschichte der griechischen Religion*[2], 2 vols (Munich 1969, 1951).
North, H., *Sophrosyne: self-knowledge and self-restraint in Greek literature* (Cornell 1966).
Nussbaum, M., *The Fragility of Goodness: luck and ethics in Greek tragedy and philosophy* (Cambridge 1986).
Ogilvie, R.M., *Livy i-v Commentary* (Oxford 1965).
Ogilvie, R.M., & Richmond, I. (eds), Tacitus, *Agricola* (Oxford 1967).
Ostwald, M., *Nomos and the Beginnings of Athenian Democracy* (Oxford 1969).
'Diodotus, son of Eukrates', *GRBS* xx (1979) 5ff.
Page, D.L., 'Thucydides and the great plague at Athens', *CQ* iii (1953) 97ff.
Parke, H.W. & Wormell, D., *The Delphic Oracle*[2], 2 vols (Oxford 1956).
Parker, R., *Miasma: pollution and purification in early Greek religion* (Oxford 1983).
Parry, A., 'The language of Thucydides' description of the great plague at Athens', *BICS* xvi (1969) 106ff.
'Thucydides' use of abstract language', *Yale French Studies* xlv (1970) 3ff.

'Thucydides' historical perspective', *YCS* xxii (1972) 47ff.

Logos and Ergon in Thucydides (N.Y. 1981).

Pauly-Wissowa (eds), *Realencyclopädie der Klassischen Altertums-wissenschaft*, 83 vols.

Pearson, L., 'Real and conventional personalities in Greek history', *Journal of the History of Ideas* xv (1954) 136ff., reprinted in *Selected Papers of Lionel Pearson*, ed. D. Lateiner & S. Stephens (California 1983) 110ff.

The Lost Histories of Alexander the Great (N.Y. 1960).

Peter, H., *Historicorum romanorum reliquiae*, 2 vols (Leipzig 1914², 1906).

Pohlenz, M., *Aus Platos Werdezeit* (Berlin 1913).

Poole, *see* Holladay & Poole.

Popper, K., *The Open Society and its Enemies*, vol.i, *The Spell of Plato* (London 1966).

Poppo, E.F. & Stahl, J.M. (eds), *Thucydidis de bello Peloponnesiaco*²⁻³, 2 vols (Leipzig 1875-1886).

Pouilloux, J. & Salviat, F., 'Lichas, Lacédémonien, archonte à Thasos, et le livre viii de Thucydide', *CRAI* (1983) 376ff.

Powell, C., 'Religion and the Sicilian expedition', *Historia* xxviii (1979) 15ff.

Powell, E., 'Puns in Herodotus', *CR* li (1937) 103ff.

Lexicon to Herodotus (Cambridge 1938).

Pritchett, W.K., 'The Attic stelai', *Hesperia* xxii (1953) 225ff. and xxv (1956) 178ff.

The Greek State at War, 4 vols (Berkeley 1971-1985).

Dionysius of Halicarnassus on Thucydides (California 1975).

Radermacher, L., *Artium scriptores (Reste der voraristotelischen Rhetorik), Sber. Öst. Akad. Wiss.* 227.3 (Vienna 1951).

Raubitschek, A., 'Andokides and Thucydides', in *Classical Contri-butions (Studies in honour of M.F. McGregor)* ed. G.S. Shrimpton and D.J. McCargar (N.Y. 1981) 121ff.

Rawlings, H.H., *The Structure of Thucydides' History* (Princeton 1981).

Renault, M., *The Praise Singer* (London 1978).

Rhodes, P.J. 'Athenian democracy after 404 BC', *Classical Journal* lxxiv (1979-80) 305ff.

Commentary on the Aristotelian Athenaion Politeia (Oxford 1981).

Robert, J. & L., Bulletin épigraphique, *REG* xcvii (1984) 314.

Roberts, J.W., *City of Sokrates* (London 1984)

Robertson, M., *A History of Greek Art*, 2 vols (Cambridge 1975).

Robinson, R., Aristotle's *Politics*, books iii and iv (Oxford 1962).

Romilly, J. de, *Histoire et raison chez Thucydide* (Paris 1956).

The Rise and Fall of States according to Greek Authors (Ann Arbor 1977).

'Sur un écrit anonyme ancien et ses rapports avec Thucydide', *Journal des savants* (1980) 19ff.

Roy, J., 'The mercenaries of Cyrus', *Historia* xvi (1967) 287ff.

Rubincam, C.R., 'Qualification of numerals in Thucydides', *AJAH* iv (1979) 77ff.

Ruschenbusch, E., *Untersuchungen zu Staat und Politik in Griechenland vom 7-4 Jhdt. v. Chr.* (Bamberg 1978).

Russell, D.A. (ed), Longinus *On the sublime* (Oxford 1964).

Russell, D.A. & Winterbottom, M. (eds), *Ancient Literary Criticism: the principal texts in translation* (Oxford 1972).

Russell, D.A. & Wilson, N.G. (eds), *Menander Rhetor* (Oxford 1981).

Rusten, J.S., 'Two lives or three? Pericles on the Athenian character (Thucydides 2.40.1-2)', *CQ* xxxv (1985) 14ff.

Rutherford, R.B., 'At home and abroad: aspects of the structure of the Odyssey', *PCPhS* 211 n.s. 33 (1985) 133ff.

'The Philosophy of the Odyssey', *JHS* cvi (1986) 145ff.

Ste Croix, G.E.M. de, 'The popularity of the Athenian empire', *Historia* iii (1954/5) 1ff.

'The constitution of the Five Thousand', *Historia* v (1956) 1ff.

The Origins of the Peloponnesian War (London 1972).

'Aristotle on history and poetry (Poetics 9,1451a36-b11)', in *The Ancient Historian and his Materials: essays in honour of C.E. Stevens*, ed. B. Levick (Farnborough 1975), 45ff.

'Herodotus', *G. and R.* xxiv (1977) 130ff.

The Class Struggle in the Ancient Greek World (London 1981).

Salmon, J.B., *Wealthy Corinth* (Oxford 1984).

Schadewaldt, W., *Die Geschichtsschreibung des Thukydides²* (Zurich 1971).

Schepens, G., 'L'information complète chez les historiens grecs', *REG* lxxxviii (1975) 81ff.

Schneider, C., *Information und Absicht bei Thukydides* (Göttingen 1974).

Schrödinger, E., *Nature and the Greeks* (Cambridge 1954).

Schwabacher, W., 'Lycian coin-portraits' in *Essays in Greek Coinage presented to Stanley Robinson* ed. C. Kraay & G. Jenkins (Oxford 1968) 111ff.

Schwartz, Ed., *Das Geschichtswerk des Thukydides²* (Bonn 1929).

Gesammelte Schriften vol.ii (Berlin 1956).

Seager, R., 'Alcibiades and the charge of aiming at tyranny', *Historia* xvi (1967) 6ff.

'After the peace of Nicias: diplomacy and policy 421-416 BC', *CQ* xxvi (1976) 248ff.

'Neu sinas Medos equitare inultos', *Athenaeum* lviii (1980) 103ff.

Segal, C., 'Sophocles' praise of man' in Woodard, T. (ed.), *Sophocles* (N.Y. 1966) 62ff.

Sharples, R., 'Knowledge and courage in Thucydides and Plato', *LCM* viii (1983) 139ff.

Shorey, P., 'On the implicit ethics and psychology of Thucydides', *TAPA* xxiv (1893) 66ff.

Siewert, P., 'The ephebic oath in fifth-century Athens', *JHS* xcvii (1977)

102ff.

Smart, J.D., 'Athens and Egesta', *JHS* xcii (1972) 128ff.
 'Thucydides and Hellanicus' in *Past Perspectives*, ed. I.S. Moxon, J.D. Smart & A.J. Woodman (Cambridge 1986) 19ff.

Snodgrass, A.M., *Archaic Greece* (London 1980).

Solomon, J., 'Thucydides and the recognition of contagion', *Maia* xxxvii (1985) 121ff.

Stahl, H.-P., *Thukydides: die Stellung des Menschen im geschichtlichen Prozess* (Munich 1966).

Starr, C., 'Thucydides on sea power', *Mnemosyne* xxxi (1978) 343ff.

Steiner, G., *Antigones* (Oxford 1984).

Steppler, C., *The Nature of Athenian Politics 432/1-322 BC*, Oxford D. Phil. thesis 1986.

Strasburger, H., *Studien zur alten Geschichte*, 2 vols., ed. W. Schmitthenner & R. Zoepffel (Hildesheim 1982).

Stubbs, H.W., 'Thucydides i.2.6', *CQ* xxii (1972) 74f.

Stroheker, K., 'Zu den Anfängen der monarchischen Theorie in der Sophistik', *Historia* iii (1953/4), 381ff.

Syme, R., *The Roman Revolution* (Oxford 1939).
 Tacitus, 2 vols (Oxford 1958).
 'Thucydides', *PBA* xlviii (1962) 39ff.
 Sallust (California 1964).

Tarn, W.W., *Alexander the Great*, 2 vols (Cambridge 1948).

Täubler, E., *Die Archäologie des Thukydides* (Leipzig 1927).

Thompson, W., 'Thucydides 8.20.1: Astyochos' office', *CQ* xxxiii (1983) 293ff.

Tod, M.N., *International Arbitration Amongst the Greeks* (Oxford 1913).
 Greek Historical Inscriptions, 2 vols (Oxford 1946², 1948).

Toynbee, A.J., *Hannibal's Legacy*, 2 vols (Oxford 1965).

Trédé, M., 'Akribeia chez Thucydide', *Mélanges Delebecque* (Paris 1983) 407ff.

Turner, E.G., *Greek Papyri²* (Oxford 1980).

Veyne, P., *Les grecs ont-ils cru à leurs mythes?* (Paris 1983).

Vickers, B., *Towards Greek Tragedy* (London 1973).

Vidal-Naquet, P., *The Black Hunter* (London 1986).

Wade-Grey, H.T. 'Thucydides' in *Oxford Classical Dictionary²* ed. N.G.L. Hammond and H.H. Scullard (Oxford 1970) 1067ff.
 Essays in Greek History (Oxford 1958).

Walbank, F.W., 'Speeches in Greek historians', Third Myres memorial lecture (Oxford 1967) 1ff., reprinted in *Selected Papers* (Cambridge 1985) 242ff.

Webster, T.B.L., *Athenian Culture and Society* (London 1973).

Weidauer, K., *Thukydides und die hippokratische Schriften* (Heidelberg 1953).

Welles, C.B., *Royal Correspondence in the Hellenistic Period* (Yale 1934).

Wells, C., *The Roman Empire* (London 1984).

West, M.L., 'Melica', *CQ* xx (1970) 205ff.

West, S., 'Herodotus' epigraphical interests', *CQ* xxxv (1985) 278ff.

Westlake, H.D., *Individuals in Thucydides* (Cambridge 1968).

Essays on the Greek Historians and Greek History (Manchester 1969).

'Thucydides and the uneasy peace', *CQ* xxi (1971) 315ff.

'Thucydides on Pausanias and Themistocles – a written source?' *CQ* xxvii (1977) 95ff.

'Thucydides, Brasidas and Clearidas', *GRBS* xxi (1980) 333ff.

'Tissaphernes in Thucydides', *CQ* xxxv (1985) 43ff.

Whitehead, D., *The Ideology of the Athenian Metic* (Cambridge 1977).

'Competitive outlay and community profit: *philotimia* in democratic Athens', *Cl. et Med.* xxxiv (1983) 55ff.

The demes of Attica (Princeton 1986).

Wilamowitz-Moellendorff, U. von, 'Die Thukydideslegende', *Hermes* xii (1877) 326ff., reprinted in *Kleine Schriften* vol.iii (Berlin 1969) 1ff.

Antigonos von Karystos (Berlin 1881).

Griechisches Lesebuch 2 vols in 4 (Berlin 1902).

Wilkinson, L.P., 'The language of Virgil and Horace', *CQ* ix (1959) 181ff.

Willink, C.W., 'Some problems of text and interpretation in the *Bacchae*, II', *CQ* xvi (1966) 220ff.

Wilson, J., ' "The customary meanings of words were changed" – or were they? A note on Thucydides 3.82.4', *CQ* xxxii (1982) 18ff.

Pylos 425 B.C.: a historical and topographical study of Thucydides' account of the campaign (Warminster 1979.)

Wilson, N.G., *see* under Russell, D.A.

Worthington, I., 'A note on Thucydides 3.82.4', *LCM* vii (1982) 124.

Woozley, A.D., *Law and Obedience: the arguments of Plato's Crito* (London 1979).

Wyse, W. (ed.), *The Speeches of Isaeus* (Cambridge 1904).

Zahn, R., *Die erste Periklesrede* (Diss. Kiel 1934, with notes by F. Jacoby).

Zimmern, A.E., *The Greek Commonwealth*[5] (Oxford 1931).

Ziolkowski, J.E., *Thucydides and the Tradition of Funeral Speeches at Athens* (Salem, New Hampshire 1981).

Zucker, F., 'Anethopoietos', *Sber. Berl. Akad.* 1952 (4), 3ff.

Zuntz, G. *The Political Plays of Euripides* (Manchester 1963).

Index of passages in Thucydides

General index